DAME SARAH'S LEGACY

An Inventory or Schedule of the Rents

belonging to ye Trustees of ye late Lady Crowley's Charity for one whole year ending at Lady Day and Whitsontt 1719. viz.

The Trust Estates in ye City of York and in Fraya park Broarton and Fusanes Conistrop and West-Ayton in the County of York. which Mr Alexr Harrison hath in charge (N.B. The Rent daies are Wtitias & Lady Day.)

At West Ayton	£ s d	In or near ye City of York	£ s d	£ s d
Wm Allanson	4.10.0	Mr Tolford	23.0.0	
John Blackburne	3.0.0	John Long	4.10.0	
Wid Boyes	6.16.0	John Ward	1.15.0	£ 33.16.0
Eliz Bovill	0.4.0	John Hodgson	2.13.0	
Wm Collinson	9.6.0	John Allison	1.18.0	
Anne Coltas	1.10.0	**At Fraya park**		
Wm Davidson	5.6.0	Matthias Atkinson	4.0.0	
Drakehill field	17.6.0	Wm Andrews	14.0.0	
Robt Fox	1.10.0	Widow Barbor	15.0.0	
Wid. Fox	7.17.0	David Bland	47.0.0	
Robt Fearnes	0.10.0	Richd Bruo	18.0.0	
Tho.Hoddonp Thorntos	0.14.0	Mr Coates	53.0.0	
Grace Harrison	16.0.0	Execrutrs of Mr Casse	6.13.4	
Jno Hall	6.15.4	Thomas Crook	74.16.0	
Wm Jefferson	0.12.0	Francis Dukenson	17.0.0	
Lion King	2.10.0	Wm Elmsley	57.0.0	
Robt Lillay	4.4.0	Mrs Ingham	25.14.0	£ 472.10.8
Tho: Lillay	1.4.0	John Holdgate	36.13.8	
Jno Wyles	2.18.0	Geo: Johnson	26.8.0	
Wm Mattison	8.6.0	John English	25.0.0	
Mrs North	2.0.0	Jo Jennings	0.1.0	
Anne ponnock	0.10.0	Thomas Slingsby	1.0.0	
Jno Roads	2.16.8	Richd Sissons	15.15.0	
Mr Mettalf	12.0.0	John Symson	2.13.0	
Mary Spencer	0.8.0	Richd Titty	6.16.8	
Tho: Storke	2.4.0	**at Conistrop**		
Mr Storr	12.14.0	Matthias Atkinson	2.0.0	
Tho: Thompson sen	1.0.0	**At Broarton & Fusanes**		
Wm Thompson	0.12.0	Martin Grondall	24.0.0	
Tho Thompson jun	0.15.0			
Wm Wood	1.15.0			
Richd Warrop	4.0.0			
CWood & S Matthews	60.7.0			
Anne Walker	7.0.0			
Wm Wintorsdale	2.10.0			
John Warrop	17.0.0			
Sr A Caley's free rent	0.3.3		£ 308.13.11	

£ 815.0.7

DAME SARAH'S LEGACY

A History of
The Lady Hewley Trust

By Richard Potts

To Dame Sarah Hewley, without whose life, example and generosity this history could not have been written.

'Love the Lord your God with all your heart ... soul ... strength, and ... mind'; and 'Love your neighbour as you love yourself.'

(Luke 10, 27, Good News Bible)

Published by The Lady Hewley Trust

The Lady Hewley Trust

Lady Hewley's Charity is no. 230043 in the Charity Commission Register, and was registered on 25 October 1963. Its governing document is derived from the schemes of 6 May 1976 and 3 October 1983, as amended on 3 April 1992 and 23 May 2000. The purpose of the Charity is described as (a) the Relief of Poverty and (b) Religious Activities. It makes grants and loans to individuals and to organisations. The Lady Hewley Charity Trust was incorporated as a Limited Company on 18 December 1991 and, on application to the Lord Chancellor's Department, became authorised to act as a Trust Corporation from 16 January 1992 (no. 2672189).

Two other charities have origins stemming from Dame Sarah Hewley's generosity. The first of these is 'Lady Sarah Hewley's Charity', one of forty-six 'York City Charities', no. 224227, registered on 5 February 1964, and governed by schemes dating from 5 July 1956 to 2 July 1972; the objects of York City Charities as a whole are for (a) the benefit of such deserving and necessitous children living in the city of York as the Trustees select, (b) the provision of almshouses and pensions to poor persons of good character who have resided in the city for not less than four years, and (c) the benefit of the poor of York generally or of such poor persons dwelling there as the Trustees think fit. The second is no. 529724, 'Lady Hewley's Charity for Schools', registered on 30 January 1964, whose governing document is the scheme of 19 January 1976, and whose objects are to advance the education of persons under the age of twenty-five who are (or have a parent) resident in the County of North Yorkshire, and who are in need of financial assistance.
Both these other charities are outside the scope of this study.

©The Trustees of the Lady Hewley Charity

Published by The Lady Hewley Trust, 2005

ISBN: 978 0 9551588 0 3

A catalogue record for this book is available from the British Library.

Printed by Elanders Hindson, North Tyneside.

Prologue

THE DUTY OF A TRUSTEE is a hard one. The duty of a chairman is made more complex still by a perhaps unwritten duty towards the other Trustees. Their best judgements must be drawn out. The best appraisal of the imminent changes in the Trust's environment – political, legal, commercial, beneficiary – must be made. To help to lead the Trustees is a great responsibility, but it is a great honour to be allowed to discharge that duty.

All the fellow-Trustees and chairmen who preceded us must have felt the same. They took many opportunities to manage the investments entrusted to them (and the saga of iron-working on Teesside is part of our Trust's history). They developed their charitable activities and protected the Trust from what we might today call an illegal take-over (the creation of the Charity Commission was at least in part the result of the Trust's persistence in the highest courts of the land).

Today, we look forward with careful optimism to continue meeting the obligations laid upon us by our Founder, Lady Sarah Hewley. We shall conscientiously manage her – and our – investments and respect her intentions though in a very different context from when she was alive. The Trust has shown that it can outlive and survive change. But we must move ahead and grasp those opportunities that allow us to respond to changing needs.

My hope is that you will enjoy this, the first detailed and authoritative history of the Trust. We are most grateful to Richard Potts for his extensive research and to Anna Flowers for its excellent design.

John Lumsden, Chairman, The Lady Hewley Trust

WHILST THE OVERALL RESPONSIBILITY for the Almshouses lies with the Grand Trustees, they are assisted by a group of Sub-Trustees who all live in York, where the Almshouses are situated. This is very much a mutual arrangement, each group keeping in close touch with the other, so that a seamless level of supervision and support can be given to the running of the Houses and the welfare of the residents.

The Sub-Trustees are drawn from the memberships of the City Centre Baptist and United Reformed (a union of two previously Congregational and Presbyterian) churches. They are led by the Ministers of the two congregations, with five other members, one of whom acts as Clerk and one as Treasurer.

The Sub-Trustees perform a vital role (particularly fulfilled by the

Clerk) by being able to have close contacts with the residents, assisted in this by the Resident Supervisor. They are responsible at the outset for handling all applications from prospective residents and, by personal interview, to ensure as far as is possible, that the applicants fulfil the conditions of eligibility as originally indicated by Lady Hewley (subsequently amended by the Charity Commissioners) and that they will fit into the community of existing residents in a harmonious manner. Living in what is, in effect, a small community brings with it the benefit of mutual support – and also some of the frictions of daily life! When advanced years bring inevitable health problems, residents are often able to continue in their homes with the help of the Statutory Bodies. The existence of the Sub-Trustees means that in all these matters the changing needs of the residents are appreciated and, where appropriate, guidance is given or action taken.

As with any dwelling, repairs and renewals frequently require attention, and the property needs of individual residents sometimes change. The Sub-Trustees are charged with the general oversight of this, and now have the expert involvement of the Property Manager of the York Conservation Trust, who regularly visits the properties, instigates maintenance work and reports directly to the Grand Trustees on any significant matters. The Grand Trustees take a lively interest in all aspects of the running of the Almshouses and at their half-yearly meetings reports are given and information exchanged, and every two years the properties are visited by the group as a whole. Thus it can be seen that by a close working together of Grand and Sub-Trustees, effectively knitted together over the years, the wish of Lady Hewley to be of help in providing a good standard of home and pleasant living conditions to those who need it, is ensured and still maintained after 300 years.

Mrs Cathy Halliday, Clerk to the Sub-Trustees

IN 1710 SARAH HEWLEY, a Yorkshirewoman of means and title, left a fortune in trust for 'poor and godly preachers of Christ's Holy Gospel'. Her trust, like her Ladyship, was Presbyterian but by the nineteenth century her Trustees had become Unitarian. That transition was gradual. It was natural without being inevitable and it had many parallels. It also aroused the critical attention of legally-minded and alert evangelicals, amongst them George Hadfield, a Manchester solicitor and Congregationalist. Issues like this, indeed, launched him on a long political career and if at

Westminster Hadfield never got beyond the back benches he nonetheless became a powerful fixture as one of Sheffield's Liberal MPs. As for the Hewley case, that was resolved in 1842, after twelve years of litigation, when the House of Lords gave judgement against the Trustees. Their Lordships' reasoning was clear: a Trust could not be held for any purpose which was illegal when that Trust was established, and in 1710 Unitarianism had been illegal. The implications were encouraging for historically-minded Congregationalists but alarming for Victorian Unitarians who now feared for their title to the chapels in which they worshipped. Developing the attractive, if specious, Open Trust theory (that some Trusts were deliberately left open by their founders to allow for changing circumstances) they promoted the Dissenters' Chapels Bill which passed into law in 1844. Unitarian chapels were saved, but the Hewley Charity celebrated here by Richard Potts had been set fair on its present course, and justice was somehow done to all parties.

The issues at stake were important. For a certain sort of mind they were compelling. The processes set in train were often unedifying. Given the social, religious, and political passions of the 1830s and 1840s, they were probably bound to happen. Lady Hewley and her charities have their place as much in the nineteenth-century as in late seventeenth- and early eighteenth-century history. In fact their significance is greater than that of a test case in charity law. It reminds us of the formative role of religion in English life, of the importance of the provinces (in this case York and its leading citizens), of the part played by charitable bequests in the shaping of social attitudes and in enlarging the boundaries of what people believed to be possible, of the place of law in chapel affairs, and of the interaction of all these factors with politics. The story of the Lady Hewley Trust is that of the evolution of English society and of the particular role of dissent in testing the weave and colouring the design of the social fabric.

Clyde Binfield, Professor Emeritus in History, University of Sheffield,
and President of the United Reformed Church History Society.

SARAH LADY HEWLEY'S GENEROSITY has had a long and benevolent effect. Amongst other charitable aims, the Lady Hewley Trust has sought to provide support for poor ministers – especially those for whom either government support or formal pension schemes has been insufficient. It has also, on occasion, taken the opportunity to help individual churches or synods in their ministries to what Lady Sarah referred to as 'poor places'. That concern reminds us of our present responsibilities to those who, for whatever reason, have fallen into hardship and poverty. That, lest we forget, is how Jesus promises to distinguish the sheep from the goats. This history is therefore to be welcomed, not only as a much-needed account of a singular charity, but also as a reminder of the priorities of the people of God.

The Revd. Dr. David Cornick, General Secretary, United Reformed Church

THE LADY HEWLEY TRUST has long been respected for its support to the Dissenters of Northern England. In her will, Lady Hewley sought to bring financial relief to 'godly persons in distress' and her wishes have been faithfully carried out by her Trustees for three centuries. The Trust today continues to assist those in financial need, bringing relief to widows, orphans and those training for the ministry. This assistance is as important today as it has ever been. I commend this history of the Trust and hope that the valuable work of the Hewley Trust may continue for many years to come.

The Revd. Christopher Damp, Congregational minister, London

THE LADY HEWLEY TRUST has a long and honourable history among the Dissenters of the North of England. We celebrate 300 years of positive work by the Trust. As a young first-generation Baptist experiencing the call to Christian ministry and being set aside by my church, I benefited by grants from the Trust enabling me to study at the Northern Baptist College. I represent many young people assisted in this way and I am delighted to commend this history to you as we rejoice in the munificence of Lady Hewley which has enabled the forming of People for Christian Ministry.

The Revd. Keith G Jones, Rector, International Baptist Theological Seminary, Prague, Czech Republic, and former Deputy General Secretary of the Baptist Union

THERE ARE TWO REASONS for those of us engaged in ministerial education to welcome this history of the Lady Hewley Trust. The first is that denominational history is little understood today and often dismissed as irrelevant. The matters which divided Christians in the past have a habit of resurfacing under new guises in every generation. Today's students need to understand that balance between the principles of charity and justice which are exemplified in the personal history of Lady Hewley and in the subsequent history of contention over her charity. The second is that in celebrating the history of the Trust the accumulated generosity of the benefactor to generations of students is commemorated. Each year I see at first hand the difference that a grant can make to the finances of students for ministry. Most of them today are mature people who have given up well-paid jobs to come into the service of the Church, and who still have family obligations competing for the limited financial support which is available to them. To be given a grant wholly committed to study is to be given a kind of freedom, wholly in the spirit of the foundress. Our thanks are due to the current Trustees, who not only continue the traditions of the Trust but give up their time voluntarily to do so. On behalf of today's beneficiaries I am glad to record our gratitude and commend this history.

The Revd. Professor Stephen Orchard, Principal, Westminster College,
Cambridge

The Grand Trustees, Lady Hewley Charity, in 2004.
Left to right: Stephen Gorton, Philip Thake, John Lumsden (Chairman), Gordon Simmonds, Muriel Proven, Bryan Herbert, Dr. James Porteous.

Author's acknowledgments

The Grand Trustees, Sub-Trustees and Officers of the Hewley Trust. Alan Goldfinch, former Clerk to the Sub-Trustees. The Revd. John Durell. The Revd. Professor Stephen Orchard and Mrs Margaret Thompson, Reformed Studies Centre, Westminster College, Cambridge. Mrs Jennifer Thorp, formerly archivist, Regent's Park College, Oxford. The Revd. Margaret Kirk & Mr Alfred Fletcher, St. Saviourgate Unitarian church, York.

The staffs of North Yorkshire County Council Record Office, Northallerton; the Borthwick Institute of Historical Research, University of York; York City Archives; Tyne and Wear Archives, Newcastle upon Tyne; Reference and Local Studies Sections, Central Library, Newcastle upon Tyne; York City Reference Library; Beverley Shaw and the Archaeological Resource Centre (ARC), St. Saviour's church, York; York Minster Archives; Cambridge University Library; State Library of Western Australia, Perth; Northern College, Manchester; Dorman Long Technology.

Ian Drake, YAYAs. Mrs Elizabeth Ellis, manager, Electoral & Civic Services, and Richard Pollitt, Business & Collections manager, Mansion House, both York City Council.

Anna, Catherine & Tony Flowers, Vanessa Histon, Tim Addison, Beth Pilley, Darren & Rachel Pedley; Jean, David & Fiona Potts.

(It should be added that any errors or infelicities are mine! RP).

A note on dating

This commemorative history might be thought to be late in making its appearance as Lady Hewley is said to have created her Trust in 1704. However, prior to 1752 this country observed Old Style (Julian) dating, with each calendar year starting on 25 March and running through to 24 March of the following year. In 1752 Britain changed over to our present and more accurate New Style (Gregorian) system, falling into line with most of Europe. New Style dating was first introduced by Catholic countries from 1582 and then gradually adopted over the years by Protestant states. Because of the chronological disparity between England, Scotland and the continent in the years leading up to the changeover in 1752, the period between 1 January and 24 March increasingly came to be expressed in England and Wales in both Old and New Style terms, for example, 13 January 1704/5 (*i.e.* 13 January 1705 and the date of Lady Hewley's first Foundation deed). Dates prior to 1752 in the text are all rendered in New Style.

Contents

Illustrations

Colour illustrations

Background

1 Dissent and Nonconformity

The Elizabethan Settlement establishing the Church of England sought to be inclusive, but alienated both Roman Catholics and, progressively, those who preferred a simpler form of worship, who became the 'Separatist' or Dissenting element. There was persecution of both extremes when they failed to conform, and some Catholics and Puritans lost their lives for their beliefs or fled to the continent.

By the middle of the seventeenth century, there were four main Dissenting bodies: Baptists, Independents (later known as Congregationalists), Presbyterians, and the Society of Friends (Quakers). The last were the most radical in their theology and quickly became a distinct group primarily because of their continued resistance to the State on matters of conscience, for which they suffered most. The other three groups were broadly Calvinist in theology, with the Baptists split between the more numerous Particular Baptists (orthodox Calvinists who believed any possibility of redemption was reserved for the predestined or 'elect') and General Baptists (who were Arminian, maintaining that salvation was 'general', i.e. open to everyone, if they cared to avail themselves of it).

Both Independents and Baptists, while differing over infant and adult baptism, held that the essential unit was the local congregation of believers, autonomous in its own right and not subject to higher ecclesiastical authority. The Presbyterians, on the other hand, recognised the importance of the individual congregation but regarded this as the lowest rung of a ladder of 'courts'. Each group of Presbyterian meeting-houses, often geographically scattered, was organised into a 'Presbytery' governing its

Maling's Rigg Chapel, the interior of a typical Presbyterian meeting house.

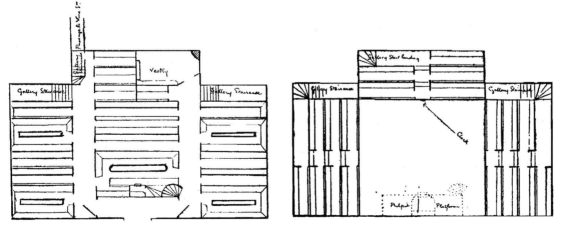

constituent congregations, attended by ministers (and later by lay representatives as well); each Presbytery was represented at an annual national Assembly, where the denomination's major decisions were made.[1]

After the Civil War, when first Presbyterians and then, under Oliver Cromwell, Independents, were in the ascendant, Dissent ruled. When Charles II returned in 1660, the Independents feared there would be a Royalist and High Church backlash which would affect them adversely. Many Presbyterians however thought there would be a new Established Church incorporating elements of Presbyterian authority and organisation. The Independents were the more realistic, for the new Government and its supporters in the Restoration Parliament were determined to put the clock back to pre-Civil War monarchist times, suppress Puritan rule and belief, and make everyone conform to an unchanged, unswerving, Church of England. It was with this in mind that the Restoration Parliament passed a series of punitive Acts collectively known as the Clarendon Code. Fortunately for Dissenters and the nation as a whole, these statutes were only patchily enforced. The Corporation Act (1661) compelled all members of Corporations to take Communion according to Anglican rites and swear an oath not to bear arms against the Crown. The Act of Uniformity (1662) forced all clergy in England and Wales to use the Book of Common Prayer and be ordained by a bishop, and all schoolmasters to be licensed by a bishop before they could teach.

Together with those who resigned at the time of the Restoration, about 2000 ministers in all (Independents, Presbyterians and Baptists) were ejected as a result of the Act of Uniformity, while about 11,000 remained in their parishes. The Conventicle Act (1664) forbade attendance at religious services other than those of the Church of England, with fines for first and second offences and transportation for a third.[2]

In 1665 the Great Plague, in London and beyond, resulted in many inhabitants, including clergy, fleeing the capital and churches being closed 'when people were in a ... disposition to profit by good sermons; whereupon some ... Nonconformists went into the empty pulpits, and preached with great freedom, reflecting on the vices of the court and the severities ... they ... had been made to suffer ...'[3] The Five-Mile Act (1665) forbade ministers and schoolmasters to come within five miles of any town without an undertaking to refrain from trying to alter Church or State. The Clarendon Code was draconian legislation and severely inhibited Dissenters, although they continued to meet, albeit illegally: '[Which] severity, in a time of war and public calamity … drew hard censures on the promoters … raised a compassion for the recusants, and occasioned many plentiful contributions for the relief of their necessities'.[4]

In 1672 Charles II, seeking to help Catholics (including his brother, later James II), issued a Declaration of Indulgence, permitting limited religious liberty under licence to both Catholics and Dissenters. Parliament reacted to the proclamation in fury, forced the king to change his mind, and passed the Test Act in 1673, compelling everyone holding public office to repudiate Roman Catholic doctrines and conform to Anglican doctrine; this also had severe implications for Dissenters. The Test and Corporation Acts were not repealed until 1828, just before the Catholic Emancipation Act was passed. The Tory stance held sway for many years, although in 1689 the Toleration Act, passed within a year of William & Mary's accession, allowed Protestant Dissenting congregations to build their own meeting-houses and worship freely, subject to certain conditions. As a result, the Dissenters in York were able to erect their meeting house in St. Saviourgate, shortly before Sarah Hewley founded her Almshouses. However, by the time she settled estates on her first Trustees, Queen Anne had come to the throne and it was the era of the vicar of Bray and Dr Sachaverell's hysterical sermons against Dissenters, and a period when Parliamentary Bills were introduced in the hope of suppressing the Dissenters still further.

The Independents and the Presbyterians were on terms 'of friendly intimacy' and attempts were made in the 1690s to bring about closer co-operation with the 'Happy Union', which started in London and soon fanned out into the Provinces, including the north. Some of those later associated with the Hewley Trust, such as Richard Stretton, were involved in this initiative. Unfortunately, however, this first attempt to work together proved abortive. In the 1730s further efforts were made to collaborate, this time also involving Baptist congregations.[5]

In the early eighteenth century Daniel Defoe, himself educated in a Dissenting Academy, implausibly reckoned that the total number of Dissenters in England exceeded two million people. The Government estimate in 1689 was 111,000 but this was probably an attempt to make the Toleration Act more acceptable to Royalists. The correct figure lies somewhere between the two, but it is clear that in the period between the Restoration and 1689 there was a substantial growth in Dissenting numbers despite the persecution suffered during that time.[6]

During the eighteenth century, Unitarianism (Arianism or Socinianism), whose origins can be traced back in this country to the sixteenth century, emerged as a major Dissenting force for civil and religious freedoms and saw its most rapid growth when Dr Joseph Priestley (a Hewley beneficiary) was one of its main proponents. It was a liberal and rational faith and as such did not have the same impact or motivating force as the Evangelical Gospel.

In 1719 Presbyterian congregations comprised about two-thirds of Dissenting numbers, but thereafter the denomination suffered a steep decline. After the contentious vote that year at the Salters' Hall conference, narrowly favouring or at least tolerating holders of Arian doctrines, Trinitarian doctrines increasingly vanished from Presbyterian pulpits. While some Presbyterian churches became Independent, many decayed and others closed. However, Presbyterianism remained strong in Scotland, with an influence extending southwards into Cumbria and Northumbria.[7]

The General Baptists had probably never been entirely free of Arianism, but Independents and Particular Baptists had adhered steadfastly to a strict Calvinist creed. Although the Toleration Act of 1689 specifically excluded Roman Catholics and those of non-Trinitarian persuasion, the burgeoning of the Unitarians saw them become a strong and virtually separate denomination, achieving legal status in 1813. The new movement was strengthened by former members of the Church of England, notably its eventual leader, Theophilus Lindsey, the former vicar of Catterick, who became minister of the flourishing Essex Street congregation in London. It would appear that when the minister of a meeting-house became Unitarian, his congregation tended to follow, and in due course nominated a successor from Unitarian ranks, thereby perpetuating the loss to the original denomination of both people and buildings. When part of the congregation wished to remain orthodox, those members were obliged to leave and found a new meeting-house elsewhere in the locality, usually organised along Independent lines.[8]

Those who became Unitarians seem to have been drawn mainly from the ranks of the more educated and intellectual Presbyterians and Old General Baptists.[9] The Presbyterians were further weakened as their notions of church government became increasingly harder to achieve and consequently many of their congregations became Independent. In addition, the exclusion of Dissenters from the two universities led to a decline in the supply of educated ministers; it was to meet this need that

Dissenting Academies, such as Dr. Philip Doddridge's famous college at Northampton, came into being to provide an adequately-informed and trained ministry. These Academies in certain respects, and partly through their choice of new subjects, offered a superior standard of education to that available elsewhere. The Unitarian Dissenting Academies, such as Hackney and Warrington (where Priestley, and later another chemist, Dalton, taught) were also notable centres of learning as well as of religious and social enlightenment.[10] The Warrington Academy later moved to Manchester and then York, where its principal was the Revd. Charles Wellbeloved, the minister of St. Saviourgate chapel and a Hewley Sub-Trustee.

In 1715 there were said to be 59 Presbyterian congregations in Yorkshire alone, including two or three Independent causes with Presbyterian sympathies. By 1730 this number had shrunk to about 40 and as the century progressed it diminished still further, mostly in rural rather than urban areas. By 1834 the Presbyterians had only about 20 churches remaining in Yorkshire.[11]

The eighteenth century also saw the success of John and Charles Wesley's extensive travels, and the rapid growth of Wesleyan Methodists and General Baptists of the New Connexion (both Arminian), as well as the Countess of Huntingdon's Connexion (Calvinist) and the Calvinistic Methodists in Wales. All of these experienced spiritual revivals and broke with many of the practices of older denominations (both Anglican and Dissenting) taking their message to a hungry people (often in new industrial areas where there was no church or meeting-house). The energy and progressive growth of the Evangelical Revival eventually led to a renaissance of Old Dissent, especially for Baptists and Independents, who displayed a parallel revival of mission. The Calvinists who rejected evangelism as pointless (believing God had already selected those to be saved) now found their views replaced by more generous and acceptable doctrines of the extent of God's love. It was as a consequence of this change that the first foreign missions organisation, the Baptist Missionary Society, was founded by William Carey in 1792. One of the long-term effects of the revival was denominational resurgence, including the Presbyterians later in the nineteenth century.[12]

The Methodists and the Quakers were both well-organised and strictly controlled, but the Independents and Baptists (by conviction) and the Presbyterians (by geography) remained loose in organisation. As the nineteenth century dawned, the Baptists and Independents recognised the need for individual congregations to work more closely together, support the ordained ministry, foster evangelistic effort, and co-ordinate publications development. To achieve this, they began to organise into more formal county unions, governed on a federal basis, with the first attempts at a national structure.[13] The Unitarians also sought to strengthen their organisation through the creation of 'Societies' or important committees.

Following the Reform Act in 1832, there were many Dissenting electors. No less a person than the Duke of Wellington wrote: ' ... a new democratic influence has been introduced into elections, the copy-holders and free-holders and lease-holders residing in towns which do not themselves return members to Parliament. These are all dissenters from the Church, are everywhere a formidably active party against the aristocratic influence of the Landed Gentry. But this is not all. There are dissenters in every village in the country; they are the blacksmith, the carpenter, the mason etc ...'[14]

The religious census of 1851 showed that, out of a total population of almost 18 million in England and Wales, only $7^{1/4}$ million attended any form of public worship, yet the Protestant Dissenting churches alone had sufficient accommodation for 26% of the population. The approximate estimated attendance was: Church of England $3^{1/4}$ million; Methodist (all branches save Calvinist) about 1,400,000; Independents (or Congregationalists) 800,000; Baptists (all branches) 600,000; Calvinistic Methodist (Welsh, Countess of Huntingdon's Connection) 180,000; Scottish Presbyterians (all branches) 60,000; Unitarians 37,000; Society of Friends 18,000; Moravian 7000. In the light of modern analysis of the 1851 census, a significant conclusion may be drawn: 'there were few cloth caps in the churches and chapels'.[15]

2 York

The Romans came to York in AD71, and stayed for approximately 340 years. Under them the place became a key military settlement in the occupation of Britain, the capital of their northern English province, and a centre of importance in the Roman Empire, visited by several emperors. It was from York that the emperor Constantine the Great went to Rome and converted the Roman Empire to Christianity. The Romans were followed by the Saxons, whose king became a Christian in 627 and was baptised in the small wooden church which became the first Minster. In 876 York was captured by the Danes and under them became a great trading

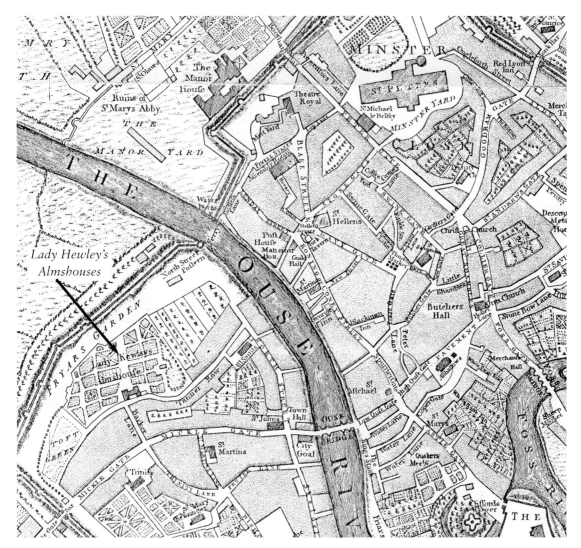

Lady Hewley's
Almshouses

*Thomas Joffrey's
plan of York,
1775. The
almshouses are
bottom left.
(York Reference
Library.)*

centre. A devastating fire in 1069 virtually destroyed York but provided the
Normans, who recognised its strategic importance, with the opportunity
to build a greater city, complete with new defences and city walls.[16]

In medieval times York had the second largest population in the country and became the capital for the King's Council in the North (which
continued until 1641). The city possessed churches and craft guilds, its
monasteries and religious schools flourished, and it was the political, religious and commercial centre of northern England.[17] The move of the
wool trade away from the city and the dissolution of the monasteries then
reduced York to a long period of poverty and stagnation.[18] By the later
seventeenth century, it was clear the city was not well-affected to policies

pursued by the country's rulers: the 'factious party' in the city was led by its Members of Parliament, Sir Henry Thompson and Sir John Hewley, supported by all but two aldermen, and even by the Minster clergy. The city's anti-monarchical stance and the frigid reception shown to the Duke of York when he visited in 1679, offended Charles II, as did its choice of MPs and its petition for the recall of Parliament. When the Duke became James II in 1685, he took steps to purge the corporation, especially as the city had failed to make an expected address in favour of his ecclesiastical policy (in favour of Roman Catholicism) but his unpopularity in the country soon led to York's charter being restored. A period of calm ensued after 1688 with the accession of William and Mary.[19]

During the seventeenth century there was much artistic and intellectual activity in York. Theologians, teachers and lawyers had long been established in the city, and by 1700 physicians and surgeons formed another important professional group, including Martin Lister (1638-1712), a prominent doctor, antiquary and naturalist; another medical practitioner was Lady Hewley's chaplain and one of her first Trustees, Thomas Colton, described as 'M.D.'[20] at her funeral service and as 'Doctor of Physic'[21] in several other documents. Literary interests were stimulated by the presence of the king's printer in York from 1642 to 1644, and later by Thomas Broad whose press produced Parliamentary orders and Puritan tracts. In 1660, the printing trade was quite exceptionally authorised to continue, the only other permitted centres at the time being London, Cambridge and Oxford. Later still, John White of York was appointed royal printer for the northern counties, as a reward for printing William of Orange's 'Declaration' in 1688. Amongst craftsmen, plasterers from York travelled as far as Edinburgh castle to decorate the king's lodgings and silversmiths made intricate domestic pieces as well as chalices for churches throughout the north. The country gentry, the Hewleys amongst them, provided patronage to eminent local painters, engravers, woodcarvers, sculptors and glass-painters.[22]

In the early eighteenth century the city enjoyed a minor revival and, as it was still a major staging post on the coach roads, York became a fashionable resort, and the residential centre for many county families attending race meetings, theatres, assemblies and social gatherings. York was by this time not one of the more populous cities and towns; London, Bristol, Manchester, Liverpool, Birmingham, Norwich and Leeds were all much larger. Much of the medieval architecture was removed during this period, to be replaced by fine Georgian buildings, as in St. Saviourgate. Daniel Defoe, himself once a student at the famous Newington Green Dissenting Academy, described York around 1725 thus:

'there is ... abundance of good families live here, for the sake of the good company and cheap living; a man converses here with all the world as effectually as at London; the keeping up assemblies among the younger gentry was first set up here ... No city in England is better furnished with provisions of every kind, nor any so cheap, in proportion to the goodness of things; the river being so navigable, and so near the sea, the merchants here trade directly to what part of the world they will; for ships of any burthen come up within thirty mile of the city, and small craft from sixty to eighty ton, and under, come up to the very city. With these they carry on a considerable trade; they import their own wines from France and Portugal, and likewise their own deals and timber from Norway; and indeed what they please almost from where they please; they did also bring their own coals from Newcastle and Sunderland, but now have them down the Aire and Calder from Wakefield, and from Leeds ... The old walls are standing, and the gates and posterns; but the old additional works which were cast up in the late rebellion, are slighted; so that York is not now as defensible as it was then ... York ... is a spacious city ... the buildings are not close and thronged as at Bristol, or as at Durham ... But as York is full of gentry and persons of distinction ... and have houses proportioned to their quality; and this makes the city so far extended on both sides the river. It is also very magnificent ...' [23]

In the nineteenth century the city was 'inhabited almost entirely by shopkeepers' and played second fiddle to many younger and less noted towns[24] until its economy was massively reborn, largely through the efforts of the entrepreneur, George Hudson, who made York a great railway centre and helped to generate an industrial boom, eventually attracting major firms such as Terrys and Rowntrees.[25]

George VI is said to have remarked: 'the history of York is the history of England'.[26]

Sir John and Lady Sarah Hewley

Although it is said that the Hewleys were a Cheshire family,[27] what is more certain is that John Hewley's grandfather accompanied his employer, the quarrelsome Cumbrian Edwin Sandys (successively Bishop of Worcester and then London) back north in 1576 when he was translated to the Archbishopric of York.[28] For his services the grandfather was given the manor of Wistow, near Cawood on the Ouse near Selby, which the family continued to hold over several generations. It was here that John was born in 1619.[29] At the relatively young age of about twenty, he was entered at Gray's Inn on 4 February 1639 to read for the Bar.[30] He suspended his legal studies to play an active part in the Parliamentary struggle against the Crown, and there is a tradition that he fought as a volunteer in 1644 in Cromwell's victorious detachment at the battle of Marston Moor, six miles west of York, resulting in the capture of the city.[31]

By the time of the Commonwealth, John Hewley seems to have been doing well in his chosen profession, and it was probably around 1649 that John married Sarah Woolrich, and they then settled in York where they became members of the Revd. Edward Bowles' congregation.[32] It was while studying law in London that John Hewley is said to have met Sarah, 'the little lady who was to become more famous than he'. It seems likely that John was an associate and perhaps a protégé of Robert Woolrich (Wolrych, Wolrich, Wolridge, Ulrich), a prominent Ipswich lawyer and Gray's Inn barrister, and a substantial landowner in Yorkshire, and his wife Sarah.[33] Robert's wife's maiden name was Mott, and she was the widow of a Mr Tichborne (possibly a member of the Tichborne family of Tichborne, Hampshire) inheriting his considerable fortune, which on her remarriage passed into the hands of Robert. Their only daughter, also baptised Sarah, was born in 1627 and after her mother's death she became heiress to her father's substantial wealth.[34] Sarah's father, Robert, would not have permitted his only child to marry a man without excellent character, some money and splendid prospects (but perhaps being a girl of considerable wealth and spirit, she was made a ward of the Chancery court; nevertheless, family tradition asserted that, the Lord Chancellor not looking with favour on the young lawyer's suit, Sarah and John decided to elope, she insisting on sitting in front of him on their horse, so it could never be suggested that he abducted her!)[35] By his marriage, John

Sir John and Lady Sarah Hewley, painted by an unknown artist, probably around 1660.

was guaranteed future wealth and status, enhanced on the death of Robert in 1661.[36]

The Hewleys' marriage was characterised by a religious and professional compatibility linked to a strong sense of public duty, with both holding strong puritan convictions. Oliver Heywood, the famous Nonconformist divine and a close family friend, revealed in his diary 'glimpses of a tranquil, well-regulated household, where serious talk flowed freely, godly men, the poor and the persecuted were ever welcome, and good fare was plentiful for all'. During his frequent visits to York he often stayed with the Hewleys, enjoyed their generous hospitality, and worshipped with them.[37] John and Sarah's like-mindedness and unity facilitated their prominent role in public affairs from the 1650's. The couple were by all accounts devoted to each other, and blessed with a long, happy and mutually supportive marriage although, sadly, both their sons, Wolrych and John, 'barely survived babyhood'.[38] The two infants are said to have been buried at St. Martin's, Coney Street, York, which may indicate that the Hewleys lived in that part of the city before moving to St.

Saviourgate.[39] It would seem that following the loss of their children, the couple determined to help relatives and extended family such as Hewley Baines, Thomas Woolrich and Mercy Mott, but resolved to devote the bulk of their great wealth to charitable and benevolent purposes.[40]

John and Sarah's lives extended over the traumatic events of the Civil War Commonwealth and Protectorate, the Restoration and the difficult period through to the Glorious Revolution of 1688 and beyond. They watched a variety of parties and sects rise and fall, and during their lifetimes experienced considerable change, reaction, persecution, panic, pestilence and war, the passing of regimes and the start of new eras, and the re-emergence of England as a European power.[41] Yet despite passing through all these changing scenes of life, John and Sarah seem to have remained for the most part on very good terms with their neighbours who, between them, held a variety of political and religious opinions.[42] Although grounded in the Presbyterianism typified by the likes of Richard Baxter and Edward Bowles, neither of the Hewleys were extreme in their views. Sir John encouraged the biblical commentator Matthew Poole, the constant advocate of a comprehensive broad Church, and his name appears in the list of those who assisted in the writing and printing of the celebrated *Synopsis*. The couple maintained connections with the educator, industrialist and charity pioneer, Samuel Hartlib, and his circle, while their literary contacts included the antiquary Sir William Dugdale, the influential public servant and political historian John Rushworth, and the poet and satirist Andrew Marvell, the last two perhaps having met the Hewleys at Sir Thomas Fairfax's home at Nun Appleton when respectively secretary to the general and tutor to his daughter Mary.[43] The Hewleys are also said to have been on good terms with the conscientious Archbishop of York, John Sharp, and his wife.[44]

John first came to significant public notice in York in 1656 when he was employed by the Corporation to manage the purchase of the Dean and Chapter jurisdiction, as directed by Parliament, although he had been intermittently active in county affairs since 1646.[45] During Commonwealth times, he was Recorder of Doncaster but soon resigned this post because of the growing success of his practice at the Bar. However, he became Recorder of Pontefract and represented that Borough with distinction in the House of Commons, 1658-1660.[46] At the Restoration he was automatically excluded from public office, but was knighted on 30 June 1663 for his services in helping to bring back the monarchy. Charles II's court and government was not however a congenial environment for a sober-minded gentleman intent on preserving his nonconformist and liberal connections.[47] Nevertheless, Sir John still possessed parliamentary ambitions and during the next fifteen or so years unsuccessfully contested a number of Yorkshire seats. In 1679 he fought his home seat of York mainly on an Exclusion ticket (to prevent the Catholic Duke of York eventually succeeding to the throne) in the Whig interest; this time he was elected, enabling him to re-enter the Commons, where, during the three Exclusion Parliaments to 1681, he proved to be an extraordinarily-active Member, involved in three out of every four committees. As well as supporting moves to protect the country from 'popery', he also backed Bills designed to prevent drunkenness, swearing and Sabbath breaking.[48] After this busy but short stint as a Member, he had little to do with national politics. Notwithstanding this, when William & Mary came to the throne, he accepted two Government posts in Yorkshire (Commissioner of Aids and Receiver of the Poll) although he was by then almost 70 years of age.[49]

John Hewley's role as a distinguished advocate, politician, local administrator, magistrate, and freeman of York has probably been underestimated.[50] Although frequently mentioned in the Journals of the House of Commons he has come down to us mostly as the husband of his munificent wife. He emerges as a typical eighteenth-century gentleman, a founder of modern England, intent on playing his part on the national and local scene. In one respect, however, he was different from his contemporaries, for whom hereditary wealth and position usually played a major part in the careers and unions of local magnates; his father seems to have been too insignificant a local squire to hope to compete in their league.[51] Sir John was a self-made man who succeeded at his chosen profession, was conscientious in his dealings with others, and was fortunate enough to fall in love with a helpmate who was able to add substantially to the money he was earning at the Bar, enabling both of them to help others less fortunate than themselves. John and Sarah subscribed to many good causes, including money for the poor of Naburn parish[52] and silver and furnishings for the Corporation of York, including a fine ornamented wooden fireplace still resplendent in Committee Room 1 in the Guildhall.[53]

Although John Hewley emanated from Wistow, it does not seem the couple ever lived there.[54] In Commonwealth times, John began, like many another seventeenth-century gentleman, to consolidate his position by

Bell Hall, Naburn, York, from a photograph in Country Life, 1922.

buying up land.[55] In 1650 he bought Newby Manor, while through his marriage he was to acquire large though scattered pockets of land throughout Yorkshire.[56] In 1654 he purchased land at Naburn, four miles south of York, and around 1662 bought the Bell estate there, with another 80 acres the following year.[57] This purchase may have come about as a result of John and Sarah selling off lands in Kent and Sussex inherited after Robert Woolrich's death in 1661.[58] In 1680 John and Sarah had Richard Bell's century-old house at Naburn demolished and Bell Hall built on its site to serve as their principal residence.

Bell Hall still stands and is a fine example of a seventeenth-century brick-built house, with stone dressings. It has two main storeys, but also a basement, attics and dormers. Five bays long and three deep, the house has imposing stepped entrances on the south and west sides. It is said to contain a painted room of seventeenth-century date and many seventeenth-century fittings, including a re-set fireplace and decorated wooden panelling, possibly the work of Huguenot refugees (and behind which Sir John and Dame Sarah are reputed to have hidden religious refugees from France and Holland as well as English Dissenters, when sheltering them from discovery and prosecution). The architect is said to have taken the precaution of incorporating into his design a 'priest's hole' or emergency hiding place, but this may refer to the area behind the wooden panelling. The Hewleys used the large attic at the top of the house as a private chapel, where they, their servants and guests, would have worshipped in comparative safety, ministered to by Dissenting ministers despite the restrictions of the Clarendon Code; after Sir John's death, Dame Sarah had the chapel heavily draped in black for many years. Originally, there was a roof-top balustrade and a lantern tower; a service wing erected in the nineteenth century was also later removed.[59]

It is through the protection that Sir John and Dame Sarah gave to the nonconformists of northern England that they particularly deserve to be remembered. The Hewleys were amongst a small number of elite families who helped the ejected ministers of 1660-1662, and their dependents; these benefactors included the Earls of Anglesea and Denbigh, the Countess Dowager of Clare, the Countesses of Exeter and Manchester, and the Lords Wharton, Holles and Delamere; 'Lord Wharton and Lady Hewley in particular [gave] generous financial support to Presbyterian ministers and congregations'.[60]

Despite Charles II's initial overtures to the Dissenters in 1660, the revitalised Tory (Royalist) Party soon prevailed on the new king to introduce the harsh measures known as the Clarendon Code, discriminating against those unwilling to adhere to the doctrine and teaching of the Church of England, affecting both Catholics and Dissenters, many of them the virtual controllers of the country's wealth, and forcing them into separatist and potentially dangerous factions. These divisions should have weakened the English political and commercial fabric fatally, but the danger was averted by men and women like Sir John and Lady Sarah Hewley, who, in the midst of repression and persecution, built up strong nonconformist networks which extended throughout the country. Among country gentlemen Presbyterian and Independent doctrines had already gained a firm hold, especially in the north, and these could not easily be eradicated. It was this class which bore the weight of local administration, acting as liaison officers between central government and the population at large, interpreting the law with much tact and mercy, softening the rigidity of royal edicts and the Westminster legislature.[61] To help in this process, men such as the Presbyterian Sir John were officially Anglican and 'occasional conformists' attending the local parish church, but Dissenters by inclination and conviction, whose first loyalty was to their meeting-houses. By this ambiguous behaviour such men, and their families, were able to serve the cause of Dissent in many branches of public life, while escaping overt persecution.[62]

Fortunately, for late-seventeenth and early-eighteenth century Dissenters, the cost of building meeting houses and paying ministers was partially offset by their rising prosperity, despite the privations caused by discriminatory legislation.[63] Fortunately, too, Sir John and Lady Sarah were amongst the most active and generous patrons of Nonconformity, mostly in York and Yorkshire.[64] As a woman, Dame Sarah was unable to hold public office, but that did not prevent her being as influential as her politically-active husband.[65] She has been described as 'the first and most powerful patron of Nonconformist meetings in York after the Restoration',[66] 'a mother in Israel to the Presbyterian Church'[67] and 'an eminently pious and benevolent woman [who] was a chief supporter of the Presbyterians in the north of England. Her personal charity to ministers seemed to know no limit'.[68] Dissenting ministers were always welcome to stay at either of their two houses, where a small congregation was able to gather in the private chapel, with services conducted by the Hewleys' domestic chaplain. The Hewleys not only 'maintained an elegant hospitality, receiving the families of chief account in the North of England' but were also at the centre of religious and legal circles which had direct political significance, as demonstrated during the Exclusion Crisis (1679-1681), when Yorkshire Nonconformists assembled to pray in the homes of the Dissenting leaders in York before voting for the Whig platform at the shire elections at York castle.[69] When Oliver Heywood and Richard Frankland discussed the foundation of a school, the Hewley's domestic chaplain since 1682, Timothy Hodgson (later a Sub-Trustee of the Hewley Charity), expressed a wish to concentrate on this work, and was ardently encouraged by Sir John.[70] Ministers in distress could always rely on the assistance of the Hewleys, who not only offered hospitality and succour in their town and country houses but also visited and consoled those imprisoned 'for conscience sake' in appalling conditions in York Castle and the Ouse Bridge prison, the latter so near the river line that when in flood, water poured into the cells.[71] One remarkable aspect of their care, concern and patronage of Dissenting friends was that the Hewleys seem to have escaped direct persecution themselves.[72]

Sir John died at Bell Hall in 1697, appointing his wife sole executrix of his will. In that document he requested the cost of his funeral should not exceed £50, leaving bequests to his and his wife's relations, the Baines, the Wards and the Woolriches, and to the poor of the parish 'wherein I depart this life £10'.[73] He was probably neither a saint nor a hero, but a man of above average ability, active, conscientious and God-fearing, generous, perhaps not of outstanding virtue or greatness, possibly even a shade unscrupulous in politics and slightly unsound in religious doctrine; he was an everyday man in an everyday world, concerned for his neighbours and for his country.[74] An occasional conformist to the last, he was buried in his local parish church in York, St. Saviour's, next door and to the immediate west of the Hewleys' town house, not far from their chapel, also in St. Saviourgate.[75]

After Sir John's death, Dame Sarah largely seems to have given up using Bell Hall, apparently preferring the town house in St. Saviourgate 'one of the neatest and best-built streets in the city', to be near to her chapel and concentrate on her charitable activities.[76] After her husband's decease, Lady Sarah became increasingly infirm, so much so that she frequently had to be carried in a chair the short distance from her house to the pleasant little chapel in St. Saviourgate where she worshiped.[77] In her widowhood, Dame Sarah did not relax her efforts for the Dissenting cause, and during this time she was one of the foremost supporters, donating £200, for Archbishop and Mrs Sharpe's establishment of the Blue (Boys) and Grey (Girls) Coat Schools in York, while in her will she left money to the Lord Mayor and Aldermen for the maintenance of a recently-erected boys school (£100) and for the building and maintenance of a girls' school (£100) in York, as well as £500 to provide coal for deserving poor people in the city.[78]

Thirteen years after the death of her husband, Dame Sarah Hewley also died, requesting that her body be disposed of with as little ceremony and cost as possible. She 'was laid to rest beside him, leaving the world the poorer for a generous and devout woman, the richer for her plentiful endowments'.[79] It may seem strange that the Hewleys were buried in St. Saviour's rather than the little burial ground in front of the Dissenting chapel across the street, but at that time, despite the persecution and sufferings of Dissenters, Presbyterians such as Sarah Hewley and her husband may not have given up hope of eventual reconciliation with the Church of England, and of some element of Presbyterianism being included in a reformed national Church.[80]

Tim Addison

The inscription over their grave (at the east end of St. Saviour's), discovered beneath the sanctuary steps during restoration work in 1850,[81] is Puritan in thought but theologically non-committal:

Here lies interred the body of Sir John Hewley late of the City of York, Knight, who departed this life the 24 of August 1697 aged 78. In the same Bed of Dust are deposited the Remains of Dame Sarah Hewley the virtuous consort of the said Sir John Hewley ~ She exchanged this life for a better on the 23 day of August 1710. Among the dead in Christ that shall rise first. 1 Thess. 4. 16.[82]

The tombstone of Sir John and Dame Sarah Hewley in St. Saviour's Church, York. Redrawn by Tim Addison from a rubbing by York Archaeological Research Centre. The original tombstone is approximately six feet square.

On Lady Hewley's death in 1710, Bell Hall and the Wistow estate were inherited by Sir John's deceased sister Margaret's grandson, Hewley Baines (1693-1760).[83] The Baines family continued to live at Bell Hall until recent times, and at least one descendant, Hewley Mortimer Baines (1788-1874), deplored Dame Sarah's generosity in his memoirs, clearly resenting the fact that by her charitable actions, she had impoverished the Baines family and deprived them of an income that he considered rightfully theirs.[84]

From the sermon preached at Lady Sarah Hewley's funeral at the chapel in St. Saviourgate by her chaplain, Dr Thomas Colton, a picture emerges of a conscientious, dutiful, pious, humble and generous woman 'to whom many had recourse for wise counsel, and by whose means many were nursed for heaven'. Although wealthy, she appears not to have been materially-minded but especially concerned for the welfare of others: 'her charity was universal and extensive ... relieving the necessitous ... If her private charities were all well known they would truly amaze you'. Her health was apparently not strong: 'she spent almost half her life in the valley of the shadow of death ... ' and 'would often speak feelingly of the good of affliction' ... 'Nothing could keep her from the public worship of God, but absolute inability. How often has she come hither on the wings of her desires than upon her own legs' ... 'She was daily retired for secret

THE

FUNERAL SERMON

FOR

DAME SARAH HEWLEY,

RELICT OF SIR JOHN HEWLEY, KNIGHT,

PREACHED AT ST. SAVIOURGATE CHAPEL, YORK, 1710,

BY THE REV. THOMAS COULTON, M.D.

TO WHICH IS ADDED,

The Rev. Edward Bowles's Catechism,

APPOINTED TO BE REPEATED BY THE INMATES OF HER
LADYSHIP'S HOSPITAL, TANNER ROW, YORK.

⁓⁓⁓⁓⁓

LONDON:

HAMILTON, ADAMS AND CO.

MANCHESTER: BANCKS AND CO.; W. ELLERBY. LIVERPOOL: D. MARPLES AND CO.
LEEDS: J. Y. KNIGHT. YORK: J. SHILLITO.

1836.

Frontispiece of sermon preached by Dr. Thomas Colton at the funeral of Dame Sarah Hewley, 1710, reprinted 1836. Hewley MSS.

devotion, even when, by reason of her weakness, it was not safe for her to be left alone' ... 'but now heaven has received her sanctified soul, and there she lives without pain or sickness'.[85] Despite her frailty Sarah Hewley was a woman of considerable character and sound business ability, ready to listen to others and to rely heavily on the best spiritual (and, in worldly matters, professional) advice she could obtain. She was also in many respects ahead of her time, for she is said to have 'died in the hope that divisions among God's people would be healed'.[86] From other sources we learn that she was barely five feet high (her coffin was 5 feet 8 inches long and barely one foot wide across the shoulders). She had many splendid qualities and seemingly a strong personality. She had also earned the affection and respect of people beyond her own religious and immediate social circle, evidenced, for example, in the bequest to her by Marmaduke Rawdon of £500 and 'my great jewill of gold with King David his picture offering his heart to God' – 'as a token of the great love [and] service I have always had towards her'.[87] The letters that Dame Sarah wrote to her Presbyterian friend and intended executrix, Lady Ursula, widow of Sir Thomas (Judge) Rokeby, reveal the deep piety shown during her life and by her character, while the style suggests that she was no more educated than was usual at that time even for ladies 'of superior station'; in her will, however, she mentions what appears to be an extensive library.[88]

St. Saviourgate Chapel

Although York was the focal point of an archdiocese, there is strong evidence to suggest the influence of Puritanism was felt in the city at least as early as 1607, while John Hewley's grandfather's patron, Archbishop Sandys (1576-1588), was labelled 'an obstinate and conscientious Puritan'.[89] By the 1630s Puritan clergy were entrenched in central parishes of the city, and several of them, including John Birchall, were prosecuted for non-adherence to the prayer book, failure to catechise or baptise, administering communion to non-parishioners, and for conducting conventicles in York and elsewhere. There was much support for the Puritan clergy (who were 'not lacking in ability, zeal and scholarship') from laypeople, and the Corporation encouraged these preachers both before and after the Civil War.[90]

The origins of Presbyterian nonconformity and discipline in York date back to about 1645, when the Corporation successfully petitioned Parliament for £600 to be granted annually out of sequestered chapter revenues to maintain four preaching ministers in York. These four men (including the Revd. Edward Bowles, of whom more later) were the principal religious leaders in the city throughout the Interregnum, and so popular that the Corporation agreed to maintain them even if Parliamentary funding was reduced and as late as 1661 approved their offer to continue working and opened a subscription list to support them. The four were all Presbyterians and in 1646 the city urged its citizens to sign the Covenant and petitioned for the establishment of a Presbyterian system of church government. With the ascendancy of Cromwell's Independents in the country as a whole in the 1650s, Presbyterians were forced into a subsidiary role, but apparently continued to rule in York. Only the four preaching ministers and one other clergyman were forced out under the Act of Uniformity of 1662.[91]

Despite repression, nonconformity spread in York after that date, with the Corporation itself appointing a 'city preacher' intermittently to 1676.[92] This energetic growth was led and fostered by ejected clergy, the most notable being the Revd. Ralph Ward, forced out of Hartburn parish, Northumberland, in 1660 and who then came to York to be the Hewleys' chaplain. By 1676 there were said to be 161 Dissenters living in York, out of a population of 3806.[93] Under Charles II's brief 'Declaration of

Indulgence' in 1672, licences were granted for Presbyterian, Independent and Baptist preachers, teachers and gatherings; in York six licences were issued for particular houses and Dissenting preachers, including Peter Williams (one of the four former city preachers) and Ralph Ward.

Prominent York citizens who were members of these Dissenting meetings included the Hewleys, Sir John Brooke, the Rokebys, ex-Alderman Brian Dawson, Lady Lister and Lady Watson, the widow of a former Lord Mayor, Stephen Watson. Although the Hewleys are normally thought to have been Presbyterian, Ward was one of four preachers licensed as an Independent teacher (although originally ordained as a Presbyterian). The houses licensed in the city for Independent worship included that of the wealthy merchant Andrew Taylor, in Micklegate, the main meeting-place; Brian Dawson's, in Ousegate; and Lady Watson's in St. Saviourgate, all of whom were Independents; and that of the Presbyterian preacher, Peter Williams. For the Baptists, Theophilus Browning's and William Wombwell's houses in York were also licensed in 1672. Oliver Heywood later wrote in his diary that he was at the house of Andrew Taylor, in Micklegate: 'where the Nonconformists met before St. Saviour's Gate Chapel was erected'. In 1673 Heywood lodged at the Hewley's town house in York, heard Peter Williams preach at Lady Watson's house, and the following day he and Ralph Ward preached at Andrew Taylor's house.[94]

Ward amongst others was arrested and brought before the courts in 1682 for absenting himself from worship in the Established Church and not receiving the sacrament there, but the leniency with which they were all treated aroused suspicion that some magistrates were overly sympathetic to the accused. Then, on 22 June 1684, Ward and Andrew Taylor were again arrested and a deposition was heard at the Castle before the Lord Mayor 'that a conventicle was held at the house of Andrew Taylor in Micklegate, Ralph Ward the minister', followed by a list of those present, and the names of three informants.[95] The case was tried before the dreaded Judge Jeffreys and the two of them were each fined £50 and committed

Record of the registration of St. Saviour's Meeting House in the Court of Quarter Sessions, York, 1693. York City Archives, House Book.

to the Ouse Bridge prison.[96] Jeffreys spoke of the 'black list of damned fanatiques whom I am resolved to scour'. It was probably at this point Ward wrote to his congregation 'If you suffer with Christ, you shall reign with him'.[97] Ward was released in 1686 and was thereafter assisted by the Revd. Noah Ward (no relation), who had been licensed in 1672 as a Presbyterian preacher at Little Askham near York.[98] The congregation they served does not seem to have been either primarily Presbyterian or Independent. Sir John and Lady Sarah, together with

St. Saviour's Meeting House. Reproduced from 'A York Miscellany'.

Lady Watson, Lady Lister and other prominent individuals in York, used their influence to protect Ward and other Dissenting ministers, favouring Independents and Presbyterians equally. In some documents Dame Sarah is described as a Calvinist which might infer either Presbyterian or Independent loyalty at this time but, while there is no proof that the Baptists had as yet formed a united front with other Dissenters in any public matters, the Presbyterians and Independents were on terms of fairly friendly intimacy and, when their interests coincided, they were glad to act as one body.[99]

After an active ministry in the city of almost 30 years, Ralph Ward, worn out by his sufferings, died in 1691, and was succeeded 'as pastor of the Dissenters at York' the following year by his son-in-law, Dr. Thomas Colton, who had been educated at Leiden where he may have known Edmund Callamy, the nonconformist divine and historian.[100] Oliver Heywood noted in his diary that on 24 August 1692: 'In the chamber of Andrew Taylor, Mr Noah Ward, Mr Timothy Hodgson chaplain to Lady Hewley, Mr John Lister … with a goodly company, proceeded to the ordination of Dr. Thomas Colton. Service began at 10 a.m.'[101]

The Toleration Act of 1689 allowed Dissenters to become a little less surreptitious and permitted them to build their own meeting-houses and places of worship, subject to proper registration. In 1692 the congregation, led by Colton, set about building 'a small and commodious chapel' on the site of Lady Watson's house in St. Saviourgate, and sometimes known as 'Lady Hewley's chapel', perhaps because she advanced the bulk of the cost (£90) for a building close to their town house but on the other side of the street.[102]

Completed by December 1692 and licensed at the Court of Quarter Sessions on 28 April 1693 for Independent worship, this is accepted as the first nonconformist chapel to be built in York (although in 1658 a building, whose site is now unknown, was erected for the use of Protestant Dissenters at the instigation of Dame Priscilla Brooke, while in 1674 dwelling houses in Friargate were adapted for Quaker worship).[103] Oliver Heywood describes in his diary for 1693 a journey to York where 'I preached the Lecture in the New Meeting Place ... for Mr Colton; travelled to Bell Hall and discoursed with Lady Hewley and prayed for her and her sick family', and again during July 1695 'Preached at the new chapel at St. Saviour's Gate, York; a large congregation, although the Archbishop preached the same day in the same street. The ministers were Mr Noah Ward and Dr. Colton'.[104] As one of the original benefactors of the chapel, Lady Sarah seems to have made a special allowance during her lifetime to the minister, and by an article in her second charity deed, in 1707, made provision for this to be continued after her death, one of the three main bones of contention in subsequent major litigation in the next century.[105] She is said to have had 'a spacious pew directly fronting the pulpit'.[106] A broad seventeenth-century chair, known as 'Lady Hewley's Chair' and supposedly also used by her, is still kept in the building.[107]

The first minister of the chapel, Thomas Colton, was perhaps closer to Dame Sarah in her later years than anyone else. Thomas Baxter, one of three sons of another ejected minister, Nathaniel Baxter, acted for some years as Colton's assistant.[108] Some time after 1698, the Revd. John Hotham, who had also spent some time abroad, returned to his native city to work amongst the Dissenters, becoming Colton's assistant sometime between 1698 and Baxter's death in 1710.[109] When Dr. Colton died, on 15 December 1731, aged 73,[110] John Hotham succeeded as senior minister. The Revd. John Brook of Norwich, was Hotham's assistant from 1732 until his early death in 1734, being followed by the Revd. John Root, who died in 1755.[111]

In 1743, there were an estimated 42 Presbyterian, 23 Quaker and 65 Roman Catholic families, out of a total of 1985, in York; and in St. Saviour's parish there was a meeting house of the 'Presbyterian sort': 'They assemble every Lord's Day and Wednesday. In number I have observed on the Lord's Day about 300 ... the teachers are Hotham and Routs [Root] ...'[112]

The St. Saviourgate chapel was one of just 2418 buildings registered for public worship by Independents, Presbyterians (who built perhaps two-thirds of the total), Baptists and Quakers between 1689 and 1700, all of them of 'a modest, retiring and domestic nature', without spires, but with interiors planned so that the preacher could be seen and heard by every member of the congregation. In contrast to the panelling of the gallery front and the pews, the walls were usually whitewashed. This charming building is brick-built, with a tiled roof, described as designed in the form of a Maltese or Greek cross, the area of each limb being equal to that of the central intersection, with a small 'tower' rising above the latter. Drake describes it as 'a pile of building, erected about thirty or forty years ago, as a meeting house for dissenters of the Presbyterian perswasion'.[113] Hargrove described the interior of the chapel as 'not spacious, but neat and comfortable; being properly aired with stoves and well lighted'.[114] A pleasing feature of the building is the simple elegance of the wall monuments to Unitarians later associated with this chapel, including the ministers Newcome Cappe, Charles Wellbeloved and his son-in-law John Kenrick, as well as Varley Beilby and Robert Driffield, all of whom served as Sub-Trustees of the Lady Hewley Trust. Some of the church plate is engraved with the names of Thomas and Mary Colton, and there is a record of the Hewley Trustees purchasing a piece of plate for around £25 in 1761, perhaps for this chapel.[115]

Despite major alterations mainly made in the nineteenth century, including refitting most of the interior, the chapel remains important for its unusual cruciform shape and as the earliest surviving nonconformist building in York. In 1851 it was felt safe to erect the present iron railings and gate that form the frontage to replace the original high boundary wall erected to discourage frequent attacks made on Dissenters. The chapel is approached through a small garden. There is a small burial ground in front of and behind the chapel, and this includes the grave of the Revd. Charles Wellbeloved.[116]

Establishing Dame Sarah's Charities

Lady Sarah Hewley was not unique: after the Restoration, Philip, Lord Wharton, for example, laboured in Parliament to protect Dissenters and further their interests. He made a regular financial allowance to a number of ministers, both Presbyterian and Independent, including Oliver Heywood, and provided employment for several ejected ministers as estate agents and managers of the family lead mines in Yorkshire. He drew up a plan to help friendly justices who wished to avoid dispensing the full rigours of the law when dealing with Dissenting ministers and laypersons. He enabled meeting houses to be built, including one in Swaledale for miners. Today he is perhaps best remembered for the charity he created for the distribution of Bibles and catechisms amongst children in the counties associated with his family, Yorkshire, Cumberland and Buckinghamshire, appointing Dissenting ministers and laymen as his Trustees. In his will he bequeathed large sums of money for charitable purposes.[117]

Dame Sarah seems to have been making charitable grants to ministers and others during her lifetime and as her health deteriorated she probably sought advice on how her benevolent wishes could be safeguarded in the future. One of the first people from whom she sought advice was her minister, Dr. Thomas Colton, but he seems to have felt himself unfit to proffer adequate counsel and suggested she consult the Revd. Richard Stretton, ejected in 1662, who was for a time chaplain to the Fairfaxes in Yorkshire, where he became a friend of the judge, Sir Thomas Rokeby, whose wife was one of Dame Sarah's closest friends. Stretton was granted a licence in 1672 as a Presbyterian teacher at Cawood under the Declaration of Indulgence, but later returned to London. Dame Sarah probably obtained advice from other close friends too, ministers and those acquainted with the law amongst them.[118]

So it was that by deeds executed on 12 & 13 January 1705 and 25 & 26 April 1707, Dame Sarah put in place the grand project that had almost certainly been in her mind for several years. Both Colton and Stretton were amongst her first 'Grand' Trustees, as was the London lawyer, Thomas Marriott, who probably drew up the deeds and was certainly much relied on by his colleagues in the early days, as he pursued two suits on behalf of the Trust. One Trustee, Nathaniel Gould, was a member of a wealthy merchant family in London, while another London Trustee, Thomas Nesbitt, had commercial interests in York as well.[119] By these deeds, she created two charities, conveying, firstly, lands at Haya Park (Knaresborough) and West Ayton (near Scarborough) and, secondly, her 'newly-erected' almshouses or hospital for poor people in York together with lands at Eston in Cleveland, to seven male Dissenters, the Grand Trustees, these trusts and charities to be operated by them from the time of her death, which occurred on 23 August 1710.[120] It is clear that Dame Sarah maintained a powerful discretionary influence over her charities until about a year before her death. Annual sums were to be paid out of the residuary rents and profits of properties which had been purchased mainly by her father Robert Woolrich, and then inherited by Dame Sarah and her husband. These Trust estates were to provide financial assistance for:

1. Poor and Godly Preachers of Christ's Holy Gospel;

2. Poor and Godly Widows of such Preachers;

3. Godly Persons in Distress 'being fit objects of charity';

4. Encouraging and Promoting the Preaching of Christ's Holy Gospel in such Poor Places as the Trustees deem Necessitous;

5. Exhibitions towards the Education of up to five Young Men (at any one time) designed for the Ministry of Christ's Holy Gospel;

6. The continuation of charitable allowances made by Lady Hewley before her death;

7. Supporting the Almshouse at York, and the Poor People therein; and supplying them with Catechisms;

as the Trustees (or a majority) see fit, giving preference to York, Yorkshire and the six Northern Counties, but not necessarily exclusively so.[121] Although a Presbyterian, she placed no sectarian limitation on the application of either these or any of her other charities; indeed much of her own charitable giving was made in secret.[122] The annual value of her charitable Trust funds was in 1710 said to be in the region of £4000.[123]

However, within a year her will and her charitable wishes were being challenged in the courts. A Mr Ady Mott (son of Mark, son of Adrian, the uncle of Sarah Hewley) claimed to be her legitimate heir and therefore entitled to the whole of her real and personal estate at her death. On her deathbed, Sarah Hewley is said to have blamed herself for being too gen-

This Indenture made the Thirteenth Day of January, In the third year of the Reigne of our Soveraigne Lady Anne, by the Grace of God, of England, Scotland, ffrance, and Ireland, Queene, Defender of the ffaith &c. Annoq Domini 1704. **Between** Dame Sarah Hewley of the City of York, Widow, Relitt and Executrix of the last Will and Testament of Sr John Hewley, late of Grey's Inne in the County of Middx, Knt, her late husband decd, and daughter, heir &c Administratrix of the Goods and Chattels of Robert Woolrich, otherwise Wolrych, late of Greys Inne aforesaid Esqr deceased, of the one part, And Richard Stretton the Elder of Hatton Garden in the said County of Middx, Gent, Nathaniel Gold of the parish of St Mary Newington in the said County of Middx, Esqr, Thomas Marriott of Grays Inne in the said County of Middx, Esqr, John Bridges of Hatton Garden aforesaid, Merchant, Thomas Nesbitt of London, Merchant, Thomas Colton of the City of York, Gent, and James Winlow of Yarme in the County of York, Gent, of the other part. **Whereas**, by Indres of Lease and Release, the Lease bearing Date the Day next before the Day of the Date of these presents, and the Release bearing even Date herewith, and made or mentioned to be made betweene the same partys as are to these presents, The said Dame Sarah Hewley, for the Considerations therein respectively mentioned, **Hath** Conveyed unto the said Richard Stretton, Nathaniel Gold, Thomas Marriott, John Bridges, Thomas Nesbitt, Thomas Colton and James Winlow, and their heires, The Mannors of Killinghall and Brayment, with their Rights, Members, and appurtenances in the said County of York, And the Parke or Inclosed Ground some

Copy of part of the deed between Dame Sarah Hewley and the first Trustees, establishing her first Trust, 13th January 1705. From the Hewley MSS, North Yorkshire County Council Record Office.

erous to Ady but her attitude to her relatives was that they were 'persons needing her kindness', although she complained they had behaved 'disobligingly' towards her. Dame Sarah's mother (also Sarah) had married Robert Woolrich, following the death of her first husband, a Mr Tichborne, who had bequeathed his estate to her. At her death Dame Sarah considered it had been her mother's wealth that was the foundation of her father's, husband's and then her great fortune. Dame Sarah's mother was the daughter of Mark Mott of Braintree, Essex, who was the great-great grandfather of Ady Mott. Ady died soon after Sarah and his younger brother Nathaniel, an Anglican clergyman in Weathersfield, Essex, then took up the cudgels in the Court of Chancery in July 1711, on behalf of himself and his sisters Barbara (the wife of a York lawyer, William Ward, and the guardian of Hewley Baines, who had been left Bell Hall) and Mercy, Dorothy and Anne, all of whom were now said to be Dame Sarah's next of kin. They claimed that Dame Sarah's minister, Dr. Thomas Colton, had exercised undue influence on a frail old lady 'who by the misfortune and prejudice of education had been bred up and to her death continued a Presbyterian or Dissenter from the Church of England', whose real intentions had been to pass on her wealth to her immediate family – the Motts – and then as the surviving executor of her will Colton was to ensure this was put into effect.[124]

It has been suggested that the Motts were seeking to take advantage of the prevailing feeling against Dissenters: the plaintiffs deplored the fact that all the Trustees were Dissenters, that Dame Sarah had settled her property to benefit Dissenters and Dissenting institutions and that Colton was 'a person dissenting from the Church of England and pretending to be in Holy Orders and a preacher or teacher of some congregation of dissenting Protestants within the said city of York'. Nathaniel's lawyers asserted that her landed estate was worth £50,000 and her personal estate £30,000 – enormous sums by today's values; it has been estimated that a truer valuation would be about £20,000 all told, still probably well into seven figures today. What is also rather sad to observe is the alliance of several people named in Lady Sarah's will who seem to have turned against her once she was no longer alive. At any rate Thomas Colton made a strong rebuttal, advancing the true facts about the charity foundations and that although elderly when she created her trust settlements Dame Sarah was 'a Lady of clear understandings and discerning judgement'; furthermore the Motts were not the sole or closest relatives (there were also Woolrich heirs; Sarah's grandfather Arthur Woolrich had several brothers whose descendants were still alive). The case seems to have collapsed for want of firm evidence that the Motts were legitimate claimants. Nevertheless, the Trustees were obliged to spend almost £200 in fighting this claim.[125]

At the same time, the new Trustees felt obliged to go to law with the minor, Hewley Baines, who had been bequeathed Bell Hall. In her will Dame Sarah had charged Barbara Ward with the responsibility of looking after the Hall until Hewley Baines was twenty-one. His guardians appear to have occupied Hewley estates at Killinghall and Braycroft. Initially, the case was heard at two successive Assizes in York before transfer to the law courts in London (Exchequer and Chancery). Despite expending almost £250 more on this additional litigation, it appears that the Trustees lost the case for the land seems never to have been within their control.[126]

Lady Hewley's Almshouses: Tanner Row

York has had the benefit of many almshouses over the years. Three almshouse charities were founded in medieval times, and another eight in the seventeenth century (including one by Sir John Hewley's Parliamentary colleague, Sir Henry Thompson). Six more came into being in the eighteenth century (including Dame Sarah's Almshouses, as well as those founded by her devoted minister, Dr. Thomas Colton, and his wife Mary, in 1717 and 1729, which until 1909 stood on the corner of Rougier Street and Tanner Row). The remainder came in the nineteenth century.

Part of deed between Sir Godfrey Copley and Dame Sarah Hewley for the land in Tanner Row, the site of the first Almshouses. Hewley MSS.

The Tanner Row Almshouses in the eighteenth century. From an illustration in the possession of YAYAS.

By 1946 there were still 20 almshouse charities in York, providing accommodation for 177 older people, together with four foundations formerly associated with almshouses but which were by then paying out regular pensions instead.[127]

In 1699, Lady Sarah bought six houses, a stable and a dovehouse, a kiln, a garden with fruit trees, and a close and grass plots, collectively known as The Friary. This was another display of her customary shrewdness for she paid just £520 (a previous owner had had to spend £815) for these lands and tenements called the 'Black Fryars' (the site of an old Dominican property), with Toft Green, and fronting onto Tanner Row, all within the city walls and near Micklegate.[128] She then had the Almshouses built for her and these opened in 1700.[129] The new buildings were at the top of Tanner Row, facing the end of Barker Lane, and just off the present North Street and south west of the Lendal Bridge. Her minister, Dr. Thomas Colton, is said to have resided at the Almshouses for a time.[130]

By the title deeds of her second charity, dated 25 & 26 April 1707, Sarah Hewley conveyed to her Trustees 'all that new-erected house … used for an Hospital, Almshouse or habitation for some poor people, with the buildings, curtillages, outhouse, courts, easements and boundaries, with all the fruit trees and other trees therein and … appurtenances whatsoever situate within and near unto the walls of the city of York …'[131]

Francis Drake, whose history of York was published in 1736, wrote: 'Lower down in Tanner-row stands a neat but small hospital founded …

by the lady Hewley, relict of Sir John Hewley of Bell-hall, some time member for this city. This lady died a Presbyterian, and the hospital was designed for ten old women of that persuasion, who have ten shillings paid them every first Monday in the month, and coals allowed'.[132]

William Hargrove, writing in 1818, described Lady Hewley's Hospital as:

'a neat brick building raised above the street three steps; with wings at each end, both in front and behind; whereby a small courtyard is formed in each. Over the front entrance are the arms of the donor, below which is the following inscription:

This Hospital was founded and endowed by Dame Sarah, the Relict of Sir John Hewley, of the City of York, Knight, Anno Domini 1700. Thou, O God, hast prepared of thy goodness for the poor – Ps[alm] 68, x.

The institution is for ten old women … to be approved by the trustees. Every woman is allowed two rooms and they originally had also six pounds per annum … In the courtyard behind, is a small distinct building, that is by them called a chapel; in which, prayers are read three times every week, by a person appointed for the purpose. Behind this hospital are very extensive gardens, now in the occupation of Messrs. T. and J. Backhouse, called Friars Gardens … the site of a Monastery, erected by a Christian fraternity, called "The Friars' Preachers", from whom the gardens derive their name'.[133]

In 1709 Dame Sarah had rules and orders drawn up for the future government of the Almshouse, which were provided to accommodate ten (preferably Dissenting) poor people (nine widows or unmarried women, and, if possible, one poor old man to act as chaplain, all over the age of 55). She stipulated that each almsperson should be able to repeat by heart the Lord's Prayer, the Creed, the Ten Commandments and the Revd. Edward Bowles' *A Plain and Short Catechism*, first published in 1676.[134]

Edward Bowles (1613-1662), whose father Oliver had been a member of the Westminster Assembly of Divines, was a Parliamentary army chaplain.[135] Following the surrender of York to the Parliamentary forces on 15 July 1644, he seems to have moved into the city as chaplain to Sir Thomas Fairfax, and may have helped the Fairfaxes save the Minster from iconoclasm and helped to preserve the library and archives there.[136] He soon became the most important of four special preachers appointed by

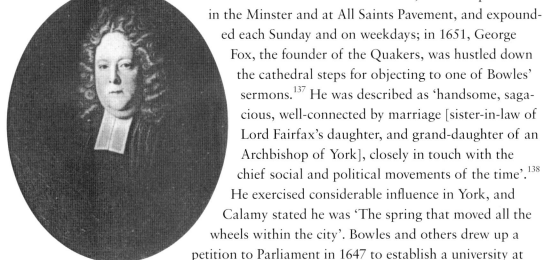

Reverend Edward Bowles.

Parliament in 1645 to minister in York, where he preached in the Minster and at All Saints Pavement, and expounded each Sunday and on weekdays; in 1651, George Fox, the founder of the Quakers, was hustled down the cathedral steps for objecting to one of Bowles' sermons.[137] He was described as 'handsome, sagacious, well-connected by marriage [sister-in-law of Lord Fairfax's daughter, and grand-daughter of an Archbishop of York], closely in touch with the chief social and political movements of the time'.[138] He exercised considerable influence in York, and Calamy stated he was 'The spring that moved all the wheels within the city'. Bowles and others drew up a petition to Parliament in 1647 to establish a university at York, so that the north might lose its 'stain of rudeness and incivility'.[139] Without being 'a forward man',[140] he enjoyed much more than a local reputation, being invited to preach at St. Paul's in 1648 before the Lord Mayor and Aldermen of London, who ordered his sermon to be printed.[141]

Bowles was a confidant of the non-sectarian but Calvinist Fairfaxes at nearby Bilborough, and of General Monk, responsible for restoring Charles II to the throne. He was one of the Parliament's five Commissioners (three of whom were from York, the others from the city being the veteran General Fairfax and the young Brian Fairfax) who travelled to Breda in Holland to negotiate the King's return, incurring odium amongst some fellow Dissenters for doing so, although not from the Hewleys; John Hewley was knighted for his work in securing the King's return. There is a strong suggestion that Bowles spent many hours with Monk during his five days in York, pressing him to declare for the Restoration.[142] When Richard Baxter declined the Bishopric of Worcester, he suggested Edward Bowles as a suitable candidate. Bowles subsequently declined the offer of the deanery of York, despite the efforts of leading members of the Established Church, including the Yorkshireman, Tillotson, later Archbishop of Canterbury, and Stillingfleet, afterwards Bishop of Worcester, to persuade him to accept and conform.[143] Asked during his final illness what he disliked about the Church of England, he is reputed to have replied: 'the whole'.[144] Nevertheless, Bowles apparently believed, like many Presbyterians, that a spirit of compromise would

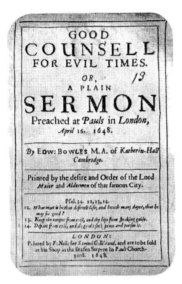

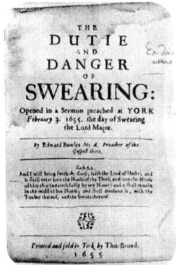

Frontispieces of two sermons by Edward Bowles.

ensue after the Restoration and his denomination would in some way be included within a reorganised Established Church. Aged just 49, he died disconsolate on 21 August 1662, appalled at the bitter outcome of the Restoration he had done much to bring about, three days before the Royalists' retributive Act of Uniformity came into force, and mass ejections and resignations occurred.[145]

Bowles' *Catechism* is supported, in all bar one instance, by scriptural references. The 59 questions and answers are all brief, concise and, within the language of the day, reasonably clear. The doctrine is orthodox, moderate and Trinitarian, clearly intended for religious instruction rather than theological exposition. The Hewleys, being resident in York, would have had frequent opportunity to hear Bowles preach, and would have known his *Shorter Catechism* well, and may have been involved with him in Dissenting matters.[146]

Substantial efforts were made over the years by the Trustees and Sub-Trustees to make the Almshouse a welcoming and attractive dwelling, and to keep it in good repair. The value of money was very different then, so the cost of building repairs might seem slight to us today; it was not. The first mention of extensive work was in 1714 when more than £21 was spent, with another £25 in 1718, a further £28 in 1723, almost £16 in 1728 and £37 in 1746, with smaller sums intermittently. In addition, there were the minor tasks such as 'Mending the pump at the hospital', while in 1754 a total of £18 was paid to a painter, a bricklayer, a whitesmith, a plumber and for general repairs.[147] In 1747 we find a 'Mr. Burnet to be employed ... to build a fireplace and chimney in the house in Lady Hewley's Hospital inhabited by Mrs Ann Hasbert',[148] and in 1763-1764 the large sum of £52 was spent in repairs.[149] In 1769 it was 'Agreed a convenient little room be erected ... for such poor persons in the Hospital to perform their devotions.[150] In 1781 £6 was spent on glazing, while in 1804, 1808 and 1813 further repairs cost £12, £21 and over £31 respectively, and in 1817 more than £40 was spent out on repairs to the Hospital. Between 1819 and 1828 further remedial work was undertaken at a cost of nearly £75, involving Robert Gray bricklayer (the lion's share), George Lockey carpenter, Brown & Kirlew painters, Coates & Son joiners, and other unnamed workmen.[151]

The Trustees normally paid the annual stipend of £60 for the year ahead to the Sub-Trustees on the anniversary of Dame Sarah's death, 23 August, until 1805, when they decided that Lady Hewley's monthly stipend of ten shillings to each Almswoman was no longer sufficient, and doubled this sum, with a further increase six years later and again in 1818.[152]

In 1824, the Trustees leased the gardens around the Hospital to Messrs. Thomas & John Backhouse for 15 years at £90 per year. These gardens had been in the hands of the Telford family since 1710, latterly working as nurserymen; the Trustees offered to let Mr John Telford live in the dwelling house and have the attached garden there for life, if he wished.[153] In 1826, 'It having been represented' that a supply of mains water from the Water Works Company in York piped into Lady Hewley's Hospital would be a great boon to the poor people living there, the Trustees ordered this to be done with the consent of the Sub-Trustees, and it was implemented shortly afterwards. [154]

Around 1835, by which time the Trust was being administered by the Court of Chancery, plans were announced, on the initiative of the 'railway king', George Hudson, soon to become a prominent member of York Corporation and later its Lord Mayor, to promote a York & North Midland Railway and other connecting lines to and from York. In 1838 the announcement came that the city's first railway station would be built within the city walls and that land in the 'Quayside' area would be requisitioned for this purpose. This included the Almshouses and other nearby premises. It was inevitable that permission for the railways and their station would be granted, as apart from Hudson, York's Town Clerk was deputy chairman of the two railway companies concerned, the main company's banker became City Treasurer, the company engineer was a city councillor, the company architect served as the city's Sheriff, while Hudson's brother-in-law was also a city councillor.[155] Most of the property required for the railway station and its frontage belonged to the Corporation and was readily ceded to Hudson, while the area needed for access roads included the Hewley

George Hudson, the 'railway king'.

Almshouses, Toft Green and some of the old Friary area, with Backhouse's Gardens, all of which were compulsorily purchased by Hudson's railway companies. Under the powers granted in the Act of Parliament for the line, the York & North Midland purchased the Almshouse site for £5105.[156]

When the first York and North Midland Railway train to leave York departed and returned amidst much celebration on 29 May 1839, a temporary station was used outside the city walls. Joseph Blower, a partner in the London firm of solicitors, Vizard & Blower, and the Receiver appointed by the Court of Chancery to administer the Trust estates during the protracted legal wrangling, now moved quickly and by Chancery order and deeds executed on 25 & 26 June 1839, procured an alternative site for the Almshouses for £1410 from John Ickeringill, a city councillor and builder, who had purchased the land to the immediate east of St. Saviour's parish church in St. Saviourgate in March 1834.[157] The remainder of the money paid by the railway company into Court funds at this time, for the Almshouse site and new building, was used by Joseph Blower to purchase six closes of arable land (about 45 acres) at Whixley, a new estate for the Trust, between York and Knaresborough. The deed conveying this property notes that the purchase was to be 'for the benefit of the said Hospital or Almshouse'.[158]

By 18 July 1839 an archway, seventy-feet wide, had been built in the city walls, near the North Postern, so that trains could run into the intended permanent station to be built on the old Friary gardens site, with a frontage facing onto a realigned Tanner Row. The York & North Midland Railway advertised in the spring of 1840 for a contractor to construct the new station, to start work that June. The old Almshouses and the old House of Correction in Tanner Row were then demolished. York's first railway station opened to passengers on 4 January 1841.[159]

York's first station, 1841, from W.W. Tomlinson's 'North Eastern Railway', 1914.

Administering the Charity: the Ancien Regime

The first Trustees were described as all Presbyterian (although at least two of them enjoyed close relations with the Independents), and grants appear to have been made to ministers and beneficiaries in all three Dissenting communions: Independent, Presbyterian and Baptist.[160] During her lifetime, Dame Sarah was a generous contributor to the Presbyterian Fund, administered from London, whereby strong congregations helped the weak; soon after her death and the establishment of her charities, the Presbyterian fund transferred support of the northern churches and 'their' ministers and families and deserving poor to the Hewley Fund.[161]

As the first Trustees died, replacements were invited and elected by the remainder of their colleagues.[162] In accordance with the original provisions, new Trust deeds were executed, but usually not until every third vacancy had been filled, the new Trustees serving in the meantime (often some years) as 'Managers' until a new deed conveyed all the property and possessions into the hands of the surviving and new Trustees. Interestingly, while this was the original requirement, faithfully observed in recurring Trust deeds, the minutes from 1762 to 1830 suggest that those filling vacancies during that period were as often as not accorded both Manager and full Trustee status simultaneously, often long before their names appeared in a new Trust deed. The surviving deeds show a a complete chain of Trustee title from 1705 down to 1830, when the Hewley Trust entered into a long period of litigation. When the Trust recommenced in1849, a different system of Trust deeds came into being, changed most recently in 1976.[163]

Initially, the Trustees normally met two or three times, exceptionally four or five times, each year. Sometimes these meetings took place over a couple of days. When they met in York they enjoyed the hospitality of James Wyndlow on occasion.[164] To start with, they seem to have met either in York or London, the majority of the Trustees living in the capital. By 1762 the Trustees had settled down to a pattern of two meetings each year, with the occasional visit by some or all of them to one or other of the estates. By that date business meetings were always held in Wakefield, the first around May, with an annual audit meeting in September. It is unclear why the venue was altered, perhaps to suit the convenience of particular Trustees, or simply to facilitate journeys. Down to the mid-eighteenth century most travellers still went on horseback, but by that time turnpike roads were becoming increasingly numerous.[165] However, some indication of the speed and difficulties of travel then is perhaps gleaned from the Treasurer, James Wyndlow, whose expenses in 1711 included 'being away from home about 65 days' or Richard Wyndlow seeking reimbursement in 1748 'for shoeing two horses … ale, and for a barber in Knaresborough'. The Wakefield venue was 'The Strafford Arms', one of the town's coaching inns, and then from 1772 to 1830, 'The White Hart', Wakefield's principal post house, in Westgate, near to the Unitarian chapel. Occasionally, the date of the September meeting was brought forward or put back because of Wakefield's Race Week, presumably because accommodation would then have been at a premium. This was not a problem after 1794 when the races ceased to be run.[166]

When the Trust started to function after the death of Dame Sarah, the Trustees appear to have worked well and harmoniously for many years. This ceased in 1755 when a major dispute occurred, brought about to some extent by the election of three new Trustees: Samuel Shore, Aymor Rich and Thomas Lee, all of whom were Unitarians. This does call into question the continuing Trinitarian beliefs of the Trustees who appointed the three newcomers.[167] A change in the smooth running of the Charities soon made itself apparent. An 'orthodox' Trustee, Robert Moody, of York, had wished two well-known London ministers to be elected, the Revds. Dr. Jennings and Samuel Hitchin, but he was overruled. Thereafter, and perhaps because he failed to have his own way, he exhibited growing impatience and despair with his colleagues. In 1756 he strenuously resisted a half-year grant of £30 awarded to the Revd. Newcome Cappe. Cappe briefly succeeded the Revd. John Root before he was appointed sole minister of St. Saviourgate on the death of the Revd. John Hotham in 1756.[168]

Cappe was the son of Joseph Cappe, the eminent Presbyterian

The White Hart Inn, Wakefield. From J W Walker's 'History of Wakefield', 1939.

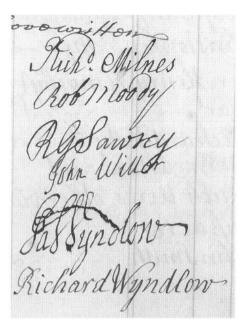

Signatures of Trustees including that of Robert Moody, 1744. Hewley MSS.

minister of Mill Hill chapel, Leeds (where Joseph Priestley later served as a Unitarian minister). Newcome Cappe had been educated at several Dissenting Academies, including Northampton, where its famous principal, Dr Philip Doddridge, had a high opinion of his student's abilities. However, Cappe had become a decided Unitarian and it seems that a majority of the Hewley Trustees selected him to become the sole minister of St. Saviourgate, apparently in opposition to the wishes of a majority of the congregation.[169] Newcome Cappe introduced Arian doctrines as a result of which 'many … left the place as they could not profit under his ministry. Some attended the preaching of the Methodists, others a serious practical preacher of the established Church', although Cappe's stipend continued to be augmented by the Hewley Trustees. They, observing the decline in his congregation, gave Cappe and his immediate followers oversight of the Hospital 'so that the rules of the Hospital are totally neglected and the character of the people put in the almshouse different from Lady Hewley's design'. Cappe had quickly built up a scholarly reputation in Unitarian circles and in York as a man of serious literary tastes, going on to found a Literary Club in the city in 1771.[170]

Robert Moody would have known that the minister of St. Saviourgate chapel had since the time of Dame Sarah (and at her express wish) received a much larger grant from the Trust than any other minister. The surviving accounts from 1711 to 1760 make it quite clear that the St. Saviourgate minister consistently received generous supplements twice a year. However, Moody probably resented the Unitarianism of both Cappe and other Trustees. Furthermore, it seems likely that Cappe was already in receipt of a handsome stipend of between £100 and £200 per year, so Moody felt that any increment by way of a Hewley grant was contrary to the spirit of the founder's wishes. Moody was put out, too, because the Trustees had, the previous year, agreed to make grants only to those ministers whose income was below £60 in a market town and £40 in a village. In 1756 Moody eventually agreed to sanction the grant to Cappe, but only on the understanding that it was a one-off payment to a man who had begun his ministry in York in debt. When his co-Trustees proposed a renewal of the grant to Cappe the next year, Moody again objected and was appalled to learn that they intended to make this a permanent annual charge of £60 (that was paid until Cappe's death in 1799). Robert Moody subsequently refused to authorise any of the distributions that included Newcome Cappe ever again, noting that 'I could not consent to rob so many necessitous families in order to gratify an aspiring boy to keep a Footman at the expense of Charity', observing simultaneously that there were some ministers with incomes of as little as £6 who were being ignored by the Trust. Matters had deteriorated to such an extent by 1760 that Moody refused to execute a new Trust deed, and for the remaining seven years of his life took virtually no part in the affairs of the Hewley Trust, although it has to be added that since his election in 1744 he had not been especially conscientious in attending meetings.[171]

Moody's principal complaints were not only the other Trustees' partiality to Newcome Cappe and other Unitarian ministers or the deliberate disregarding of Dame Sarah's rules for the Almshouses, but also the wilful neglect of Trust property leased to tenants at lower rents than those prevailing on comparable neighbouring farms. When he first saw the Haya Park estate near Knaresborough, he was surprised at the excellent quality of the land, which seemed markedly at odds with the rents expected. At the Trustees' next meeting on 8 September 1756, Moody suggested that the rents be doubled (to bring in £895 a year), which he believed could be done without hardship to the tenants, who, he thought, had neglected field drains and 'fence ditches' to the detriment of themselves and the Trust. The meeting authorised Moody to negotiate new terms but none of the tenants would agree, so he ordered that those who failed to accept the new rents by Lady Day 1757 should be ejected. However, other Trustees were in the meantime making alternative suggestions, undermining Moody's position. It then emerged that outside parties had offered to take the Haya Park estate for £600 per year and then sub-let it to the tenants at considerable private profit. One Trustee valued the estate rental at £595, while another, Samuel Shore, a prominent campaigner for Dissenting liberties, said he did not care how low it was let for. When Moody persisted with his argument for realistic rents, 'Instead of having any rational reply one of them threatened to break every bone in my skin'. The other Trustees eventually told him to reduce his valuation or they would carry out their own proposals for Haya Park. Moody believed that the other Trust estates were also let too low, and offered to resign if anyone could

An example of the treasurer's accounts, 1743-1744, including paying grants to 'the Beneficiaries in the North', annual maintenance grant for the Almshouses, rents and rent arrears. Hewley MSS.

The Charge in Mr Richard Wyndlow's Account } £1126 - 9¾
Brought over }

The Discharge continued   £368:19:3¾
Paid to Mr Hugh Boag his travelling }
Charges in paying the Beneficiaries } £ 2: : :
in the North
Paid for Ink, Coach-hire, Porter and }
Carriage of Post-Letters & parcels --- } £ : 17: :¾   } £886 16 3¾
Allowed to this Accountant for a }
Clerk and for his Trouble as Treasu- }
rer for the year which ended --- } £15 : :
July 22d 1744

        November 21st 1744 There Remains   £239 4 6

Sundry Accounts Dr to Mr Richard }
Wyndlow as by the above State of his } £148:16:3¾
Account appears
    viz
51 Lady Hewley's Hospital for the wonted } £ 60: : :
    Allowance
48 And Loss and Gain for the said other }
50 Allowances and Expences --- } £ 88:16:3¾   £148 16 3¾

The Account of the Trust Estates in General Stated
        The Charge
By a debt owing from Chris. Hudson £8:10: }
and Arrears of Rents due at Lady } £144: 2: 9} £152:12:9}
day 1743   } £1258 19 6
By a whole year's Rents at Lady day 1744 --- £1106: 6: 9}
Deducting the yearly Allowance to the hospital £ 60: : : }
And Balance of the Account of Loss & Gain £411:15:3¾} £471 15 3¾
        November 21st 1744   There Remains - £787 4 2¼

Which Said Remainder consisteth of Hudsons }
Debt and Arrears of Rent due at Lady day 1744 £163:13:9
And clear Profits receiv'd to be carryed to the }
Account of Distributions --- } £623:10:5¼} £787 4 2¼
        November 21st 1744
The Trust-Estates in general Dr to Sundry Accounts   viz t
45 To Loss and Gain for Disbursments and Expences £ 411 15 3¾
48
45 To Distributions for remaining clear Profits received £ 623 10 5¼
47

be found who would let the properties at a realistic level. If the others continued with their policy of underletting, he would have to oppose them. They replied that, since the entire Trust estate was a freehold, they had the power to dispose of it entirely at their discretion, which Moody clearly felt was a breach of trusteeship.[172]

Eventually Moody recorded his feelings: 'I am wearied of rowing against them' and 'I have often thought, especially of late years that this Charity doth far more hurt in propagating errors than the small part that's given the contrary way does good'. But he would continue as long as he felt able: ' … but still think of the poor ministers and widows; then farewell charity'. He noted that two of the Trustees were 'so … incapable of acting' and that 'All resolutions of the trustees of matters of moment are no longer entered into the Book for that use'.[173]

Moody continued: 'It is these estates the Lady has left that supports the dissenting interests in the northern counties, and whoever lives a few years to see it in the hands of the present Trustees will find the bulk of it given to favourites that are no objects within the limits of the Settlement – even this year [with the Hewley funds £300 in debt] they have reduced the Widows list to one half that they might gratify their humours'. He was so incensed by what he saw as the other Trustees' dereliction of duty that on three occasions he sought the advice of Attorney-General Charles Pratt (later Lord Camden) who counselled a suit in the Chancery Court, agreeing that the other Trustees had a case to answer that could lead to their removal from office and a requirement to make restitution. At the same time the Attorney-General cautioned Moody that the cost of legal action was likely to be very high, and this appears to have been the reason why he did not proceed.[174]

Looking at the period from 1760 to 1830, the Hewley Trust seems to have been in the hands of a small oligarchy of leading, closely-connected and inter-related Unitarian families: the Shores, Aymor Rich and the Milnes, the Lees, the Walkers and the Heywoods (the last descended from an ejected minister, the Revd. Nathaniel Heywood, brother of Oliver Heywood).[175]

As the eighteenth century gave way to the nineteenth, the Trust's administrative systems and financial methods gradually became more sophisticated. Previously, when faced with financial predicaments, the Trustees gave or lent money as necessary (as in the case of Dr Thomas Colton who donated £170 around 1730 to cover the shortfall occasioned

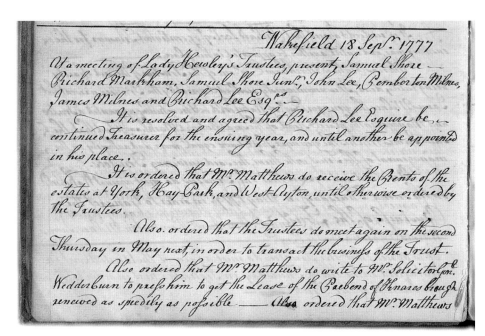

A well-preserved page from the minutes of the Trustees' meetings at Wakefield, September 1777, although little business appears to have been transacted. Hewley MSS.

by the maladministration of a deceased and insolvent Treasurer, or the loan of £200 repaid to Aymor Rich who had lent this sum to the Trust to tide it over in 1760). When the Trustees were hit by a large bill in 1795-1796 for the costs of the Hutton Buscel and West Ayton enclosure, the funds were utterly insufficient to meet the additional charge and so several of the Trustees advanced money out of their own pockets, receiving interest at 5% per year until the capital could be repaid to them.[176]

From around 1810, when Benjamin Heywood took over as Treasurer, there was greater reliance on banking services, thereby attracting further income by way of annual interest (from Messrs. Leatham Tew & Co. of Wakefield). In 1813 the Trustees asked Heywood to purchase the first of a series of Exchequer Bills (for about £1000 each) to be kept by Messrs. Joseph Denison of London, and these also yielded useful interest. At the same time the Trustees accepted a Promissory Note from the previous Treasurer and his son, Richard and Thomas Lee, who owed the Trust almost £800, to be repaid over the years 'with legal interest'.[177]

The Trust in Chancery 1830-1849

While there is evidence to suggest the Unitarians spent much time, energy and money on charitable objectives, it is clear that in the late eighteenth and early-to-mid nineteenth centuries Parliament, the Church of England, Methodists, and the other Dissenting denominations had few kind words to say about them. Their publications were on occasion ordered to be burnt, and non-Trinitarians were specifically excluded from the Toleration Act in 1689 until finally winning statute approval in 1813, as a result of rapid numerical growth.[178] The Unitarians' Act of Parliament that year had the effect of giving them both respectability and renewed vigour.

When the Revd. John Grundy, minister of Manchester's Cross Street Unitarian chapel ('a powerful centre of reform, with a congregation largely composed of families of prosperous manufacturers and professional men', and where several Hewley Trustees were Presidents in the early nineteenth century) accepted a call in 1824 to Paradise Street chapel, Liverpool, a public farewell dinner was held on 24 August that year. After the meal, one speaker, the Revd. George Harris, supposedly descended from Oliver Cromwell, and conspicuous for his fiery espousal of the Unitarian cause, ridiculed the evangelical doctrines of other communions and strongly criticised 'the spirit of orthodoxy' for being 'mean, cruel, vindictive and persecuting' as well as 'direful and demoralizing' in its effects. Most of those present were unaware of the journalist in their midst, until they saw his account of the proceedings reproduced in a local newspaper, especially Harris' vitriolic comments. As a result, a keen and lengthy correspondence ensued (the Socinian Controversy'), principally in the pages of the *Manchester Gazette*, exciting a wide and lively interest. The principal protagonists in the debate were the ardent Independent, George Hadfield, stung into a reply (a Manchester solicitor, later MP for his native Sheffield) and the Unitarian, William Wood (later MP for Kendal). Hadfield used the opportunity to attack Unitarian occupation of orthodox property, and *inter alia* argued that Lady Hewley's endowments should only be applied for the benefit of Trinitarian Dissenters.[179]

Hadfield claimed the Unitarians had no moral or legal right to many of their places of worship and endowments, as most of these had formerly been Presbyterian. Furthermore, he suggested the Unitarian members of the Hewley Trust were abusing the terms of Lady Sarah's gift by diverting funds for their own sectarian purposes and that the Unitarian Trustees were exclusive holders of the Hewley properties and thus guilty of illegal usurpation.[180]

The dispute between the Unitarians and other Dissenters in Manchester was the catalyst that eventually set in motion complaints to a House of Commons Commission examining charity abuses. This was one of a series of four such commissions inspired by Henry (later Lord Chancellor) Brougham, bitterly resented at the time by many charity governing bodies. (The last of these commissions completed its work in 1837 and its final report led to the creation of the Charity Commission in 1853.)[181]

An initial and then a subsequent petition were forwarded to the Parliamentary Commission in 1826 by Rotherham Independent College (whose principal had inherited Robert Moody's account of his grievances) complaining that all the student exhibitions that should have been allocated by the Hewley Trustees for the training of Dissenting ministers throughout northern England had for many years been given only to those students attending the Manchester Unitarian College now removed to York (whose principal was Charles Wellbeloved, also the minister of St. Saviourgate chapel and a Sub-Trustee for the Almshouses, where he was expected to ensure Trinitarian teaching!) The Commission investigated the Hewley Trust and in 1829 reported its findings. The careful language suggests its members found much that was praiseworthy, but reserved their barb for the end:

> *It does not appear to us on enquiry that the administration of this charity, and examination of the books of account, &c, that the trustees are other than duly appointed in all essential particulars, unless it is considered a departure from Lady Hewley's intentions, that part of the revenues should be applied in favour of dissenting ministers who entertain and preach [a] Socinian or Unitarian doctrine of faith, or in the allowance of stipends to widows of such ministers and exhibitions to students brought up in those sentiments.* [182]

The Commissioners were nevertheless sufficiently concerned to conclude:

> *We think the question which has arisen in this case ought to be sub-*

mitted to a court of Equity, in order that a judicial declaration may be pronounced as to the proper mode and dispensing [of] the Charity, in the particular respect above noticed, and such direction may be given as the nature of the case may require, for securing its proper administration in future.[183]

In his editing of the Commissioners' Report, George Hadfield noted the existence of five Dissenting Academies in the Northern Counties: Rotherham, Airedale and Blackburn (all Independent), Bradford (Baptist) and Manchester College at York (Unitarian). Hadfield also noted that within the north of England (interpreted by him as Yorkshire, Durham, Northumberland, Cumberland, Westmoreland, Lancashire and Cheshire) there were at this time 310 Independent, 97 Baptist and 78 Unitarian chapels; of those 78 Unitarian causes, Hadfield reckoned 64 had originally been built for Trinitarian worship. Hadfield examined the history of 223 Unitarian chapels in all, and discovered 178 had been founded by Calvinists, and in an analysis of ministers receiving grants from Hewley funds calculated that out of 237 Dissenters benefiting, 39 were Unitarians. Curiously, Hadfield (an Independent) makes no direct mention of the Presbyterians, apparently regarding them as either of Scottish extraction or having over time given way to Independents. Hadfield particularly drew attention to the Hewley Trustees' grants to the Revd. Charles Wellbeloved (a supplement of £80 per year to his stipend), Manchester College in York (£120 per year), and the Almspeople (£180 per year, Dame Sarah having allowed £60 to them more than a century before!)[184]

At a meeting of Yorkshire ministers on 23 April 1830, it was decided to institute legal proceedings against the Unitarian Trustees at once. Joseph Blower, a London solicitor, was in Leeds on other business at this time, and offered to act on behalf of Hadfield and his allies on very liberal terms. An Indemnity Fund was set up, to raise £500 in Lancashire, £500 in Yorkshire and £250 in London. Later that year an 'Information' was filed in the Chancery Court by Hadfield and his colleagues, under the title of *Attorney-General v Shore and others*, arguing that over a period of time the Hewley estates had fallen into the hands of Unitarians, who had behaved improperly. Initially, the Attorney-General refused to regard this as an adequate basis for Crown proceedings, perhaps fearful the whole case was merely denominational bickering, led by George Hadfield. (Certainly, Hadfield emerges as one of the more extreme radical Dissenters, obsessed by a wish to secure justice and also advantage for the Independents. In his later Parliamentary career, he especially supported economic, legal and religious reform. A prominent Congregationalist, he offered his denomination £1000 a year for five years in 1864, on condition that 50 Independent chapels were built during this time. In association with others, he established the Lancashire Independent College at Blackburn, and gave £2000 towards its endowment in 1840).[185]

The origins of the problem went back almost to Lady Hewley's day. Gradually many, mostly Presbyterian, chapel and trusts had passed into the hands of Unitarian ministers and laymen. Indeed, Joseph Hunter, a Unitarian minister trained by Wellbeloved and later a distinguished Assistant Keeper of Public Records, said in his defence of the Hewley Trustees, published in 1834, that had Lady Hewley still been alive she too would have been a Unitarian.[186]

Parallel to the Hewley litigation was the 'Wolverhampton Chapel Case', where the John Street Presbyterian chapel erected in 1701 had eventually become Unitarian. A new minister appointed in 1812 announced that he would henceforth preach only evangelical Trinitarian doctrines. When the Unitarian trustees attempted to deprive him of his chapel and manse, he decided to defend himself in the courts. The action began in 1817, but then dragged its way painfully slowly until 1836 when judgement was postponed until the result of the more important Hewley case was known. [187]

The Hewley proceedings began on 18 June 1830 at the behest of the 'Relators' (Hadfield and other petitioners), with the approval of the Attorney-General, against the fourteen Grand and Sub-Trustees, all of whom were Unitarian with the possible exception of one Sub-Trustee who is variously described as a member of the Church of England or the Presbyterian Church of England.[188] The case was a legal marathon requiring powers of great concentration and endurance. It attracted much national attention, and along the way a bitter pamphlet war (as the four sturdy volumes relating to the Hewley controversy in York Minster library testify) was waged between the different Dissenting factions. During the almost twenty years that this case lasted, in one form or another, the Hewley Trust was efficiently administered and regulated by the courts, but it was to some extent rudderless and in a state of vacuum. The prolonged litigation has been compared to a 'grotesque boxing match', with one fighter knocked down to the canvas in each round, only for a new opponent to emerge as the contest progressed.[189]

The York Foundation provided a battle ground for Arian and Trinitarian, hinging on the intent of the donor, Dame Sarah Hewley. At no point was there any suggestion of intentional maladministration, for all the Unitarian Trustees were well-known men of honour and position.[190]

To start with, the defendants were more than willing to answer all the questions put to them with regard to their conduct as Trustees, but less than forthcoming about the essential nature of their religious beliefs. One crucial defence witness was Charles Wellbeloved, minister of St. Saviourgate chapel, a Sub-Trustee, and the principal and divinity tutor of the Unitarian College at York, founded in Manchester in 1786 and transferred in 1803. Wellbeloved was a local antiquary and archaeologist of note, and a founder of the York Subscription Library, York Philosophical Society and the York Institute. After the calamitous fire at the Minster in 1829, he took a leading part in raising funds for its restoration. As the minister of the St. Saviourgate congregation, Wellbeloved received a grant of £80 per year from the Hewley Trustees, which, with the existing stipend, made it the wealthiest Dissenting living in the north, and perhaps in the country. The York Academy was described in 1819 as a Unitarian seminary supported by endowments, with about 20 pupils, the lay-students admitted for three years and their theological colleagues for five years. In 1821 the Academy was said to be in receipt of annual grants from charities in Hull, Manchester and Liverpool, as well as £120 from Hewley funds. Wellbeloved and John Kenrick, the classics, literature and history tutor 'without question the greatest scholar of his denomination',[191] argued in 1827 that the college was open to students from any persuasion and the majority of the students were 'Presbyterians' (Unitarians frequently used this sobriquet at this time, especially when title to property was in question),[192] and that no distinctive doctrines were taught. Nevertheless, most theological students at York seem to have entered the Unitarian ministry. James Martineau, who studied under Wellbeloved at York, described him as 'candid and catholic, simple and thorough'.[193] The Relators, however, did not regard Wellbeloved as a 'Godly Preacher' within Lady Hewley's definition of the term. The question of the Manchester College endowment was one of the three main areas of enquiry in the court action.

On 23 December 1833, the Vice-Chancellor of England, Sir Lancelot Shadwell, concluded that 'the ministers or preachers of what are called the Unitarian belief … are not fit objects of, and are not entitled to partake of the charities of Dame Sarah Hewley' and ordered the removal of the existing Trustees from office and the appointment of Trinitarian successors in their place.[194] The defendants promptly appealed but on 5 February 1836 two judges, Baron Alderson and Mr Justice Patterson, with the approval of Lord Chancellor Lyndhurst, rejected this, stating the Hewley Trustees had misapplied the funds by favouring persons of their own persuasion, and again found in favour of the Relators. The parties then agreed to further proceedings held in Gray's Inn hall, at the end of which Lord Lyndhurst again upheld the Vice-Chancellor's decision. The defendants immediately decided to take the case to the House of Lords.[195]

Relations between the Unitarians and the other Dissenting denominations had already soured to such an extent that by 1835 matters came to a head after orthodox leaders pushed to prevent Unitarians holding office in the various joint bodies formed to protect nonconformist interests. Not surprisingly, the Unitarians responded by withdrawing from the ministerial committee of the Three Denominations (including Presbyterian, of which the Unitarians claimed to be a part) and from the lay Protestant Deputies.[196]

While the Hewley case continued its tortuous course through the courts, it is clear that the Unitarian Trustees continued to meet, despite the legal impediments to their activities, for we have a note of an incident in 1836. In February of that year, 'the Duke of Leeds' stagecoach was involved in a serious accident near Rochdale, on its way from Manchester to Leeds. One of the wheels came off and several of the passengers were injured, including the Revd. William Turner, the Unitarian minister at Halifax, who suffered deep gashes to the head. The report of the accident stated that 'The Rev. gentleman was returning from Manchester where he had been to attend the anniversary meeting of the trustees of Lady

Hewley's charity'.[197]

Before the case was heard in the Lords, a new scenario opened up. The Relators had negotiated with a Master in Chancery for the removal and replacement of the former Trustees, subject to the Attorney-General's approval. However, the case now became still more complicated. Somehow, several members of the Church of Scotland (the Kirk) and the Scottish Secession Church, resident in the north of England, discovered the names of the Relators' nominees as new Trustees. In the hope of benefiting from the Trust themselves, the two bodies also applied to the Master to be allowed to make nominations. This was granted in the Master's report of 16 December 1837. Under the new scheme the Relators were permitted to identify three possible Grand Trustees and three Sub-Trustees, while the Kirk and the Seceders were each allowed to propose two Grand Trustees and two Sub-Trustees.[198]

On 5 August 1842, the case reached the Lords. Six of the seven judges found for the Relators, and the Lord Chancellor reiterated that as all the former Trustees and Sub-Trustees had concurred in the misapplication of funds, they were all without exception disqualified, mostly on the grounds of their Unitarianism which was contrary to Lady Hewley's religious beliefs. The Vice-Chancellor's decision, nine years before, was now declared final. Lord Henley, one of the Masters in Chancery, was asked to proceed without delay in choosing new Trustees. The 1837 report was then re-examined and found wanting, for it had been largely negative. The various nonconformist denominations, who had previously combined in a united front against the Unitarians, now divided to fight their own corners for sectarian advantage.[199] The Independents, who had first challenged the old Trustees, now began to think seriously about monopolising the Hewley Trust and its funds for their denomination alone, maintaining that while Dame Sarah may have been a Presbyterian, they were the modern lineal descendants of the Presbyterians, and accused those who called themselves Presbyterians of being either Unitarians or Dissenters whose origins lay within the Scots Kirk, thereby rendering them ineligible even if they lived in the northern counties of England.

Before the denominational wrangling was finally resolved, however, there was another twist to the long-running saga. When the Hewley case went against them in the House of Lords, and soon afterwards the Wolverhampton Chapel Case, the Unitarians realised with dismay that their title to all their older (at least 200) properties and trusts had become exceedingly tenuous. Following intense lobbying by the Unitarians and those sympathetic to their cause, and to avoid a possible legal minefield, Lord Lyndhurst persuaded Sir Robert Peel's administration to table an important measure to prevent the endowments of Dissenting communions from being despoiled by one another. The law at that time held that the faith of the founder was held to be binding on successive generations of Dissenters; a change or development of creed might forfeit an endowment, and what one sect forfeited another might claim. The Government measure proposed instead that 'when there is no trust deed at all, or none determining the doctrine, polity, or worship, a usage of twenty-five years should be taken as conclusive evidence of the right of any congregation to the possession of their place of worship, and the schools, burial grounds, and endowments thereto'. Despite vigorous opposition in the country and fierce debate in both Houses, the Government Bill had a straightforward passage, and passed into law as the Dissenters' Chapels Act on 19 July 1844, relieving much of the immediate and potentially devastating threat to Unitarian property and trusts, whereby they retained St. Saviourgate chapel in York (but whose minister ceased to receive a Hewley grant).

Gradually, too, the confusing appellation 'Presbyterian' disappeared from most Unitarian places of worship.[200]

A new case, *Attorney-General v Wilson*, based on Lord Henley's deliberations and findings, was heard before the Vice-Chancellor in May and June 1848. The Vice-Chancellor's decision this time was to some extent counter to the 1843 proposals for new Trustees, and it would seem that over the intervening years there were a number of contradictions and changes of heart by judges, lawyers (and the parties they represented). The Vice-Chancellor nominated a fresh set of new Trustees, but there was immediate concern from the various interests. An appeal was lodged in the August of that year, requesting the Vice-Chancellor to reconsider, and the different parties were given time to negotiate, compromise and agree.

The final hearing was held before the Attorney-General on 25 January 1849, when a variation on the previous year's judgement was made, and the basis for much of the Trust's present practice established, and then confirmed by the Lord Chancellor, Lord Cottenham. Dame Sarah's emphasis on qualifying beneficiaries living primarily in York, Yorkshire and the other five Northern Counties was confirmed. The term 'godly preachers of Christ's Holy

Gospel, mentioned in both the 1705 and 1707 Foundation deeds of the Trust was now interpreted to apply only to orthodox (*i.e.*) Trinitarian English Dissenting ministers of Dissenting churches and congregations essentially the same in doctrine and discipline as those in Lady Hewley's time. This was understood to encompass only Baptist (not until then represented in any of the Hewley law suits or subsequent negotiations), Independent (by then increasingly known as Congregational) and Presbyterian persuasions, and specifically excluded those under the control of or in communion with the Church of Scotland or the Scottish Secession Church. Similar interpretations were made in respect to the remaining Hewley Charity categories: minister's widows, encouraging the Gospel in poor places, helping godly people in distress, the poor people admitted to the Almshouses, and exhibitions to assist students training for the ministry, all of whom had to be members of one or other of these three denominations. The funds were to be distributed amongst the three participating bodies in the following proportions: Baptists two ninths, Presbyterians three-ninths and Independents four-ninths. The seven Grand Trustees (and the Sub-Trustees managing the Almshouses) were henceforth to be drawn from the three denominations in the ratio of one Baptist, three Independents and three Presbyterians. When an Independent or Presbyterian vacancy occurred, the two surviving representatives of that denomination were to appoint a successor, while Baptist replacements were to be selected by the remaining Grand and Sub-Trustees, presumably by soundings within that communion. The appointment of new Sub-Trustees was to be subject to the approval of the Grand Trustees. Six of the fourteen nominated in 1848 as either Grand or Sub-Trustees declined to serve and were accordingly discharged from that responsibility.[201]

The total cost of the whole sad struggle between 1830 and 1849, but whose antecedents went back to the time of Robert Moody, is said to have amounted to £23,453.[202] In 1849 the Accountant-General for the Court of Exchequer held £21,425 in trust arising from the cause *Attorney-General v Shore and others*. This was ordered to be used to meet the costs incurred by the various parties in the civil case *Attorney-General v Wilson*, and any surplus or dividends paid over to the the new Treasurer of the Trust.[203]

The former Grand Trustees who were still alive (Offley Shore, Peter Heywood, Daniel Gaskell, and John Wood) conveyed the Hewley Trust estates into the hands of the new Grand Trustees on 11 March, 1850, by which time they had been at work almost a year.[204]

The New Dispensation

The new Trustees met for the first time at Wills' Coffee house in Lincoln's Inn Fields on 25 April 1849, just three months after the end of the long litigation. The Baptist representative, distinguished nonconformist and outstanding businessman, Samuel Morton Peto, was elected to chair this first meeting. William Vizard was in attendance and read the Decree of the Lord Chancellor of 21 January, declaring the objects of the Charity. The Trustees resolved that the Trust Deeds and the Rules made by Lady Hewley, together with the Decree, should be printed for the use of the Trustees and to guide intending applicants to the Trust.

Vizard was appointed Receiver (*i.e.* Secretary or Clerk) for the next year, to manage the estates and collect the rents, to report at the half-yearly meetings, take minutes, receive applications for grants and send a schedule of these to each Trustee. An advertisement to be inserted in Northern newspapers inviting applications from poor ministers and widows would insist on applications being made on a printed form available from any Trustee.

At the next meeting, a month later, valuations of the properties were ordered to be bound up, and schedules of deeds and archives entered in the minutes. At the September meeting that year, the Trustees resolved to strengthen their hands by applying to the Court of Chancery to transfer the Trust's funds into their names.

In 1853 the question of obtaining the portraits of Sir John and Lady Sarah Hewley, then in St. Saviourgate chapel, was considered and an attempt made to secure these for the Trust; however, the minister, still the Revd. Charles Wellbeloved, was understandably reluctant to part with them.[205]

From 1849, it was normally the policy until most of the estates were sold off, to have one of the two Trust meetings each year in London, and the other in a suitable location near the Almshouses or one or more of the estates. So we find meetings taking place not only in York, but also at Scarborough, Saltburn, and Knaresborough or Harrogate, and the Trustees then visited either the Almshouses or one or other of the estates.[206] After 1849, the Trustees of the new regime also adopted a more stringent attitude towards administration, receiving income from bank accounts, and also investing heavily in Consols (Government Securities)

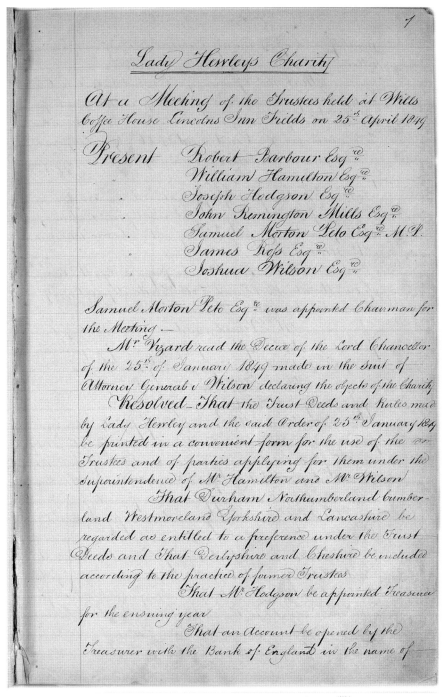

when this proved possible (particularly mining royalties).[20]

On 21 June 1878 the Charity Commission introduced new arrangements for the better administration of charities generally. After much discussion, the Hewley Trustees applied on 27 May 1879 for the establishment of a Scheme for the future regulation of the Trust estates and the distribution of Hewley charity funds.[208] The Commissioners advertised their intention to approve a Scheme with detailed notices at the Almshouses in York and in the local and national press.

The Commissioners' Order had two schedules, the first noting the different estates (with tenancies and acreages), investments and financial holdings, and the second specifying the rules governing the future administration of the Charities, many of which were merely a continuation of existing practice. The Scheme included the vesting of all real estate in 'The Official Trustee of Charity Lands' and all financial estate in 'The Official Trustees of Charitable Funds'. The present Trustees were to continue in the same ratio as before: three Independents (Congregationalists), three Presbyterians and one Baptist, but disqualification would occur in the event of the bankruptcy, incapacity or non-attendance (for two years) of any of them; Trust vacancies were to continue to be filled according to the court directions made in 1849. The Grand Trustees were to hold at least two meetings, plus any special meetings, each year, the Clerk to give at least 21 days notice to each Trustee; a quorum at meetings would be constituted by a minimum attendance of four Trustees; all matters were to be determined by a majority vote; and the Trustees were empowered to appoint sub-committees.

Robert Barbour of Manchester, businessman and one of the first of the New Trustees in 1849. From the original portrait at Westminster College, Cambridge.

One Trustee was to be elected Treasurer, with power to appoint a Treasurer's Clerk at a salary not then exceeding £50 per year; the Trustees were to employ an Auditor each year at an appropriate fee. The Trustees were to appoint a Clerk (at a salary then of no more than £150 per year) who was to keep the accounts, summon and attend (and keep the minutes of) all Trustees' meetings, forward copies of accounts as required under the Charitable Trusts Acts, and discharge other administrative duties as necessary, save those requiring the services of a legal advisor; if the Trustees appointed someone else to keep the accounts, they could pay that person a proportion of the Clerk's salary. The Trustees could appoint a Land Agent and Collector to manage their lands and estates and receive the rents due to the Trust, being paid no more than 3% of the gross amount of the yearly rents. Every appointment of a paid officer was revo-

cable by the Trustees, and no Trustee was to receive any salary or remuneration other than that stipulated in 1705.

Account and minute books were to be provided by the Trustees, with
the appointment of each new Trustee and all Trust proceedings properly
recorded in the minute book, which was to be signed either by the chairman at the end of that meeting or subsequently. Full accounts were to be
kept of the income and expenditure in account books provided, with the
accounts stated for each year, and examined and approved at the first
meeting of the ensuing year, and signed by the Chairman. Sufficient
accounts of the endowments, receipts and outgoings of the Hewley
Charity were to be forwarded to the Charity Commissioners, and published in compliance with the Charitable Trusts Acts. The Trustees were to
arrange for a fire-proof box to be deposited in some secure place for the
safe-keeping of deeds, archives, minutes, accounts and other Trust documents, together with a list of these signed by the Clerk. All monies not
required for immediate Trust use were to be deposited at a Bank appointed by the Trustees; all cheques and money orders were to be signed by
three Trustees, one of whom was to be the Treasurer. All unoccupied
estate lands were to be let or otherwise managed by the Trustees, adequate public notice being given in the parish in which the property lay. Net
proceeds arising from timber sales and mining royalties and income were
to be regarded as capital and invested in Government funds in the name of
'The Official Trustees of Charitable Funds', save in exceptional cases
authorised by the Charity Commissioners.

All the proper costs of administering and managing the Trust (including discretionary subscriptions, of not more than £100 per year, to local
religious and secular projects in the localities where the Trust has property) were to be defrayed first out of current Trust income after the charity's
objects had been met: payments to or for (1) poor and godly preachers of
Christ's Holy Gospel (2) poor and godly widows of such preachers (3)
encouraging or promoting the preaching of such Gospel in such poor
places as the Trustees think fit (4) providing up to 50 exhibitions in any
one year for the education of young men designed for the ministry of
Christ's Holy Gospel (5) relieving 'godly persons' in distress (6) necessary
repairs and insurance of the Hospital or Almshouse in York, and providing £250 in addition for the support and maintenance of its inhabitants.
In the selection of recipients of Trust benefits, preference was to be given
to those living in York, Yorkshire and the Northern Counties, while the

definitions of those qualifying for benefit was to accord with the court judgement of 1849. The distribution of the charity's benefits was to be made by the Trustees together and not by any Trustee individually; no Trustee was to hold or occupy, directly or indirectly, for his or anyone else's use, any of the Trust's lands, or be engaged in the supply of goods or work at the cost of the Trust.

The Grand Trustees were to elect and appoint seven Sub-Trustees to be managers of the Almshouses, three each from the Independent and Presbyterian denominations, and one from the Baptists. No Sub-Trustee was to continue in the event of bankruptcy, incapacity or non-attendance (for two years); vacancies amongst the Sub-Trustees were to be filled in the same manner as the Trustees [in practice the Sub-Trustees made recommendations which were then confirmed by the Grand Trustees].

The full number of almspeople to be ten, elected and ordered in accordance with Dame Sarah's instructions in 1707 and 1709, and the rules and regulations approved by her for the government of the Almshouse, apart from the variations in this Order. The annual allowance to the Hospital, not exceeding £250, to be fixed by the Trustees, with each almsperson being paid a weekly or periodic payment (or payment in kind if preferred) as the Sub-Trustees saw fit, having regard to the needs and circumstances of each individual there. No almsperson was to let or part with their part of the property, or allow any other person to occupy their Almshouse without the express permission of the Sub-Trustees. Each application for admission as an almsperson was to be in writing and accompanied by sufficient qualifying testimonials; and no appointment was to be made until sufficient notice of the vacancy was given within the city of York, and every appointment was to be made at a special meeting of the Sub-Trustees, held not less nor more than one month after a vacancy arose. The Sub-Trustees were to keep a register of the names, ages and descriptions of all almspeople admitted, the date of each vacancy and a note of all applicants. The Sub-Trustees were permitted to introduce such reasonable regulations as they considered justifiable for the running of the Almshouse and for looking after the almspeople, provided that these did not conflict with the provisions of the Scheme.

A copy of the Scheme was to be kept with the Trust's archives. Any person interested in the Trust would be allowed to take copies of all or part of the Scheme. Any questions about the validity of any proceedings specified under the Scheme were to be determined by the Charity

Commissioners, and if the Trustees were to have any doubts or questions as to how to interpret any of the Scheme's provisions or the management of the Charity, they could apply to the Charity Commissioners for opinion and advice which, when given, would be binding on the Trustees and anyone else affected. The Trustees were acknowledged to own the freehold of the Almshouses in St. Saviourgate, adjoining St. Saviour's church and rectory, in York. The Almshouses were occupied by ten poor old women all aged over 55, who had to repeat a *Catechism*. There was a resident 'chaplain' who looked after the inmates and the buildings.

By a further Order, dated 5 July 1881, The Lady Hewley Trust and its estates were brought more immediately under the direct jurisdiction of the Charity Commissioners of England and Wales. This formulated and established a Scheme for the future administration and management of the Charity that embraced most of the elements outlined in the previous Order or Scheme. All the Charity's lands and estates were to continue to be vested in 'The Official Trustee', and all stocks, shares, funds and securities belonging to or held in trust on behalf of the Charity were directed to be transferred into the hands of 'The Official Trustees of Charitable Funds', together with all cash not required for current expenditure.[209]

In the first schedule of the Scheme, details are set out of the estates and funds belonging to the Charity in 1881. 'The Official Trustee' was to be a party and give consent to any dealings involving either land or investments.[210] In the event of the Trustees wishing to acquire property, the report of their surveyor approving the purchase was to be submitted to the Charity Commissioners, who would, if agreeable, authorise the acquisition, which when completed had also to be vested in 'The Official Trustee of Charity Lands'. If and when the Trustees intended to sell lands, a similar procedure was to be followed, with 'The Official Trustee' made a party to the conveyance, and with all sale receipts invested in his name on behalf of the Charities. All minerals and the right to work them were to be reserved to the Charity's Trustees on any sale, and any mining leases were also subject to the approval of the Commissioners, rents paid under mining leases being regarded as capital income.[211] Separate registers of the Trust's sales, purchases and exchanges were to be kept henceforth for each of the estates, and added to as and when such transactions occurred. A complete record of all the Charity Commissioners' Orders was then kept at the Hewley Trust's solicitors, Messrs. Vizards, who also kept a record of all the long leases and assignments granted by the Trustees.[212] Since that time there have been updates and variations on Charity Commission Orders and Schemes affecting the the Lady Hewley Trust, as set out at the start of this publication.

In 1935, the Trustees considered their investment policy, receiving advice from Messrs. R J Tilney of Liverpool, the present Investment Advisors. However, when the Charity Commissioners were approached about the Tilney proposals, suggesting the sale of some Government stocks and public securities and the purchase of equities, the response was stern but understandable: only the Official Brokers were permitted to act through the Bank of England to invest the funds of charities.[213] In 1953, the Almshouses Association suggested charities with substantial investments should seek the guidance of a stockbroker, but it was pointed that the Charity Commissioners had a decided viewpoint about this. In the following May, Tilneys were again asked to provide advice and suggested a change in policy but in line with institutional and trust investors in the United Kingdom, transferring some of the capital sum into top-class equities and insurance shares. After due consideration, the Trustees decided not to make any alterations for the moment. Nevertheless, Tilneys provided further guidance the following year, valuing stocks at their then median value and recommending the purchase of equities.[214] The response from the Charity Commissioners continued to be obdurate; they could not agree to charity money being invested in equities, however well-known, and stated the brokers would have to be the Bank of England, although they would have no objection to Tilneys advising from time to time. In 1958 the Trustees were concerned at the advice received from the Official Broker, expressing strong disapproval at the idea of undated stocks for their Charity.[215] The Charity Commissioners had a change of heart in 1967, and stated that the Trustees could now use the advice and services of local financial advisors and stockbrokers if they wished.[216]

The Hewley Almshouses: St. Saviourgate

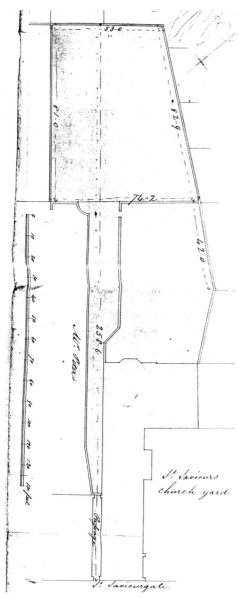

Site plan accompanying purchase deed for Hewley Almshouses, 1838. Hewley MSS.

In June or July 1840 (accounts differ), the new Almshouses opened in St. Saviourgate, the inhabitants apparently transferred direct from Tanner Row without the need arising for interim quarters.[217]

The new Almshouses were in two senses like coming home: the newly-built Hospital was virtually on the site of the Hewley's town house, and a few feet away, on the other side of the east window of St. Saviour's parish church, lay the mortal remains of Dame Sarah and her husband Sir John.[218] The buildings were to the design of a leading Yorkshire architect, James Pigott Pritchett, much of whose varied work, such as York's Assembly Rooms and the Savings Bank, still survives. His most impressive work is perhaps Huddersfield railway station. He was for a time architect to the Dean and Chapter of York Minster, and for 50 years surveyor and architect at Wentworth Woodhouse. A prominent local Congregationalist, he subsequently served as a Sub-Trustee for the Hewley Charity.[219]

Exclusive of the price of the site, the cost of building the almshouses was £1711 12s 8d.[220] Originally intended for nine widows and a married couple, these nine stone dwellings, with a former chapel converted into an additional dwelling, and a caretaker's house, are still in use today, although substantial interior alterations and improvements have been carried out over the intervening years, particularly in more recent times. The main building 'has a more spread-out style commonly found in rural establishments of this kind. A long stone-faced range in Tudor style has a series of doorways giving access to the individual dwellings. The warden's [or supervisor's] house is a separate block, double-fronted but with the gable-end to the street and in the same style as the almshouses'.[221] In the end wall of this house, and fronting onto St. Saviourgate, is a large square stone tablet with the sculptured arms of the Hewley family and the original wording brought from the old Tanner Row Almshouse; these have been reset, together with an inscription which reads:

This hospital (removed from Tanner Row) was erected in 1840 under the order of the Court of Chancery in the cause 'Attorney General v Shore and others'
Pritchett & Son Architects

Joseph Blower
Receiver
61 Lincolns Inn Fields

This noble Almshouse, transferred from the original building, built and exactly paid, nine or ten years before she died where in the space of that time, she expended above £1500[222]

While the entire Trust property was the responsibility of the Court of Chancery from 1830 to 1849, care was still taken during this time to ensure that the Almshouses, first in Tanner Row and then in St. Saviourgate, were kept in a reasonable state of repair. For example, William Vizard, the Receiver for the Hewley estates after the death of Joseph Blower in 1845, spent about £16 the next year (1846) on bricklayers, carpenters, ironmongers and on glazing work, painting the outside of the building and the chapel interior, and on gravel for the paths.[223] The new Trustees and Sub-Trustees were also quick to meet the needs of the almspeople from 1849. Expenditure up to £50 was authorised in 1850 for painting, papering and colouring 'in accordance with Mr. Pritchett's estimate',[224] and over the next ten years they paid out almost a further £100, clearly a concern for the welfare of the buildings as well as the residents.[225]

The Sub-Trustees have customarily, but not invariably, met at the Almshouses, to consider the health and well-being of the residents, vetting applications and filling vacancies (and occasionally allowing relatives and friends to live with them), giving Christmas bonuses and other grants (from the annual sums allocated to them by the Trustees), regularly reviewing the condition of the buildings and initiating redecoration, maintenance and repairs when needed, as well as recommending names to the Trustees as replacements when one or more Sub-Trustees have resigned or died.

In 1875 the Sub-Trustees 'representing the greatly increased cost of all the necessities of life' requested the Grand Trustees to increase their grant to the almswomen. The Trustees agreed to increase this from £180 to £250 per year, and in 1920 the Sub-Trustees asked that in view of the increased cost of living this might be further increased. When this was referred to the Charity Commission, the response was that the almsfolk could each be allowed up to £40 per year and, if any of them were in receipt of other income, the annual total should not exceed £46.[226] In 1927, the amount allowed for the ten inhabitants of the Almshouses was fixed at £400 in total each year, and in 1946 pensions of ten or fifteen shillings per week, according to means, became payable.[227] Since 1984, because of the high level of maintenance of the Almshouse dwellings, it has been necessary to ask residents to pay a notional contribution or rent toward the upkeep of the premises, offset to some extent by the development of state pension provision, as well as other living allowances.

The Sub-Trustees also had to arbitrate and help the residents on occasion: for example, in 1925 one resident's large number of cats had become a nuisance to the other almswomen and the Sub-Trustees decided that in future residents should be allowed only one cat each. The following year the offending woman was still 'harbouring' her cats which had become insanitary; after ignoring repeated warnings, the Sub-Trustees, acting in conjunction with the local Health Officer, finally evicted her. Her house was then ordered to be cleansed and redecorated, although it should be stated that redecoration of cottages later became standard practice to be carried out in any interval between tenants.

We see the Sub-Trustees keeping a careful watch over the Almshouses and the residents, concerned when there was sickness, injury and death, and making arrangements when necessary for care in the Infirmary or elsewhere (including one case in 1936 where an almswoman had to be removed there after serious illness brought about by an over-fondness for whisky), and organising a home help for a resident having to sleep downstairs. In 1875 a doctor's certificate was submitted on behalf of one resident who was suffering from 'a weak and nervous condition which rendered her liable to violent paroxysms of excitement succeeded by depression, so that it was unsafe for her to live alone'. The Trustees gave a grant so that a carer might be employed to live with her. In 1913 the Sub-Trustees again contacted the Trustees enquiring about the arrangements to be made when the services of a nurse were needed. It was decided that an appropriate individual should be brought in when hospital care was not required.[228] From 1927 and for many years, the Sub-Trustees gave annual grants to the Percy Cust District Nursing Fund, from 1933 to York County Hospital and from 1938 to the Dispensary on account of the help received from these organisations.

In 1930, Henry Reid, who had been 'chaplain' or supervisor for the previous 22 years, died and his niece Mary Nish took over as 'overseer', living in the Chaplain's House (no.1); she was to observe rules determined in 1904, except that prayers were now to be said weekly not daily, and these were usually led in turn by local Baptist, Congregational and Presbyterian ministers, although the practice seems to have fallen into abeyance during part of World War II.[229] At the end of Sub-Trustees' meetings, Miss Nish provided tea for the gathering and reported on the health and well-being of the residents in her care, as well as the exterior and interior state of the buildings and any work required.

Over the years, innovations had to be discussed which seem very tame to us now but which were momentous then, such as the possibility in 1932 of introducing 'wirelesses'; by 1960 a television aerial had been erected over no. 2 cottage and there was serious doubt on insurance grounds as to whether this should be allowed, but two years later two other cottages had television and the Sub-Trustees accepted the situation. In 1966, one resident requested that she be allowed a telephone; this was granted provided she paid all the expenses involved; this too soon became general. In more modern times, the warden was permitted to have a washing machine, and in 1992 it was noted that one resident owned a car which she had difficulty in parking.

By 1940 the cottages had been converted from gas to electric lighting by York Corporation and the almsfolk were delighted with the change. A severe frost that winter resulted in damage to roofs, drainpipes and outside lavatories, and money had to be spent on rectifying this. From 12 March 1941, during the Second World War, Firewatchers (paid by the Hewley Trust) took up their duties, relieving the Sub-Trustees of the need to do this. On the night of 23 September 1942 an incendiary bomb fell on the Almshouses slightly damaging no. 7, but occasioning no bodily harm.[230]

In 1946 one Trustee, Mr S M Swan, suggested that as the Almshouses were in what he considered a 'depressing area' the Trustees might give some thought to moving to a fresh site. The Agent, Mr Allison, was asked

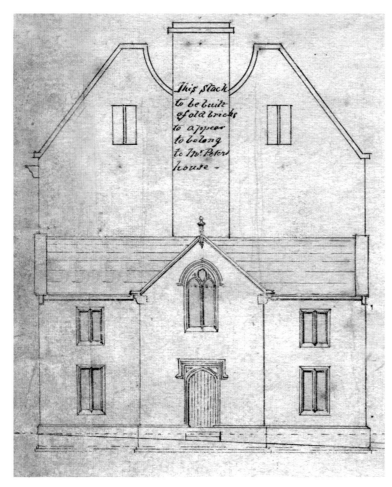

Within the drawing: *This stack to be built of old bricks to appear to belong to M.r Peter house —*

The side elevation of the Hewley Almshouses. From the architect's plan, 1839, in the possession of the Sub-Trustees.

to seek the advice of the Charity Commission, investigate York City Town Planning and Improvement schemes, and also report on the state of the Almshouse fabric. He subsequently provided a detailed statement on the buildings, which he described as 'well and substantially built of brick, with stone on front and side elevations, and roofs slated. The stonework is well preserved, the brickwork sound, except yard walls … Some eaves and gutters need repair or renewal'. He commented on the condition of each cottage and the repairs necessary, chief of which were the fractures in the back bedroom (believed to have come to rest, and unlikely to be of further trouble) in no. 1, signs of settlement in the wall of no. 7, and a leaky roof in the chapel. Mr Allison considered the Almshouse block could be maintained in a habitable condition until such time as a move might take place. The next year, York's City Council expressed interest in purchasing the site but later abandoned the idea.[231]

In 1948, Miss Nish retired and became a resident herself. In her place, Miss Christine Young, a retired assistant matron and a Presbyterian, was appointed to the overseer's post. At this juncture a bath and hot-water system was decided upon for her house; the Ministry of Works refused to sanction the work but these were installed in 1950. At the same time the Grand Trustees felt unable to accede to the Sub-Trustees' request to install a hot-water system in all the cottages. However, after a meeting with a representative of the National Association of Almshouses (to which the

Lady Hewley Trust has subscribed since 1952)[232] the Trustees agreed in 1954 to carry out these improvements, subject to a 50% grant being obtained from the local authority under the terms of the Housing Act 1949. The Trust's architect, Mr Biscombe, of Messrs. Biscombe, Ferry & Whipp, of York, prepared a scheme involving all the dwellings apart from no. 1, the lowest tender received being £2198 by Messrs. T W Taylor & Sons of York, with the total cost of the scheme being just over £2500. Under the Housing Act, the Trustees would be entitled to a grant once the Government gave the go-ahead. The original scheme was intended to include bathrooms with dormer windows to increase headroom, and indoor toilets, but the latter had to be abandoned at that stage due to cost. The local authority approved the Lady Hewley Trust as a Housing Association within the meaning of the Act, and permission to proceed was duly given by the Ministry of Housing and Local Government, permitting the work to go ahead and the first of the grants (£161 annually for 20 years) to be made, the first such scheme in York. Work began in May 1956, but was slowed considerably by bad weather and not completed until spring 1957. The final cost of the work was, with necessary repairs encountered along the way, £3519, less grant aid.[233]

Inevitably, there were disputes, as from 1933 to 1935 when the ownership of the passageway between the chaplain's (supervisor's) house (no. 1) and the adjacent York House, 16 St. Saviourgate, caused concern. The problem was that the passageway belonged to the Trustees but was held partly in common, with the York House owners and occupants having a right of entry and reasonable access, which was abused. In 1958, York House came on the market and it was suggested to the Sub-Trustees that this might be a useful addition to the Almshouse accommodation. While this would dispose of the problem of a shared passageway, the Sub-Trustees were against increasing the size and scope of the Almshouses on this occasion as they felt no. 16 was unsuitable for elderly people. The cost of conversion and modernisation into five self-contained flats was likely to be considerable and there would still be the problem of climbing stairs to the top of the three-floor building. There might also be a lack of appropriate applicants. The Trustees concurred with the Sub-Trustees' view.[234] The property was later sold by the York House Improvement Society to a private individual and then to a firm of solicitors, whose alterations to the building were expected to enhance the neighbourhood. After negotiation in 1976, the new owners took possession of the ground floor passage, and part of the basement cellar and adjacent passageway, agreeing to erect a dividing wall and reroute the gas and water supplies.[235] Unfortunately, that was not the end of the matter as the question of legal ownership of the passageway between the two properties surfaced again in 1994 and had to be referred to the Trust's solicitor.

In 1959 the Hewley Trust's increasing involvement with the National Association of Almshouses became more obvious with the first of many Christmas gifts of confectionery, distributed to the Almspeople. The NAA's *Almshouses Gazette* has proved helpful to the Sub-Trustees and Trustees and showed that the Trust was providing accommodation conforming to modern standards.

In 1967 Miss Young died and Miss Catherine Carle was appointed to succeed her and became the new occupant of no. 1, which now had to have further repairs. The next year most of the cottages were rewired, and considerable work was undertaken to eliminate damp. In addition the Memorial Plaque on the street wall of no. 1 was reincised and renovated by a local firm, and the following year York Civic Trust offered at its own cost to repaint the Hewley coat of arms in the correct heraldic colours. The Hewley arms were cleaned and further embellished in 1976.

In 1972, with the coming together of Congregationalists and Presbyterians to form the United Reformed Church, the Sub-Trustees were concerned that this might affect the appointment of residents (who were normally admitted on a denominational rota basis) as well as the Sub-Trustees themselves. This applied to the Grand Trustees as well of course, and was not completely sorted until the Charity Commission's final comprehensive ruling in 1976. At the same time the Sub-Trustees submitted that the Almshouse rules of 1849 were no longer generally applicable and required updating, spending much time over the next year or so revising these. The proposed alterations were then forwarded to the Trustees for their comments. The Charity Commission issued a new scheme in 1975, but the Sub-Trustees felt led to suggest further amendments to the Trustees, who agreed that the minimum qualification for admission to the Almshouses should be regular membership of a participating congregation (Baptist, Congregational or United Reformed Church) together with a recommendation from that person's minister.[236] The Charity Commission finally approved the revised scheme in 1976.

Further work to remove dampness from walls and roofs had to be undertaken in 1970. This was by now a constant problem, occasioning regular attention, as it was not only a health hazard but was also causing frequent damage to masonry, woodwork, the roof and guttering. In 1972, the report of the architect Mr P Ferry (of Messrs. Ferry & Mennim, York) signalled that extensive roof repairs were required, especially at the rear of the premises. He added 'These premises are of considerable architectural importance and I feel it would be a mistake to use any other material than slate'. As the building was Grade II listed it might be eligible for a grant, as the building lay within the conservation area but outside the scope of York's Town Scheme.[237] The cheapest estimate for this work was almost £3000 and an application for a Historic Buildings grant was submitted to the City Council, who sought the permission of the Department of the Environment. In the end a grant of £350 was given only for the roof of no. 1, with the remaining refelting and reslating work being paid for by the Trustees (£4170).[238] In 1975, the stonework of Almshouse no. 1 was cleaned.[239] That same year the Trustees accepted a proposal to make better use of the Almshouse property by converting the chapel into a maisonette, henceforth to be known as no. 8A.

By 1977 the Trustees were sufficiently anxious about the damp condition of the Almshouses to consider the expensive step of installing central heating but after consulting the residents it was decided to convert cottages piecemeal as they became vacant, at the same time modernising the interiors, especially the kitchens. By 1978 concern was being felt because of ominous cracks and apparent movements at no. 1 and a burst water main was at first suspected. The stone pillars at the main entrance were also badly cracked. A structural engineer was consulted who carried out test bores, which revealed serious foundation deficiencies; immediate restorative work was essential. It was said remedial work should ensure stability for many years to come.[240] By the following year the new foundation work had been completed and internal cracks filled in.

By 1980 there was trouble at no. 1 again, with more damp patches and the hump on the cellar floor more pronounced. It was felt that Miss Carle should go to a hotel for a week while the floor was relaid and a damp-proof course inserted.[241] This work was done, as well as a new leaded roof, with 25% grants each from York City Council and the Department of the Environment.

In 1981, there were signs of movement in the front wall of no. 7 cottage, and 'tell-tales' were placed there to monitor the situation; by the following year the situation appeared to have stabilised. However, in 1982 severe damp became apparent in no. 10, and it was decided to insert air bricks and treat the interior walls.[242]

It was shortly after this that the warden, Miss Carle, resigned, and was succeeded by the present incumbent, Mrs Elsie Pinder, of York Baptist church, who began her duties in February 1984, and was immediately recognised as an able supervisor. The Sub-Trustees had at this point to approach the Trustees following an application from a divorced lady; it was felt that this should not be an impediment to admission and she was consequently admitted as a resident.[243]

In 1984, following disturbing signs of settlement, the Agent, Mr Wilkinson, reported that the lower of two estimates he had received for repair work amounted to £89,700, of which £43,000 was for underpinning. The Trustees asked him for more estimates and to ascertain whether grants might be available from the local authority, the relevant Ministry or any other organisation, while the Clerk, Mr Wharrie, was asked to examine insurance aspects. Mr A E Lightly, of Messrs. Boulton & Cooper, and the York building firm of H Watson, had prepared a structural survey. By 2 October, the surveyors Stansfield, Burton & Agar had reported and were then instructed to prepare an architectural plan for the repairs. A firm of civil engineers, Messrs. Fairhurst & Son, was also appointed and their representative, Mr B E Pettinger, advised piling, at a cost of about £50,000, after a full geotechnical or subsoil survey. The Trust's insurers had been informed and, while admitting no liability at that stage, had appointed loss adjusters. No other renovation work would be undertaken until the subsidence problem had been solved.

In detail, there were serious settlement problems affecting cottages 7-10, at the Stonebow end of the Almshouses. Watson's had called in a specialist firm, Pynfold (Midlands) Ltd., who confirmed serious movement was occurring, possibly due to ground of inadequate bearing capacity or conceivably changes in ground water levels. Remedial measures would be extensive and expensive. Mr Pettinger stated that no. 8 had settled most, with a 15 cm. drop below basement floor level, and had inadequate foundations, with soft silt and water underneath. No. 7 was badly cracked; a 36 cm. trial hole revealed a very thick Roman wall and (dry) culvert. Further trial holes in the alleyway at the back of the cottages revealed another Roman drain (also dry). He concluded that his investigations confirmed historical evidence that the site lay in the midst of a bog (the adjoining parish church had reputedly been known in medieval times as

'St. Saviours in the Marsh').[244] Ordinary reinforced concrete would be use-less and any piling scheme would have to be founded below swamp level. Pettinger believed the hinge point of this broken-back problem lay on the Roman wall immediately below no. 7 cottage.[245]

At the next Trustees' meeting, on 4 June 1985, it was apparent the loss adjusters would not admit the need for extensive works. Pettinger thought they should be challenged, and it was decided to seek the help of a legal specialist, Mr Peter Knight of Vizards. In the meantime the damage was getting worse: the occupant of no. 3 cottage had recently moved out, and an examination of its foundations revealed the collapse of a subterranean mediaeval drain, causing localised settlement. By the October meeting, the loss adjusters stated they did not accept Pettinger's findings and wished to employ their own firm of consulting engineers. The Trustees agreed, and asked Pettinger to accompany their engineer when he visited the site.[246]

At the next two meetings, it was reported that Mr Knight had received counsel's opinion and had written to the loss adjusters, who now accepted liability for damage to buildings above ground level but not for rectifica-tion of the cause. The Trustees were pleased to learn of this partial shift of position but felt it was insufficient and agreed that legal proceedings should now be commenced against the insurance company. It was pointed out that since the Almshouses were Grade II listed, they could not be demolished but were eligible for various grants subject to the availability of funds. It was agreed the Charity Commissioners would have to be informed before any large expenditure was incurred on repairs. No. 7 and no. 10 cottages were deteriorating badly.

When the writ was served on the insurance company, it promptly served a defence document on the Trustees, to the effect that subsidence had been continuous since 1840 whereas the insurance policy had only been in operation from March 1975 to March 1986 at which point it had excluded this risk. Consequently the company stated that it was only liable for a small proportion of the damage, and regarded the requisite repairs as cosmetic only; the Trust was therefore offered £1500 to settle the claim! To prove their case, the Trustees now needed to demonstrate that subsidence had occurred during the period of insurance cover. To support this they had the expert evidence of Pettinger, and also that of architects, surveyors and builders who had been involved with the Almshouses in previous years, none of whom had reported subsidence while attending to remedial or improvement work. The total cost of repairs was estimated, with professional fees etc., to be between £130,000 and £200,000 depending on the outcome of the case.[247]

The Trustees pressed on with their legal case. Statements were taken from a wide range of people who had had knowledge of the property, and they supported the view that the subsidence was recent, although there was a possibility of mild settlement in 1840. The claim was then for the piling scheme, repairs, and redecoration at £106,000, with additional costs such as fees, VAT, rehabilitation and contingencies amounting to £44,000, making £150,000 in all. It was against this background that Peter Knight and the Clerk met representatives of the insurance company on 29 May 1987. The firm still resisted the claim and had recosted Pettinger's piling scheme, stating the only piling work required was beneath the worst affected areas; in consequence they would offer an *ex gratia* payment of £25,000, with a further £6000 for fees and extras, and would be prepared to re-insure the buildings if this was accepted. The Trustees declined this in the light of professional advice and, by the autumn, it was announced that the two firms of engineers acting for the Trust and the insurance company had agreed on the amount of piling needed and that the insurance company now agreed to pay half the overall costs. York City Council Planning Department had stated they would look favourably on any request for a grant of up to 40% towards approved building works. The overall cost was now reduced to just over £94,000 including rehabilitation and administration; if the insurance company met half this sum and York City Council was able to assist, this would reduce the cost to the Trust to not much more than £22,000.[248]

Work started in earnest on the Almshouses in the autumn of 1988, the residents being housed temporarily in York City property, the local Abbeyfield Home, a flat in Coppergate, and elsewhere. Gas, electricity, water and telephones were disconnected, and furniture not required by the ladies was put in store, so that all the cottages were empty. Underpinning work now began to cure the basic defects, and applications were made to English Heritage and York City Council for assistance with this major project. The first phase of the repair work was finished in January 1989, but this was then followed by the process of general making-good, and the replacement of kitchen floors. By that August a central-heating system had been installed and painting and decorating were in progress, although it was noted that there was still at this stage a considerable quantity of rubble and rubbish on site. The net cost of rehousing residents, including

The proposed elevation of the gable end of the Chaplain's house from the architect's plan, 1839.

furniture storage, removals etc. amounted to £6165. The residents began to return that autumn, with the first three moving back in September 1989 and by 1991 the cottages were again all occupied. Despite this, there was still plenty of work to be done: external decoration, door locks and general security, attention to guttering and downpipes, repointing in the back yards, joinery work and tiling in bathrooms. That year another £8000 was spent in upgrading the buildings, with £3000 in 1992 and £1500 in 1993, by which time things were quietening down on the repair front. At this point Mrs Pinder presented a garden seat for the use of the residents, and the Sub-Trustees provided a second seat.

The Grand Trustees had in 1986 requested the Sub-Trustees to provide a long-term report on the future of the Almshouses, their advantages and disadvantages, and whether alternatives should now be considered, such as sheltered accommodation. The Sub-Trustees produced a detailed report. They felt the cottages offered independence and the benefit of a small Christian community, were centrally located, and had low housing costs. However, they were old buildings, lacked central heating and suffered from some traffic noise. There was no provision for medical attention. The Sub-Trustees felt the cottages should be modernised and brought up to date, with more realistic rents being charged, believing that if this was done there would be no shortage of suitable applicants although some of these would come from outside the immediate York area.

Following damage in 1994 to one of the cottages with a small fire that might have become a major catastrophe, Mrs Pinder was congratulated for her 'expeditious work' in attending to matters so quickly, and the Sub-Trustees were quick to arrange for smoke alarms to be fitted to each cottage. The Grand Trustees were concerned about the lack of applicants and in 1998 asked the Charity Commission if men might be admitted. In 1999 the present contract was entered into with York Conservation Trust to manage the Almshouse property, with the cost of all repairs being born in future by the Trustees; this would enable the Sub-Trustees to concentrate on the welfare of the residents. Meanwhile a rolling programme to update the other cottages was carried out, with the residents moving in turn into no. 9.

Gable end of the Warden's house today.

In 1999 the Cottages were visited by the Secretary of the Almshouses Association, Major-General Anthony Leask, who raised the following points: personal alarms for residents; security lighting, the filling of vacancies; the principle of residents' maintenance payments. These would be raised with the Grand Trustees. In 2000, the rules governing the Almshouse were again revised, and these included the Sub-Trustees being given the power to arrange for medical examinations of the residents. Later that year some consideration was given by the two sets of Trustees to extending the Almshouse facilities to married couples, by converting and combining nos. 8A and 9 (this work was carried out the following year, and the new two-bedroom cottage has since been known as no. 9).

In 1882 an Eliza Margaret Taylor left an additional endowment of £90 to the Hewley Trust for the benefit of the Almshouses and their residents. The Trustees made this sum up to £100, and it was then invested in Government stock.[249] It was decided in 1984 to use the Eliza Taylor interest to supplement Christmas bonuses for the Almswomen.

In 1979 the Sub-Trustees decided to dispense with the term 'Almshouses' and substitute the term 'Cottages', having done away with 'Almsbodies' in favour of 'Residents' some years before, thereby modernising concepts and simultaneously adding to the dignity of those occupying the dwellings.

The Grand Trustees have for many years periodically invited the Sub-Trustees to dine with them in York.[250]

The Charity Estates and their Management

Acquisition The Charity lands were acquired for the most part by Dame Sarah's father, Robert Woolrich of Gray's Inn. Robert probably took advantage of the times to obtain the estates of impoverished royalists. Most of the manor of **West Ayton**, five miles west of Scarborough (renowned by 1667 as the pioneer seaside resort and soon famous for its spa waters),[251] was purchased by him and others, mostly lawyers, in a long drawn-out saga lasting from 1636 to 1657. When James Mauleverer found himself in severe financial difficulties, he mortgaged much of the manor of West Ayton to secure a lump sum of £5000, repaying at the rate of £800 per year, a commitment he was unable to maintain. Woolrich appears to have agreed to buy his partners out, and emerged with a lease for 1000 years of three quarters of the manor (yearly value £516) with the remainder being retained by the Mauleverer family. In 1739 the Trustees bought all the rights to the remaining quarter of the property from James' descendant, Timothy Mauleverer, for £300.[252] In 1877, this estate comprised 1095 acres, of which 810 were arable; in addition there were 110 acres of woodland. 1050 acres was in the occupation of the two principal tenants, James and Thomas Darrell.[253]

Haya Park, less than a mile to the east of Knaresborough, another older spa town,[254] was purchased by Woolrich from Sir William Langley, Christopher Conyers and Samuel Pearce 'for a competent sum' in 1652, 'now disparked'. The following year Henry Withes and the Darcy family sold the manors of Braycroft and Killinghall for £2700 to Robert Woolrich, who then went on to acquire Brearton and Sussacres (or Southacres) about four miles away for £416 from Francis Parker in 1661, just before Robert's death that year. In 1662 John and Sarah Hewley leased Brearton and Sussacres back to the Parker family on a twenty-one year lease at £26.5s per year. A small property at Conistrop [Coneythorpe] was purchased by Sir John Hewley from a George Tireman and his wife Anne in 1670. Brearton, Sussacres and Coneythorpe were all later absorbed into Haya Park.[255] In 1877 this estate, formerly 1588 acres, had grown through the respective purchases in 1868 and 1871 of 178 and 13 acres in neighbouring Arkendale, and in 1873 by the purchase of a further acre in Brearton, making a total of around 1780 acres, of which 1170 was arable. Seven of the 14 tenants had relatively large holdings of around 200 acres each and together occupied almost 1700 acres.[256]

In 1657 Robert Woolrich purchased estates at **Eston** (about three miles south-east of Middlesbrough) and **Margrove** (originally Maggrave) **Park** (in Skelton, approximately one mile from Guisbrorough) from George and Sir William Darcy, who later (1677-1679) attempted unsuccessfully to reclaim these lands from the Hewleys. By 1877 the Eston estate comprised 624 acres, of which 368 were arable. The two principal tenants were John Jackson and the Garbutts, with about 610 acres between them, but both these gave up their holdings and by 1877 there were more than 50 tenants all with fairly small holdings. Margrove Park at this time had 270 acres, of which 47 acres were arable. Sixteen acres of the estate was taken by the Cleveland Railway in 1861. The estate included about 16 acres of waste-land known as Stanghow Moor, and in addition there were 11 acres of woodland. The principal tenants were William Dale and the Wilkinsons, with around 200 acres between them.[257]

The estates acquired by Robert Woolrich were inherited by his daughter and heiress, Sarah Hewley, and his son-in-law John, in 1661. After Sir John's death in 1697, she became the sole owner and a very wealthy woman. The properties in Tanner Row, **York**, were then purchased by Dame Sarah from Sir Godfrey Copley in 1699 for the specific purpose of acquiring a site for an Almshouse or Hospital.[258]

In 1840, the **Whixley** estate of about 45 acres, about seven miles north-east of Knaresborough, was bought by direction of the Court of Chancery with the surplus proceeds (just under £2000) of the compulsory purchase of the Almshouse site in Tanner Row, York, by Hudson's York & North Midland Railway Company.[259] This money was the residue remaining after the cost of the site and new Almshouse buildings erected in St. Saviourgate, and the rental was to be used for the additional maintenance of the Almshouse and its residents. The property was bought from the Bailey family, and in 1877 John Bailey still continued to farm there.[260]

Management The Trust's first account book starts in 1711 with an inventory or schedule of the tenants and the rents of the lands acquired by the Trustees after the death of Dame Sarah the previous autumn. (The illustration on page 2 shows an extract from the account book for 1719.) These comprised property around the Hospital or Almshouse within the city of York (7 tenants, rental value £33.5s.6d.); Haya Park, with nearby Conistrop [Conisthorpe] and Brearton with Sussacres (23 tenants in all, rental value £468.11s.8d.);

and West Ayton (34 tenants, rental value £308.3s.8d.). The Steward for these estates was Alexander Harrison. The remaining tenancies, at Eston (7 tenants, rental value £133.7s.) and Skelton [Margrove Park] (1 tenant, rental value £50) in Cleveland were administered by a second Steward, George Matthews.

Initially, there were small abatements of rent allowed to Asculph Snowdon at Eston, Thomas Gill at Margrove Park, and George Johnson at Haya Park 'as Lady Hewley was wont to do' but these concessions did not last long. Then, in 1735, Asculph's executor, Philip Snowdon, and his under tenant, Nicholas Patton, petitioned that the farmland leased to Asculph for a further 21 years 'was let too dear' at £140 per year; the Trustees consented and reduced the rent to £120.[261]

At first the Stewards were paid a fixed annual fee for their services. For many years, the Harrisons received £30 per year, and the Matthews £10. In the late eighteenth century the Trustees decided that all the estates could be looked after by just one steward, John Matthews, who was paid an annual salary that soon rose to £110 a year.

To start with, rents were payable to Harrison at Lady Day [25 March, at the end of the winter] and Pentecost, while those to Matthews were to be paid at Martinmas [11 November, before the onset of winter] and Whitsuntide [Pentecost].[262] Because of this 'needless distinction', the rent days were changed in 1733 to Lady Day and Michaelmas [29 September]. From at least 1742 until 1913, the Trustees paid for Tenants' Dinners twice a year on the two largest estates, Haya Park and West Ayton.[263] Each year there were various deductions to pay: taxes levied by the Crown including Land Tax and towards the maintenance of the Militia; local rate assessments for poor relief, upkeep of the parish highways (and building a road from the Turnpike to Richard Waddington's farm at Haya Park), and support of the parish clerk and the parish constable; ecclesiastical levies towards maintaining the parish churches at Hutton Buscel, notably the chancel (West Ayton) and Knaresborough, especially 'the Trustees gallery' (Haya Park and associated properties) with tithes payable to the two incumbents, while in 1824 the Trustees paid £32 to purchase three pews in the 'newly erected [parish] church' at Eston for the use of the tenants; there were also free rents payable including one of £100 per year (less taxes) out of Haya Park, and a small amount to the Cayley family out of West Ayton.[264]

'Contracts' (leases) were renewed usually for the same set term of

An Account of Money received and disbursed by the Trustees of Lady Hewley's
Charity from the 10th of September 1772. to the 9th of September 1773. an Inventory or
Schedule of Rents belonging to the Trustees of the Charity of Dame Lady Sarah
Hewley late of the City of York Widow deceased for one whole Year ending at
Lady day 1773. according to the Accounts by the Stewards. —

The Charge —

The Trust Estate of the City of York and in and near Hay park, Conistrop
Brewton and Sufsacres and West Ayton in the County of York which Mr John
Harrison hath in Charge.
NB The Rent days Michaelmass and Lady Day. —

In York. —

Thomas Anderson	£2 —
John Cundall	3 —
Alexander Harrison	1 —
John Thaxby	2..5..
John Tate	4..2..
John Telford	27 —

(bracketed total: 39)

At Conistrop —
Christopher Bramley see below.

At Hay Park —

Philip Abam	£90 —
Thomas Barnet	36..10..
William Benson	91 —
Christopher Bramley	14 —
Richard Bruce	26 —
James Clarke	19 —
John East	1..10..
John Illingworth	21 —
William Howgate	98 —
Christopher Johnson	32 —
Thomas Matterson	83..9..6
Francis Moor	9..9..
George Parker	34 —
Exec. of Sir H. Slingby	
George Nitty	13..10..6
Francis Wardman	15..10..
William Wheelhouse	6..16..6
William Wilson	84 —

(bracketed total: 675)

At Brearton & Sufsacres. —

Sarah Smith	26

At West Ayton. —

Robert Acklam	£19..19..
Timothy Belt	18..8..6
John Bravener	..14..

Rents payable for York, Haya Park, part of West Ayton etc, 1773. Hewley MSS.

years and at the same time on each estate, subject to a tenant's satisfactory performance in past years.

In 1738 new leases for 30 years were awarded to the tenants at York, including Mr John Telford, gardener, for 'a messuage, dwelling house, barn, stable etc. together with garden with a variety of plants, flowers ... '[265] In 1747, when the Trustees were considering new leases for the Haya Park tenants, they may have had reservations when told that 'Beecroft of a mean character has broken up two closes of fresh ground', especially as the terms of his original lease probably forbad converting pastureland into arable.[266] In 1795, the Trustees determined that in view of the 'improper conduct' (unspecified) of Joseph Harker he should not be allowed to continue as a tenant at Eston, and the Steward was ordered to advertise his holding at not less than £70 per year.[267] In 1802, the Trustees decided to incorporate in their leases the relevant parts of a specimen document drawn up by a Thomas Trotter, and also to use part of a new lease granted to one of the Haya Park tenants, particularly with regard to what crops should be grown and ground tilled in each tenancy.[268]

In 1815, at the end of the Napoleonic Wars, the Trustees were, like other landowners, seriously concerned about the state of agriculture and land values.[269] As the agrarian situation deteriorated, the Trustees began in 1816 to allow abatements of rent, varying from 5% to 20% half-yearly or annually, to tenants on all the estates, provided all rent arrears were paid.[270] The situation slowly improved from around 1824, but the Trustees were still allowing a modest abatement as late as 1830.[271]

Over the years we find the Stewards noting that rents have been forfeited due to farms standing empty or, as in 1717 'lost the rent of Elizabeth Thornton's house fallen down'. Sometimes the Trustees were generous in their attitude to tenants who fell into arrears, and on occasion 'forgave' rent arrears.[272] In 1750 there was concern and sympathy for the tenants at West Ayton 'about their Loss by the Distemper among the Cattle', for which an allowance of £129 was given three years later, when the full extent of the ravages of the disease were known; in 1754 John Smith was also allowed £20 for his loss of cattle at Brearton and Sussacres, while the following year Benjamin Pennington was allowed money for two losses of cattle.[273] There were moments too, when tenants were at loggerheads: in 1720 the Steward, George Matthews, had to travel twice to Eston 'to view John Mewburne's farmhouses, hedges etc ... to make an end to ye difference betwixt [him] and Asculph Snowdon ... ' By the following year Mewburne had gone and Snowdon was looking after his Old Farm and a larger New Farm ('late Mewburne's').[274]

The Trustees constantly sought ways to keep themselves better informed, including the provision of detailed valuations, and later maps and plans for each member, as in 1773 when one Trustee, Robert Markham, was 'desired to get Books of Maps prepared on a small scale of each farm belonging to the Trust, for each of the Trustees, such books to be interleaved with blank paper for remarks'.[275]

The Trustees were not blind to agricultural improvements, as in 1720 when Asculph Snowdon of Eston was allowed £4 'spent on lime for tillage' and a year later his widow a further £12 for lime used on the New Farm, and in 1728 Philip Snowdon for an additional £3 for lime.[276] Nor were they were slow to allow for building, rebuilding and the upkeep of farms generally. Normally, the Stewards were sent to attend to property matters but, as and when necessary, a small group or sub-committee of

Trustees was delegated to attend to estate matters. This took formal effect in 1877 when a permanent Estates Committee comprising three of the Trustees was appointed; this group stayed in being for many years thereafter, and in 1878 was given the authority to grant 7, 14 or 21 year leases.[277]

When Tenants were genuinely beset by hardship or difficulty, the Trustees were understanding, as in 1778 when the 'Dwelling house newly erected at Haya Park near the Brown Moor intended for occupation by Mr Whalley (at a cost of £244) having been nearly burned down by accident, agreed £29 be paid to meet damage caused by this misfortune', and

Hay Park.

Philip Aham's Receipt	10.–	£232 14 3	
Mr Benson's Ditto for a year's Composition Tythe due Michaelmas 1778 to the Vicar of Knaresbrough	1..6..8		
Anthony Blanchard's Receipt for Materials for Mr Whalley's house	4.10.6		
Thomas Layton's Receipt for Tiles & for Ditto	15.12.–		
Thomas Matterson's do towards repairs	10.–.–		
Wm Wilson's do for Ditto	10..3.–		
A whole year's Fee Farm Rent paid Mr Thomas Wilkinson for James Fox Esqr due at Lady day 1779 as pr Receipt	80.–.–		
Expences &ca with Tenant to two half years	5..8..6		

Building Notes & Improvements at Mr Whalley's House at Brown Moor ——

Paid Joseph Scruton	15..4.6
Ditto	15..15.–
Robinson & Bulmer	8..8.–
Ditto	8..8.–
Ditto	10..–.–
Ditto	4..4.–
Ditto by John Whalley	3..7.–
Thomas Foster	29..6..7½
William Thompson	13..2..1
Robert Snowden	13..19..9
William Harrison	10..15.–
John Melthorpe	4..4.–

Carried forward. £136.13.11½ 1261 14 3

Whalley was not required to pay any rent for five weeks[278] and when Ralph Jackson's stable at Margrove Park was partially burnt down a few years later, the Trustees allowed him £20 towards its repair.[279]

There was much more to estate management than setting fair rents, collecting them, and ensuring the holdings were properly farmed and the buildings in good repair. The Trustees demonstrated considerable business acumen over the years in not only offsetting tenants' rents to effect improvements to farmhouses, stables, barns, granaries and outbuildings, but also encouraged regular income for the Trust by the sale of timber and bark from the different estates when possible. Tenants at each estate were particularly charged with the responsibility for looking after the woods and plantations, especially at West Ayton, Haya Park and Margrove Park. At West Ayton, Thomas Heddon (1719-1729), Richard Lillay (1754-1773) and William Hall (1774-1813) were each paid 30 shillings a year as woodmen[280] while as late as 1919 the Trustees were pleased to note that 'Raine the woodman has returned safe after three years in France, and is now working in the plantations'.[281] In the early nineteenth century, one of the tenants at Haya Park, John Lumley, acted as the woodman at the same salary as his West Ayton counterparts.[282]

The first wood sales noted in the record occur in 1724.[283] In 1767 a John Scott was given the task of numbering the trees at Haya Park with screw irons and paint.[284] In 1789 Messrs Telford, the nurserymen and Hewley tenants in York, were paid for tree-planting at West Ayton; three years later the Telfords' opinion was sought as to the practicality of creating a plantation about 50 feet deep along two sides of a moor section; Telford then planted 2½ acres of trees there. [285] In 1799, the value of the oak, ash, elm and elder trees standing and growing at the smallest estate, Margrove Park, was estimated to be £162.[286] A steady income in wood sales was being derived from the late eighteenth century.[287]

Between 1812 and 1817 a William Brown supplied 'quickwood', larch, ash and young trees for West Ayton, while in 1815 young trees were bought from a Mr Elliott of Newcastle upon Tyne, and then shipped down to Scarborough. In 1817 the Trustees obtained £243 from the sale of Haya Park timber and ordered that the timber not intended to be sold was to be marked and numbered: 'the larger trees … with white paint and smaller ones with red paint'; the following year, this one estate achieved £2188 in wood sales.[288]

Estate features All the estates had remarkable features. At West Ayton, for example, from the very time that the first Trustees took over from Dane Sarah, 'repairing the banks against the river Derwent' is a frequent entry in the minutes and accounts, with allowances made to tenants because of flooding of fields, farmhouses and buildings. 'Banking the low ground' and 'mending the banks when broken down' were common experiences. And in 1792 the Trustees ordered that the banks of the Derwent be properly 'spiled' (i.e. strengthened and protected by wooden piling). That same year a Mr Edward Cockshutt applied to renew a lease permitting him to erect a dam for the use of the Iron Forge near to West Ayton.[289] Another recurrent expense at West Ayton was the water mill, which appeared to require constant attention, with hardly a year going by without money being spent on the structure or its machinery. In 1722 the mill spindle and the milldam needed major repairs, while in 1740 a new mill stone was needed as well as remedial work on the mill itself.[290] In 1747 the Steward was to purchase a new millstone while the miller was to meet the cost of new cogs, rungs and ironwork.[291]

An eighteenth century water-mill similar to that at West Ayton.

Haya Park's distinctive characteristic seemed to be the quantity of building work carried out there, over and above all the allowances made to individual tenants to improve their properties. In 1746 the Trustees embarked on a major building, rebuilding and repair programme. Clay that had already been dug was to be made into bricks by George Poulter and John Briggs of Knaresborough, who later that year were asked to make a further 30,000 bricks 'at such place where good clay can be found' near the centre of the Park. Further work followed for the brickmakers on and off until 1760, and for George Holden the bricklayer and Robert Thompson the carpenter and their workmen, as well as other trades: building contractor, smith, tiler, woodcutter, painter, glazier, carrier ('leading materials') and suppliers of straw, laths, lime, timber, nails, iron bars, poles, stones, slates, flagstones, and stone ridges. Evidently it was thirsty work for there is an entry 'for ale for the workmen'.[292] As a result of this work there was insufficient money in the Trust Treasurer's hands in 1747 to make any distributions. Yet more reconstruction was undertaken between 1778 and 1781.[293]

Tim Addison

In 1806 the Trustees were again concerned about the condition of the buildings at Haya Park, and a Knaresborough surveyor, Mr Driffield, was asked to estimate the cost of necessary repairs.[294] In 1813 the Trustees allowed John Lumley £47 to rebuild his cowhouse 'which fell down the last winter'.[295] Then in 1817 Mr Driffield was again employed to prepare plans and estimates for a substantial rebuilding scheme, which lasted until 1826, with hundreds of thousand of bricks made and several thousand pounds spent.[296]

The Haya Park tenants were told in 1773 that if they did not repair the road through the Park sufficiently 'in the nature of a turnpike road' and properly dress the adjoining fences, the Trustees would have it done at the tenants' expense[297]

At Eston the main tenant there, Ralph Jackson, was allowed £120 towards repairing his farmhouse kitchen and outbuildings in 1806, with more if the expenditure proved greater, and the following year he was permitted another £70.[298] In 1814 he was allowed further money to rebuild a couple of cottages and in 1818 yet more to build a new granary.[299]

At Margrove Park, the new Steward, Zachary Hubbersty, reported in 1793 that considerable damage had been caused to the estate by workmen at the nearby Alum Works, belonging to a William Chaloner. The Trustees' response was to ask Hubbersty to write to Chaloner proposing the appointment of arbitrators satisfactory to both parties; two years later, the Trustees were still attempting to bring the proprietors of the Guisborough Alum Works 'to a reference'.[300]

In 1804, the major tenant, Ralph Jackson, was allowed £20 towards rebuilding a stable 'lately much damaged by fire', while in 1805 he was given permission to build a 'thrashing machine' on his farm, at his own expense, although the Trustees would consider giving him financial assistance at some point in the future.[301]

Litigation period Between 1830 and 1849, during the prolonged period of litigation, the Hewley estates were administered by the Court of Chancery, with a Receiver appointed by the Vice-Chancellor. The first such Receiver was Joseph Blower, a London solicitor, and on his death in 1845 he was succeeded by his partner, William Vizard junior, whose firm continues to be involved with the Trust to this day. Both Blower and Vizard worked hard to ensure the Hewley estates were maintained in good order, collecting rents and spending as necessary on the various properties. During the period when he acted for the Court, Vizard kept a detailed account book, indicating the names, properties and rents of tenants, together with arrears (if any), repairs and improvements to farms and buildings, including the Almshouses in York, the allowances paid to the Almspeople, the costs of tenants' dinners each April and August at Haya Park (£5. 5s.) and West Ayton (£4. 4s.), wood sales and other income, insurances and rates and other deductions. He also noted the large sums of money paid out to Mr Josiah Parkes, the Engineer to the Royal Agricultural Society, to drain the Trust estates, as ordered by the Court, and paid for by the tenants at approximately 20% per year of the cost for their holding. This account was then certified by a Master in Chancery, J W Farrar.[302]

The new Trust Once the new Trust came into being, the Trustees were keen to ensure that income was not solely dependent on the tenants' rental contributions. As early as 1849 and continuing in succeeding years, sales of wood were adding healthily to funds. For the first few years timber sales fetched £200-£300 every 12 months. In 1859 the Agent, John Parrington, was allowed £20 for over-seeing the felling, barking and chopping of more than nine tons of larch and oak trees (at 42 shillings per ton), and small amounts for felling 200 scotch fir and dressing oak timber, all at Margrove Park.[303]

In 1939 the Trustees resolved to undertake an ambitious four-year reaf-forestation scheme at Spiker's Hill (27 acres) at West Ayton, with a detailed analysis of the situation, soil, pests, climate and locality, choice of species, methods of planting, fencing and rotation from year to year, at a cost of £2655 and with an expected return of £17,830. A further detailed scheme for this plantation was commenced in 1947 at a cost of £1300, by which time grants for dedicated woodland were available from the Forestry Commission.[304] In 1950 an afforestation scheme for more than 17 acres of waste land at Margrove Park was completed, but about one acre of young trees was destroyed by fire two years later, and had to be replanted. Then in 1956 a further $3^{1}/_{2}$ acres of this plantation were burnt by a fire, caused by a spark from a railway engine; this spread over the embankment and intervening grassland to the plantation 200 yards away.[305]

During this time Joseph Blower and William Vizard were paid on an entirely different basis from former Stewards: their proper expenses plus 'Receiver's Poundage', 5% of each year's rental receipts. When the trust was reborn in 1849, William Vizard was appointed the new Steward and

Secretary at a salary of £50 plus 5% of each year's rental income, initially yielding about £300 per year. This was soon boosted by the addition of $2^{1}/_{2}$% of all the 'overworkings' by Messrs. Bolckow Vaughan on the Trust Royalty at Eston.[306]

As part of the new dispensation, the Trustees set about their task with vigour and enthusiasm, perhaps feeling that after all the previous legal hiatus they were a little on probation.

In 1849 William Vizard provided for the new Trustees his observations on the condition of the Hewley estates: 'When I first entered upon the management of the property in 1845 [for the Court], it appeared to me that many of the farms were underlet and that a new valuation was necessary. Most of the property needed draining so its value and potential couldn't be ascertained until this was done; it is generally reckoned that about three years is necessary between draining and valuation so the land can show benefit. Haya Park was mostly drained in 1847 so it could be valued next year [1850] – the tenants are well pleased and said they didn't know how they could have paid rents without it, given the present prices'.

During the period the property has been in Chancery, 'substantial Farm Buildings have been erected upon most of the Farms'. Tenants pay their rents punctually but don't farm their land as it should be done. 'They have not kept pace with the advance in the science of agriculture during the last 15 years. For example, they still keep up with the old system now exploded of having a naked fallow once in three or four years. Neither do they fat a sufficient quantity of stock to keep the land well manured and in good condition. They use lime, but liming without manuring only impoverishes the land as lime in itself contains no fertilising property, but is only instrumental in drawing out the properties contained in the land to which it is applied. I therefore recommend that in the new lettings stringent terms be laid upon the Tenants obliging them to adopt the four or five course of culture and to fat stock in proportion to the size of their Farms'.

'I cannot conclude without calling the attention of the Trustees to the remarkable (and unprecedented, I believe) circumstance of this Charity Estate after a very expensive litigation of 18 years coming out of the Court of Chancery with an Increased Income of £1000 a year and Increased Capital of £18000'.[307]

When William Vizard Junior died in 1876, he was succeeded as Secretary by his son-in-law George Augustus Crowder, and it was at that

<table>
<tr><td></td><td colspan="2">Bro.t over ———— £</td><td>101</td><td>8</td><td>11</td><td>3062</td><td>13</td><td>1</td></tr>
</table>

To paid Mr Driffield for superintending the Building &c. of y.e Farm
  House for Jonathan Andrews ... 10 . 7 . —

To p.d Tho.s Johnson for a Pair of
  New Mill Stones ... 14 . — . —

To p.d for Tenants Dinners Two
  Half Years as usual ... 10 . — . — ——— 135 . 15 . 11

Eston

To allow'd to the several Tenants an
  abatement of 10 p.Ct out of their
  whole Years rent of £611.5.6 ... ——— 61 . 2 . 6

Maggrave Park

To the like allowance to the Tenants
  out of their whole Years rent of £120.6.— ... 12 . — . 6

To p.d Jos.h Hicks for gathering Stones
  & building a Wall at the New Plantation upon the Moor ... 13 . 14 . 6

To p.d Will.m Wilson for Leading Stones
  for the said Plantation Wall ... 9 . 3 . 1½

To p.d Geo. Brigham in part for Planting the Moor with Trees ... 42 . 6 . —

To p.d for making Grips to let off the
  Water from the Moor ... — . 6 . —

To p.d for measuring the Wall in
  order to calculate the expence ... 1 . — . — ——— 78 . 10 . 1½

York

To p.d the Rev.d Cha.s Wellbeloved the am.t
  of Rob.t Gray the Bricklayers bill
  for repairs at the Hospital in 1820 ... 13 . 17 . 9

To p.d Geo. Lockey for Deals Boards &c.
  for the Hospital in 1820 ... — . 3 . 3

To p.d John Jackson for mending the
  Pump in 1820 ... — . 8 . —

To remitted the Rev.d Cha.s Wellbeloved
  the am.t of several Workmens bills
  for Repairs at the Hospital in 1819 & 1821 ... 27 . 3 . 11½ ——— 41 . 12 . 11½

To p.d Mr John Mathews for making
  the assignment of the Tithes of
  Hall &c. Park from the Earl Rosslyn
  to the Trustees of this Charity in 1819 ... 16 . 6 . 2 ——— 16 . 6 . 2

Incidents

To p.d at the Register office at Northallerton ... — . 16 . —

To p.d for Receipt stamps for one Year ... 3 . 16 . 6

To p.d for Postages & Carr.e of Parcels &c. ... 2 . 6 . 9

To „ Fox Esq.r one Years Fee Farm Rent
  due at Lady day 1822 ... £100
  deduct Stamp tax ... 3 . 4 . 2½ ——— 96 . 15 . 9½

To amount of arrears of Rent charged but not
  received at Lady day 1822 ... 107 . 10 . 2

To p.d the Subtrustees of Lady Hewleys Hospital
  at York the several binefactions up to the
  1.st April 1823 ... 180 . — . —

To p.d Mr John Mathews the Steward of this
  Trust one Years Salary due at Lady day 1822 ... 110 . — . —

<table>
<tr><td></td><td>Carr.d forward ———</td><td></td><td></td><td></td><td>3897</td><td>5</td><td>11½</td></tr>
</table>

point that the Trustees decided to have a 'competent Land Agent' in addition (who appears to have been a Mr Prior, assisted by Mr Dewes), to
advise them on any agricultural or farming matters, at the same time
appointing John Jackson of Lackenby, who had helped the Trustees in
many ways over the years as Crowder's agent at Eston and Margrove Park,
partly because of the mining interests and partly because of the possibility
of selling off building land. In 1880, as part of the new scheme the
Charity Commissioners were introducing, the Trustees decided to employ
Mr R W F Mills of York, estate agent and valuer, to supervise the estates
generally, attend to repair of buildings, set out drainage works, look after
the woods and plantations, receive the rents and render half-yearly
accounts, receiving 3% of the annual gross rental as remuneration.
Mineral and wayleave matters were however excluded. Within a short
space of time, Mills had visited all the estates and subsequently suggested
the Trustees should spend £5000 on drainage and £2000 on building
repairs over the next five years, and it was decided to seek Charity
Commission approval for this. The Secretary, G A Crowder, was now
appointed to the new post of Clerk.[308]

By 1885 Mills provided an annual report stating that there had been 'a
decided improvement in the weather since the previous May but not in the
position of the Farmer; the corn crop last year was generally light and the
prices lower than the preceding year. Because of the dry summer and a
deficiency of grass, coupled with a fall in the price of meat grazing
became as unprofitable as growing corn, so many farms had given up', but
only one Hewley tenant. More drainage works had been carried out at
Haya Park and Eston. The West Ayton tenants did not wish to bear the
cost of a piped water supply. Several of the Eston smallholdings were likely to be given up due to the diminished demand for ironstone and reduction of wages. In 1890 the new Agent Forbes commented that through the
improvement in trade in the country, agricultural prospects were much
brighter 'Barley has made a better price and there has been a slight
improvement in Oats but the price of Wheat has been lower'. Stock had
been selling well, and it was the breeder who was now getting the benefit
as grazing animals had been very expensive to buy. The following year he
reported that 'agricultural prospects are not very encouraging, as the price
of corn still continues low although there has been a slight improvement
in the price of wheat. A great loss in the past season of grazing Stock, tenants in many cases selling at the same price as they had originally bought

This Indenture Made the Thirteenth Day of January, In the third Year of the Reigne of our Soveraigne Lady Anne, by the Grace of God, of England, Scotland, ffrance, and Ireland, Queene, Defender of the ffaith, &c. Annoq: Dñi 1704, Between Dame Sarah Howley of the City of Yorke, Widow, Relict and Executrix of the last Will and Testament of Sr John Howley, late of Grey's Inne in the County of Middx, Knt, her late husband, docd, and daughter, heire, & Administratrix of the Goods and Chattels of Robert Woolrich, otherwise Wolrych, late of Grey's Inne aforesaid Esqr deceased, of the one part, And Richard Stretton the Elder of ffatton Garden in the said County of Middx, Gent, Nathaniel Gold of the parish of St Mary Newington in the said County of Middx, Esqr, Thomas Marriott of Grey's Inne in the said County of Middx, Esqr, John Bridges of ffatton garden aforesaid, Merchant, Thomas Nesbitt of London, Merchant, Thomas Colton of the City of Yorke, Gent, and James Winlow of Yarm in the County of Yorke, Gent, of the other part. Whereas, by Indres of Lease and Release, the Lease bearing Date the Day next before the Day of the Date of these presents, and the Release bearing even date herewith, and made or mentioned to be made betweene the same partys as are to these presents, The said Dame Sarah Howley, for the Considerations therein respectively mentioned, Hath Conveyed unto the said Richard Stretton, Nathaniel Gold, Thomas Marriott, John Bridges, Thomas Nesbit, Thomas Colton, and James Winlow, and their heires, The Mannors of Killinghall and Braymoft, with their Rights, Members, and appurtenres in the said County of Yorke, And the Parke or Inclosed Ground sometimes used as a Parke and now Disparked, comonly called Haya Parke, in the said County of Yorke, And divers Messuages, Lands, Tenements, Closes, Meadows, Pastures, Woods, Lodges, & Hereditaments, in the same Indentures of Lease and Release mentioned, Situate, lying, and being within the Townes, Parishes, ffields, precincts, or Territoryes of Killinghall, Ripley, Suffarnes, als Southarnes Brereton and Knaresbrough, in the said County of Yorke, To the Use of the said Dame Sarah Howley during the terme of her naturall Life, without Impeachment of Waft, And from after her Decease To the Use of the said Richard Stretton, Nathaniel Gold, Thomas Marriott, John Bridges, Thomas Nesbitt, Thomas Colton, and James Winlow, their heires and Assignes for Ever; Nevertheless under such provisoes and powers for making of Leases of the premisses, and for Revoking or Altering of the said Uses and limiting new or other Uses of the said premisses, or any part thereof, by the said Dame Sarah Howley, as in the same Indenture of Release are for those purposes Expressed and contained. And Whereas, by Indenture of Assignment bearing also even date herewith, and made or mentioned to be made betweene the same partys as are to these presents, The said Dame Sarah Howley, for the Considerations therein mentioned, Hath Granted, Bargained, Sold, Assigned, and sett over unto the said Richard Stretton, Nathaniel Gold, Thomas Marriott, John Bridges, Thomas Nesbitt, Thomas Colton, and James Winlow, their Executors, Admrs, and Assignes, All those three parts therein mentioned (the whole in ffour parts being divided) of and in the Mannor and Lordshipp of West Ayton, with the Rights, Members, and appurtenres thereof, in the said County of Yorke, and of and in the Tythes of Corne and Graine in West Ayton aforesaid, with the appurtenres, and of and in the Woods, Timber, and Timber trees Standing, Growing, and being, and which Shall Stand, Grow, or be in and upon the same Mannor or Lands thereunto belonging, And All those Grounds

1. Copy of the first Trust Deed, 1705.

2. Dame Sarah Hewley, c.1660, by an unknown artist. Original portrait in the Mansion House, York.

in, and sheep are much lower in price than last year … but no doubt the tenants on Stock Breeding Farms are turning their attention to Stock Breeding which is very desirable'.[309]

West Ayton   In 1869, the West Ayton miller, Mr Prince, appealed for a substantial reduction in the rent of his flour mill, due to the deficiency of water every year from June to October, when he could work only one out of his three stones. The Trustees asked for enquiries to be made as to steam power, and for an estimate to be obtained of the cost of installing a steam engine. Messrs. Clayton & Shuttleworth offered to erect a suitable engine to work the flour mill for £512. The Trustees felt unable to incur this sort of outlay or permit a reduction in Prince's rent. However, in 1870 after a further application from Prince, they allowed him £41 for a new water wheel and £50 towards the loss he had sustained in the summer months, and in 1873 agreed to forego his arrears (£127) and reduce his rent to £130. In 1878, it was discovered that the cause of some of the flooding at West Ayton was attributable to the Mill Sluice being out of repair so that when the water was high the miller was unable to open the sluice gate; Prince would avoid a repetition in future.[310] In 1884 it was reported that the mill wheel was almost useless, and there seemed little point in fitting a new one as, without expensive modern machinery, it was impossible to make flour that would compete with that manufactured in larger mills. The Trustees, however, preferred to arrange for repairs at a cost not exceeding £100.[311] Just after the Second World War, it was reported that the Derwent Mill water wheel was in a bad state of repair and estimates were ordered to be obtained for its renovation; two years later the wheel was giving trouble due to wear on its bearings. It was ordered the wheel be repaired and the millstones dressed.[312]

In 1852 approval was given for the erection of new cottages at West Ayton 'to be built according to plan no. 4 issued by the Society for Improving the Condition of the Labouring Classes'.[313] As a consequence, the following year, an architect, Mr Gibson, was paid £34 for superintending the construction of farm buildings and cottages on Darrell's and Coverdale's holdings. Mr Thornton, the builder, was paid £600 for his part in this work. In 1854 Gibson was paid a further £8 and Thornton another £250 towards the completion of this work. In 1855 Thornton was paid £83, the balance of the sum owing him for his work at the two farms. Unfortunately this was not the end of the matter, for soon afterwards fire destroyed part of the new buildings at Darrell's farm, and we find Thomson of the Fire Office paid for inspecting the damage, Harrison paid for new slates, Burton for fitting them and attending to the masonry, Messrs. Lord & Sons for supplying new paper for the farmhouse, and Ruddock for painting and papering, at a total cost of £46. The next year a Mr Petch was paid 15 shillings for examining the cause of the fire.[314]

Just before the First World War, the Trustees went to court against a Mrs Rachel Atkinson of East Ayton, who claimed to own half the weir serving the High Mill at West Ayton as well as half the bed of the river Derwent, and therefore entitled to remove her half of the weir as well as half the bed of the river! On investigation it transpired that Mrs Atkinson had for some time been extending her land and thereby gradually encroaching into the river. By a Chancery judgement on 18 November 1913, she and her agents were perpetually restrained from removing or otherwise interfering with any part of the weir at High Mill belonging to the Trustees, and also from placing in the river Derwent any piles, stones or other obstacles to impede its flow, and they were also to arrange for the removal of piles and stones she had previously ordered to be placed there and to restore the river to its previous condition, and pay all the costs involved.[315]

In 1918 the War Office acquired about 100 acres of Miss Darrell's land at West Ayton for an aerodrome, an early reference to flying which was still at a relatively formative stage. The land appears to have been used by the forces until cleared by the RAF around 1948.[316]

In 1932 the Trustees allowed their tenant Mrs France and her employees to work the gravel at West Ayton.[317] In 1939 she agreed to assign her licence to work the gravel pit, due to expire in 1941, to Messrs. Stephen Toulson & Sons Ltd. of Sheffield, who sought to purchase all the plant and lorries belonging to Mrs France and erect further plant. Toulsons wished to extend the licence by a further ten years. By 1943 the firm was installing electric power and expanding its business, extracting nearly 30,000 tons of gravel and had soon obtained several contracts to supply gravel and sand for making new aerodromes. In 1947, adjoining ground was added to the quarry area, and in 1948 the Trustees bought a further 2.3 acres of adjacent land, raising the assured annual royalty income to £1100.[318]

In 1883 the Trust completed the purchase of 54 acres to add to their West Ayton estate for £3553.[319] In 1889 the Trustees bought three more acres, known as the Tenter Garth, to add to the estate.[320] In 1927, the Trust sold a small parcel of the estate to Scarborough Rural District Council, but this was offset by the purchase of 51 acres of land and buildings (The Ings) in 1945, for £1659, and 91 acres with buildings, called Garth End, in 1948, for £7500. By 1949 the estate measured 1448 acres, and the gross rental had increased from £1735 to £2225 as a partial consequence of the recent purchases, with perhaps £350 of this total spent each year on maintenance and repairs. In May of that year the Trustees were told a neighbouring landowner at West Ayton, Lord Downe, wished to know if they would be prepared to sell the estate. If Downe invested in agricultural land, it was believed he might save 45% in Estate Duty as well as securing maintenance allowances and perhaps Income Tax advantages – which the Trustees could not.[321]

The Trustees investigated the question in depth and agonised over the correct decision. The Lady Hewley Trust had previously benefited greatly because of appreciation in land values, but that source of capital increment would disappear under the terms of the Town and Country Planning Act of 1947, which imposed a 100% Development Charge (later abandoned). Furthermore, the buildings on the estate were old and the standard of upkeep insisted on by County Agricultural Committees was higher than in the past. Against this, rents might be increased and repair clauses negotiated with tenants. It was noted that other corporate bodies such as Colleges were still buying up land. The Trustees' primary concern was to have sufficient income to continue to make adequate grants, which could be done if any sale monies were reinvested to bring in a yield of around $3^{3}/_{4}\%$. The estate might fetch about £49,000 plus mineral rights of about £6000 – and the sand and gravel quarry might be worked out within the next five years. In May 1950, the Trustees resolved to go ahead with the sale, including all mineral rights. The auction took place, with the authority of the Charity Commissioners, on 21 June 1951, when the West Ayton estate was sold by Messrs. Sanderson, Townend & Gilbert of Newcastle for £65,500 gross to a Bridlington man, Mr Arthur Thornton Varley. The proceeds were then invested in four Government stocks.[322]

Haya Park In September 1866 the Trustees met at Harrogate and toured Haya Park. One local builder, Mr Wilson, reported on the state of the tenant Mr Walker's house: 'walls are so damp that the paper would not hang', arising from the rain in recent storms being driven through solid brickwork and also from a defective roof. Wilson recommended stuccoing walls and stripping and re-covering the roof with blue slates overhanging the eaves. The Trustees rejected the stucco, but resolved to use best Welsh slates of a large size, with another layer of slates underneath, and with guttering and downpipes to carry off the water; all the window and door frames and sills were to be thoroughly repaired.

In that same year, there was a report of the loss by five tenants due to the 'Cattle Plague'. Compensation was given; the worst hit, Mrs Lumley, being allowed £80. In 1873 another tenant, Thomas Robinson, wrote in to the Trustees to say that as a result of the 'Foot and Mouth disease' he had lost both sheep and cattle to a combined value of £250. The Trustees allowed him just £25.[323]

In 1867 the opportunity arose to purchase about 176 acres of farmland on the neighbouring Arkendale estate, and this was eventually done at a cost of £5250 by selling investments. The farms secured were then divided between the holdings of the tenants Waddington and Snowdon. The land at Arkendale was later drained and where before 'Crops of Peas hardly worth reaping' and only six bushels of barley per acre had been harvested, in 1871 the yield was 30 bushels of barley to the acre. In 1879 a further 12 acres in Arkendale were purchased and added to the Haya Park estate.

In 1871, two fields adjacent to the tenant Walker's holding at Haya Park, and with a combined size of more than 13 acres, were also purchased.[324]

In 1879 Sir Morton Peto visited Coneythorpe and inspected new out-buildings there, completed in the following year at a cost of £420, which had received the sanction of the Charity Commissioners.[325]

In 1874 the Trustees added to their holding at Brearton and agreed to enclose this 'together with the open field Land' there belonging to the Charity, but five years later another landowner, Miss Rawdon, offered £5000 for the property, and the Trustees accepted, subject to the Charity Commission's authority to sell.[326]

After making appropriate financial arrangement to dispose of the fee farm rent of £100 gross (by this time owned by the Pitt Rivers family) subsisting in the estate, Haya Park was sold towards the end of the First World War, at the Royal Station Hotel, York, on 17 October 1918. The Charity Commission nominated a London auctioneer, Joseph Stower, who succeeded in selling all twelve lots above the reserve prices, at a total gross price of £52,524. However, the estate was not preserved as a single entity, but broken up amongst several purchasers. The Trust's Agent, Charles Forbes, reflected in May 1919 that the sale had taken place 'at just the right time as I find farmers preferring to remain as tenants under good landlords'.[327]

Eston In 1856 the Trustees first considered letting land at Eston for building purposes, because of the enormous increase in population and the consequent demand for housing. In 1857 the Trustees resolved to ask Mr John Dobson of Newcastle, the foremost architect in the North East at that time, to inspect the land at Eston and prepare a building scheme, advising the Trustees as to the 'Class of Houses most desirable to be erected … ' Dobson submitted detailed plans later that year. However it was decided to delay the scheme until the Durham & Cleveland Union Railway Act had been passed, as this line would improve communications and thereby increase land values. Unfortunately, Dobson's scheme did not reach full fruition. In 1858 Mr John Jackson was paid for putting up a notice board about the enclosure of building land at Eston, stating that the Trustees were prepared to entertain applications, but at the same time Dobson indicated to the Trustees that a great depression in the iron trade meant the demand for building land had diminished and many new houses in Eston were now untenanted. The scheme was postponed for a year. The next year Mr Dobson and Mr Blossom, a Middlesbrough land agent, commented that with the continued poor state of the iron trade it was pointless to proceed. When Blossom left the area soon afterwards, the Trustees accepted John Jackson as their agent in the area, agreeing to pay him £10 per year plus 4% of the value of any building plots he sold, yielding him £20 in 1860. However, in 1863, the Trustees accepted that there was strong prejudice about taking the building land offered, even on the 999-year leases recommended by the Charity Commissioners, and considered selling the freehold of some of the land earmarked for building purposes.[328]

In 1859 'a memorial from several working men' asked that portions of the Charity estate at Eston be let for allotment gardens; the Trustees replied that they would grant allotments to tenants who occupied cottages on the land set aside as building plots. Despite succeeding in making a few long leases, and Dobson submitting further plans for cottages at Eston, the Trustees felt it best to put the entire project on hold in 1860, but were happy the following year to let

312 acres, part of the former tenants Garbutt and Hugill's farms, to John Jackson, for 21 years, with a gradual rent increase; Jackson was not to plough the property but could sublet plots as he saw fit as 'accommodation land', with certain rights to the minerals below. After Jackson's death in 1898, another tenant, W H Ingledew, became the local agent for Eston and Margrove Park.[329]

In May 1864 letters from 'the Clergyman and the Medical Man' reached the Trustees reporting the prevalence of scarlet fever and smallpox at Eston, no doubt caused in part by the poor housing and sanitary conditions for the miners and their families; the Trustees' response was to order that sufficient cesspools be made to the several houses involved.[330]

In 1864 the Trustees agreed to an application from Eston Cricket Club for a 21-year lease of four acres adjoining 'the Brickfield' for cricket and recreation purposes for the people, including those working in the mines. The lease was restricted to 'respectable parties' and the condition that gambling would not occur. In 1872 it was reported the cricket ground at Eston let to Bolckow Vaughan was being used for pigeon shooting, cock-fighting and the sale of beer. The Trustees ordered that the ground be restricted to cricket and that no intoxicating liquors were to be sold there.[331]

In 1866 the Trustees entertained an application from George Paley and others to work for 'jet' at Eston Bank with three 'pick' men and agreed a year-on-year lease. Two years later Messrs Smith & Okey of Middlesbrough sought permission to work for gypsum in twelve fields at the northern extremity of Eston. The Trustees' Mining Agent, Mr G B Forster, was in favour, and so the Trustees proposed a 42-year lease, at a royalty of 13d. per ton and an annual fixed or 'certain' rent of £200, with certain conditions. However, the gypsum turned out to be very inferior, and Forster agreed that Smith & Okey, having come to a bed of shale at a depth of 40 fathoms, be allowed to abandon their original undertaking and take a new lease of the subsoil, paying a royalty of 1s.6d. for every 1000 bricks made and a similar amount for drain tiles, with authority to search for salt. The Trustees agreed, at a certain rent of £150 per year, the bricks to be of standard measure. In spite of this, Okey ran into considerable further difficulty and had to give up his project and lease (partly because of the provisions of the new Mines Regulation Act), filling in his shaft and restoring the land to its former state. In 1873, a Tram Road was proposed, because of the vast increase in population, from Middlesbrough to Eston, traversing part of the Hewley estate; the Trustees welcomed the idea and agreed to contribute £650 as their portion of the cost, as the Tram Road would add greatly to the value of their property.[332]

On 30 March 1941 a German bomber, a Junkers 88, was shot down and crashed on Eston Moor, just within the boundary of land leased by the Trust to Eston Urban District Council. The damage was made good by the UDC who would have been able to claim compensation from the War Ministry.[333] In September 1942 about two acres of land at Low Grange Farm (tenant J M Dale), fronting onto the Normanby Road, was requisitioned by the Air Ministry and subsequently used as an Anti-Aircraft Gun site. This was derequisitioned in 1946 and the compensation paid by the Ministry spent on removing concrete bases and air-raid shelters, and restoring the land to its original state. At the same time it was noted that Low Grange farmhouse, an old building whose walls, fabric and furniture had previously suffered severely with damp problems, had now been repaired and the damp eliminated.[334]

After the Second World War, Eston UDC expressed a desire to acquire land from the Trust to build houses 'for the working classes' and served each Trustee with notices to buy 22 acres of land south of Jubilee Road by compulsory purchase for housing purposes, potentially affecting more than 40 of the Trust's tenants. The price was to be £125 per acre and compensation would be paid for loss of crops. A further allocation of land for housing was sold to Eston UDC in 1965.[335]

In 1949 the lease of the Rifle Range at Eston, in the hands of the Territorial Army since it was granted in 1914, was surrendered before the expiration of the term, the TA dismantling the concrete butts, brick and concrete buildings, filling in trenches, removing gorse and thorn bushes, levelling and reseeding, and paying the Trustees £543 in compensation.[336]

In 1967 a pipeline to carry ethylene gas was completed, running from the new ICI works at Wilton on Teesside through to Salwick in Lancashire and on to Runcorn in Cheshire, passing through Bank Fields, Eston.[337]

In 1976 after the bulk of the Trust lands in Eston had been sold to private purchasers or compulsorily acquired (mostly by Eston UDC, or its successor Teesside Borough, for housing, public buildings, parks, playing fields and roads), the North Riding County Council (for schools, clinics and police houses), Government departments, and the Parochial Church Council (church school) there only remained Low Grange Farm (57 acres), the Bank Fields (58 acres), and premises in Barnaby Crescent, High Street and Jubilee Road, and allotments (4 acres).[338]

Margrove Park In 1859 the Agent, Mr Parrington, sent a letter to the Trustees informing them burglars had entered the house of George Storey, a Margrove Park tenant, one night and made a brutal attack on him and his family, all of them suffering serious injuries. The Trustees were disturbed to learn of this and gave Storey financial compensation, together with money to repair the window frames and place iron bars over the windows to prevent a repetition.[339]

In 1861 the Cleveland Railway, whose line passed over a portion of Hewley ground, paid for the land they had acquired from the Charity, at a rate of £100 per acre, plus £75 for small strips of land. In 1866, in line with the increasing industry of the place, Messrs. Isaac Bigland of Stockton applied for and were granted a lease of up to 14 years to take shale from three fields to make bricks. In 1871 the Cleveland Water Works Bill was proceeding through Parliament; this would give the Water Company the right to lay pipes across the Trustees' estate at Margrove Park, and it was agreed to watch the situation, which increasingly became a concern on this and other estates as various public bodies and local authorities sought wayleaves. In 1875 a George Galloway was allowed access to two fields at Margrove Park to make bricks, paying £40 per year and a royalty of 2 shillings per 1000 bricks during his seven-year lease. Galloway was evidently a man of many parts, for in 1877 the Trustees rejected his proposal to build a hotel at Margrove Park. Sadly he went bankrupt in 1880, and consequently had to give up his brickfield.[340]

There was some damage to the roofs of buildings in Margrove Park Farm in 1943, caused by bomb blast.[341]

In 1921 part of the Margrove Park estate was sold off. A further portion was sold by public auction at Guisborough on 5 July 1967 to the Clevestone Co. Ltd. of Middlesbrough for £21,150 (or £150 per acre).[342] Over the years the majority of the Trust's holdings in Margrove Park have been disposed of, so that in 1976 the Trust was left with only four acres of allotments and some wayleaves.[343]

Whixley The former owners of the Whixley property, the Bailey family, continued to farm here. The farm was relet in 1880 at 35 shillings per acre per year. Turnips there had then been sold for more than £11.[344] In 1886 the tenant at Whixley asked for and achieved a reduction in rent. The following year he gave notice as the rent was still too great. The Trustees considered the property might be difficult to relet as it was all arable land with no farm buildings. A new tenant, Theakston, offered to purchase Whixley in 1913 but the Trustees were not disposed to sell at that juncture.[345] In 1923 the Trustees leased the Whixley farm to the West Riding of Yorkshire County Council for 35 years. The 45-acre property was sold to the County Council for £1500 in 1931.[346]

Shooting, fishing Game rights were leased on several of the estates. Around 1800, for example, the trustees ruled that 'as a compliment to Mrs Osbaldeston' no person was to pursue game on the West Ayton estate; the game rights were later formally let to the neighbouring landowner, Mrs Osbaldeston and her son George.[347] Under the new Trustees, from 1849, shooting rights were granted, especially at West Ayton and Haya Park. These rights, providing further income, were usually taken by other landed proprietors but occasionally leased to tenants.[348] Fishing licences for the water at West Ayton were also granted, notably to Derwent Angling Club and Scarborough Mere Angling Club.[349]

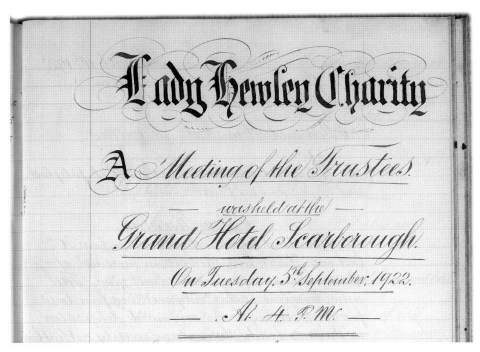

The Iron Age

Henry Bolckow was a successful accountant who moved from his native Germany in 1827 to join Christian Allhusen in Newcastle upon Tyne as a corn merchant and general commission agent. Twelve years later Bolckow was a wealthy man (with £40,000) and, when Allhusen set up a chemical manufacturing business, he then went into partnership with his brother-in-law, John [Jacky] Vaughan, to manufacture iron products. Vaughan had acquired extensive knowledge and broad experience of the iron industry at Sir Josiah Guest's Dowlais works in South Wales, and managed a small ironworks in Carlisle before his appointment in 1832 as mill manager at Messrs. Losh, Wilson & Bell's Walker ironworks in Newcastle upon Tyne. Vaughan possessed both metallurgical expertise and enormous practical aptitude. Bolckow provided £10,000 to start the firm, with all profits being shared equally between the two men.[350]

H. W. F. BOLCKOW.

Middlesbrough was, in medieval times, the halfway and crossing point for monks travelling between Durham Cathedral and Whitby Abbey, with a small Priory (St. Hilda's) and ferry. In 1801 it had a population of just 25, which had grown by 1829 to about 125; in this latter year Joseph Pease, the Darlington industrialist, and six other Quaker businessmen connected with the creation of the Stockton & Darlington and other railways, bought a 500-acre site and began to build a small town and port for the export of coal, down-river from (and more accessible than) Stockton. By 1841 the population had grown to over 5000. Soon Middlesbrough was exporting lead from the Pennines and alum from North Yorkshire, as well as dairy products, grain and flour. Small shipyards and foundries were slowly established along both banks of the Tees.[351]

Henry Bolckow and John Vaughan of Middlesbrough, ironfounders.

On 18 May 1840 Henry Bolckow and Jacky Vaughan accepted the invitation of John Harris, one of Pease's partners, to take six acres on the

south bank of the river Tees, not far from the present Transporter Bridge. The partners commenced foundry and allied ironwork on 1 May 1841, employing 150 men.[352] Over the next few years, the business expanded to include anchor, chain, cable and rail making, steam engine manufacturing and wagon building, but the works grew only slowly until 1850.[353] The site was served by the railway, bringing coal from Co. Durham and processed iron ore from Witton Park in the Wear Valley, where Bolckow and Vaughan built their first four blast furnaces. Iron ore was also available at Grosmont in the Cleveland Hills, from where it was exported through Whitby and transported by ship to Witton, but the quantity available was insufficient to meet a growing demand for iron as the railway system expanded. The new firm increasingly concentrated on iron products such as railway lines and components for the construction of locomotives and wagons. In 1846 the partners entered into a three-year contract for 12,000 tons of iron ore per year from Grosmont.[354]

John Vaughan realised there were likely to be mineral deposits closer to Middlesbrough, and it was said that he, and his surveyor John Marley of Darlington, who, in June 1850, while prospecting for a suitable place for boring, discovered traces of ironstone in an old quarry and a little further away the existence of a substantial seam, between eight and sixteen feet thick, of workable ironstone (extending, it was later said, over 200 square miles between the valleys of the Tees and the Esk) at the northern outcrop of the Eston Hills (Eston Nab). The legend is that Vaughan found the mineral deposit accidentally whilst out 'rabbit shooting, stumbled over a piece of the stuff, which he picked up, examined, and found to be ironstone', a story always subsequently denied.[355] The materials required to manufacture iron were thus all close to hand: iron ore (from Eston and other mines in the Cleveland hills), coke (from Durham collieries), and limestone (from quarries in the Pennines).[356]

The truth about the actual discovery of ironstone is a little different to the fiction. At the second meeting of the new Trustees, held in May 1849, a letter was read out from Bolckow Vaughan requesting permission to explore for minerals in the Eston Bank area. The Secretary, William Vizard, was directed to employ a local agent to ascertain the viability of the land proposed to be worked for minerals. The agent (Mr John Parrington) reported favourably on the firm's proposals and at the Trustees' meeting in September 1849 it was agreed that Bolckow Vaughan be authorised to work for minerals for a trial period, paying all expenses and restoring the land to its original state if the experiment was unsuccessful.[357]

Bolckow Vaughan were quick to exploit their find. Negotiations were entered into with the Lady Hewley Trustees, the Stapylton family and other neighbouring landowners to secure mining Royalties, and extremely advantageous leases were secured by the firm. The first seven tons of ore was extracted from the Eston mine on 13 August 1850, just a few weeks

Letter from William Vizard to John Parrington, asking him to inspect the Eston area for iron ore, 26 January 1850. Hewley MSS.

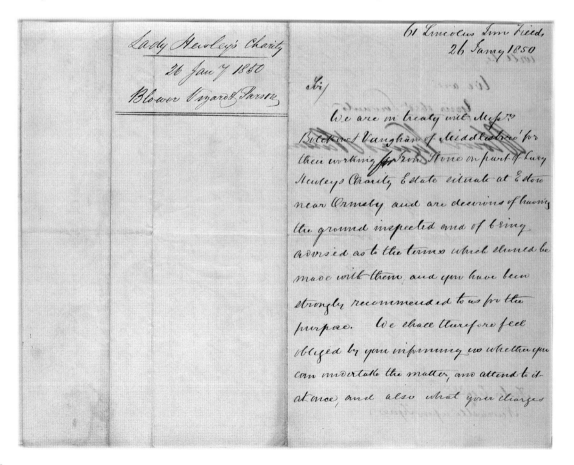

after the initial discovery, by which time the firm had already begun to build a rope-incline railway from Eston to the new mines, where a seam 15 feet 2 inches deep was now revealed. By the end of that year just 136 tons had been won. John Vaughan officially opened the Eston Mines on 6 January 1851, when he commented that the iron manufacturers of the district would soon be in a position to compete with those of other countries and, he asserted, they would shortly be able to manufacture iron more cheaply than even Birmingham. The Iron Age had begun, and the Lady Hewley Trust was soon adding substantially to its income. The rich deposits found under the then tiny villages of Eston and Normanby were to result in 'an English Eldorado', a boom not dissimilar to an Australian or American gold rush; the first ironstone worker's settlement was even named California as this unparalled industrial and social expansion took root.[358]

Vizard reported on the situation at the Trust meeting in September 1850, and a sub-committee of Trustees was appointed to consider the value of the minerals under Eston Bank, and enter into a specific contract with the firm. Initially, two Trustees met Henry Bolckow in the summer of 1851 and agreed a 7-year lease with the company, with the Trustees having sole power to appoint a person to weigh the ore, and Bolckow Vaughan paying a 'certain' rent of £300 and a royalty of 10d. a ton on the ironstone worked. The terms were varied in leases in 1852 (30 August) and then renegotiated in 1853 (18 May); these gave full authority for Bolckow Vaughan 'their agents, servants, miners, workmen and others employed or authorised by them ... to dig, bore, delve, sink, search for, raise, get, quarry and work, calcine and render for sale ... according to the Law and Customs of Mining ... used in the county of Yorkshire ... all those the mines, veins, seams or modules of iron ore or ironstone' lying in 79 acres at Eston 'and make all such ... shafts, pits, adits, fences, soughs, tunnels, headways, levels and drains and ... erect so many steam and other engines, whimseys, cranks, gins and other machines as shall be found necessary whether by underground or surface drifts ... And also to make such wagon roads, railways, tram roads and other roads and ... ways of transit and communication in, through and over the said ground'. The 1852 lease extended the term to 21 years but continued the fixed rent of £300 per year and the royalty of 10d. on every ton of $22^{1}/_{2}$ cwts, together with a further 1d. for every $22^{1}/_{2}$ cwts. gained from under adjacent properties, while the 1853 lease increased the certain rent to £800 and reduced the

Royalty that of 6 p 22½ cwt due on these Tons of 20 cwt		Wgts	Tons	cwt	Wgts	Tons	cwt
1850							
Nº 18 Pay ending Septr 7th 1850		7	21	15			
19 " 21st		81	231	14			
20 Octr 5th		23	76	8			
21 " 19th		133	412	8			
22 Novr 2		112	343	14			
23 " 16		252	762	2			
24 " 30		210	673	17			
25 Decr 14		335	882	14			
26 " 28		277	750	12	1462	4177	4
1851 1 Jany 11th 1851		52	149	6			
2 " 25th		10	29	7			
3 Feby 8th		2	6	2	64	184	13
					1526	4361	19

NB Sent to Cargo Fleet by carts — Tons 4040·7

" on to Eston Branch Rway — 321·12

Total — 4361 19

Messr Bolckow & Vaughan
To the Trustees of Lady Hewley Royalty &c

1852
July 1st To 4361 19 of Ironstone Vended from their Eston Royalty @ 6 per 22½ cwt during the experiment under the Agreement — £96·18·7

Ironstone, wrought and vended out of the Lady Hewley Royalty. Eston, 1850-1851. Hewley MSS.

royalty to 7d. on every ton of 22½ cwts.[359]

On 4 February 1852, Bolckow Vaughan had their Eston Ironworks, two miles from the mines, in full production, with six blast furnaces and a workforce of 300 men. From 1000 tons of ironstone expected from the mines each week, when the first blast furnace was blown, the tonnage quickly accelerated to reach 3000 tons daily and demonstrated the commercial success of Cleveland ore. Of course, not all the ironstone processed by the firm came from the Lady Hewley Royalty but the cluster of Royalties that formed the Eston Range. By 1855 Bolckow Vaughan employed 4000 men and its output of manufactured iron exceeded 120,000 tons (15 years later this was 1,695,377 tons). Almost overnight, the small port of Middlesbrough became an iron town of major significance, achieving borough status in 1853, with Bolckow its first Mayor and Vaughan its third, both men having helped to shape civic affairs since arriving on Teesside.[360]

In 1853 the Trustees viewed the 'Iron Stone Works' and the method of weighing ore, asking Matthew Dixon (who had taken over from Mr Parrington weighing the ore) to continue doing this task (at a starting salary of £26 which quickly rose to almost £40) and render accounts to

Vizard of the amounts extracted, which would be compared with Bolckow Vaughan's returns each quarter. Dixon's returns from 1853 to 1867 show totals varying for the most part from 2000 to almost 5000 tons per fortnight from the the Lady Hewley Royalty. In 1856 the Trustees again viewed their Royalty, and as a consequence resolved that their new Mining Agent, Mr G B Forster of Newcastle upon Tyne, who had previously advised them about applications to mine jet at Margrove Park, should visit the Eston mines and submit a report to the Trustees every six months, and also provide plans and sections of the workings and strata, and suggest the best ways for winning further ore from the Hewley Royalty. This was done regularly until the mines ceased working, with G B Forster and then his son T E Forster reporting regularly down to the 1930s, commenting on the satisfactory nature and mode of the work, the number of miners employed in the Hewley Royalty, the quantity of iron ore extracted over the previous six-monthly period, and any complications, such as mining under the railway and whether there was water present.[361]

In one report in 1859 Forster commented that everything was proceeding very satisfactorily and with great success 'but at the present rate ironstone working will be exhausted in a few years'. Work there seems to have ceased around 1867 when the seam was supposedly worked out. In 1879 Forster reported that the Eston ironstone ground contained about 255 acres in all, was triangular in shape and at the heart of the Eston range, with the Trustees' and Major Stapylton's Royalties towards the northwest. The 'Main Band' extended under the whole of Eston Moor dipping in the south and rising northwards towards the outcrop in the lands of the Lady Hewley Trust and Major Stapylton. Forster reckoned that 26 acres had been completely worked out and a further 12 acres was either waste or faulted. Of the remainder, 143 acres was standing in pillars and was about 33% worked, leaving about 74 acres untouched. Put another way, he calculated that the Trustees' Royalty alone had originally contained about 9 million tons and there were perhaps 5.4 million tons left, but due to complications in working some of this the true figure for workable ironstone was around 4.3 million tons. The seam varied from 9 to 14 feet in thickness. Two of the three outlets were in the Stapylton Royalty but passed in a southerly direction, while the other was in the Lady Hewley Royalty. The system of working was the usual one in that district of 'Bord and Pillar'. Nothing had been worked from the Hewley side for some years and he did not anticipate a quick resumption. The mine was kept clear of water with a double horizontal pumping engine, placed at the bottom of a shaft on Greenwood's Royalty. Work did not in fact recommence on the Lady Hewley Royalty until 1897, when Forster reported that it was being worked by means of a drift on the north side of the hill and that the number of miners (just 14) would soon be augmented as the mine was opened up.[362]

In 1857 Messrs. Bell Brothers of Newcastle applied to the Trustees for a trial lease of six months to extract ironstone from Margrove Park at a fixed annual rent of £350 and 6d. per ton royalty; this was referred to Forster who suggested £500 and 7d. per 22$\frac{1}{2}$ cwts; Bell Brothers accepted this and a 42-year lease, with working subsequently agreed to start on 1 May 1863, as the firm had to wait for the coming of the railway. In 1865 Forster reported that the Margrove Park workings had been discontinued by Messrs. Bell for some months due to the depressed state of the iron trade, and that while the bed of ironstone there was not as thick as at Eston he still considered that it would be a valuable and productive mine. Work at Margrove Park recommenced on 1 January 1866 and went on well; ironstone from the adjoining Walton Royalty was being carried through the Hewley Royalty. Work seems to have halted again for in 1869 Forster reported that working had recommenced at Margrove Park, but only to a limited extent. The workings were proceeding satisfactorily, with about 46 men working there producing around 180 tons of ore a day, quickly rising the next year to 240 and in 1872 to 360.

In 1872 Bell & Company asked to transfer their lease for these Margrove Park 'Spa' workings to Messrs. Gjers Mills & Co. of Middlesbrough, who were willing to pay a fixed rent of £800 per year, backdated to 1872, instead of Bell's £500. The Trustees agreed, with a new 30 year lease. In 1873 Forster considered that Gjers Mills' operations in removing about 50 acres of ironstone in Admiral Chaloner's Royalty would enable them soon to begin working a greater quantity in the Hewley Royalty. In 1875, after several previous attempts, a Mr Barningham was authorised by the Trustees to have a wayleave for 21 years for a railway through the Margrove Park estate to convey ironstone, at a fixed annual rent of £100 and a royalty of $\frac{1}{2}$d. per ton. Forster had calculated that the royalty alone could eventually bring in £12,500 for the Trust. In 1878 Forster reported that because of a further depression in the iron trade the miners at Slapewath (Margrove Park) were working short time, with just 24 men employed. In 1882 Forster reported that Admiral

3. *Sir John Hewley, c.1660, by an unknown artist. Original portrait in the Mansion House, York.*

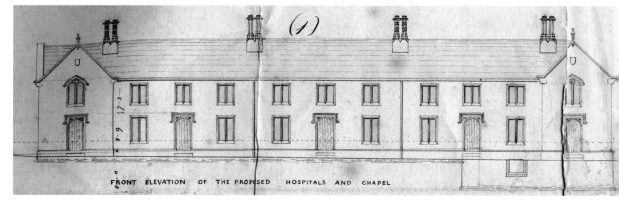

FRONT ELEVATION OF THE PROPOSED HOSPITALS AND CHAPEL

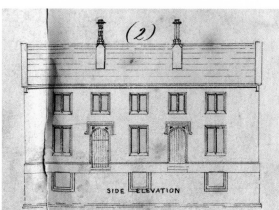

SIDE ELEVATION

4. & 5. Architect's elevations of the St. Saviourgate Almshouses, 1839. The architect was James Pigott Pritchett, one of Yorkshire's leading practitioners and a Hewley Sub-Trustee.

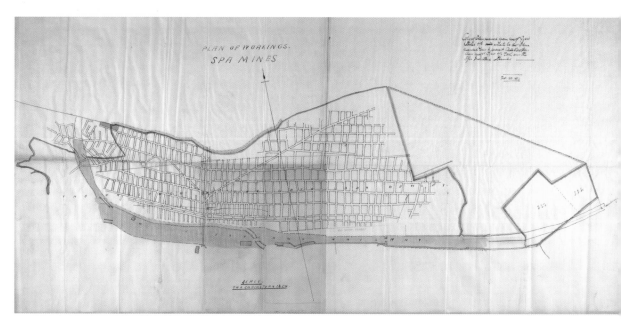

PLAN OF WORKINGS.
SPA MINES

6. Copy of the plan received from Messrs. Gjers Mills & Co. of the Spa Ironstone Mines, Margrove Park, when the firm took over from Bell Brothers. This plan is dated 1884.

Chaloner's Royalty at Margrove Park was just about worked out and that the last few miners there were now about to leave and join their 80 colleagues in the Lady Hewley Royalty. In the previous six months to 30 June 1882 almost 19500 tons had been won.[363] In 1886 Forster reported that work at Slapewath had stopped completely for five weeks in May and June due to a strike by the blastfurnacemen, but all the men employed in the mines were now working in the Lady Hewley Royalty. He had written to the lessees to restrain them from improper working as they feared 'drowning out'. Gjers Mills continued to work the Spa mines until 1904.[364]

The peak year for iron production was 1873, when the Middlesbrough district produced 374,000 tons of iron rails. But this masked a problem. By 1870, the North Eastern and other railway companies had begun to substitute steel for iron rails although shipbuilders were still asking for iron plates and other iron products. Due to a combination of inflation, foreign competition and a falling-off in demand, a downward movement in prices occurred and wages were reduced. Employers, shareholders and men suffered. Some Teesside ironmasters closed down sections of their works and laid off workmen. The men went on strike, demanding higher wages. By 1879 works output had dropped dramatically and wrought-iron manufacture by 50%. Nevertheless, in just under 30 years the area had witnessed a spectacular rise in the extraction and processing of ironstone found under the Eston Hills, the Upleatham outlier and in East Cleveland.[365]

It was steel rather than iron that was now principally in demand; Cleveland ore, because of its high phosphoric content, was unsuitable for the manufacture of high-quality steel. With the invention of the Bessemer process in 1856 to convert non-phosphoric ore, places like Barrow-in-Furness gained a marked edge. The iron trade in Middlesbrough all but collapsed, furnaces lay idle, unemployment and distress were common. Bolckow Vaughan & Co. were not to be beaten, however, and imported ore for their first steelworks, opened at Eston in 1876, producing about 1000 tons of steel each week within two years. What saved the situation for Teesside were the successful metallurgical and chemical tests of Sidney Thomas and his cousin Percy Gilchrist to eliminate the phosphorus from Cleveland ironstone. The two were invited by Bolckow Vaughan to Eston where experimental converters were built. In April 1879 the new process proved completely successful and Teesside was able to make the transition to the steel trade, using local iron ore. This became the world's most productive steel works to date. By 1888 almost all the steel made on Teesside

Eston Steel Works c.1880. From H.G. Reid's 'Middlesbrough and its Jubilee', 1881.

used the Thomas-Gilchrist process, although by 1900 this had fallen to 40%, the remainder being made with haematite. By the latter date Teesside produced 27% of the national steel output and was the fifth largest steel-manufacturing area in the world.[366]

In 1877 the Trustees decided to go back to the Court of Chancery, this time against Messrs. Bolckow Vaughan over the ownership of minerals under Eston Moor. The company were lessees of both the Trustees and Major Stapylton, the adjacent landowner, who had granted a 99-year mining lease to Bolckow Vaughan on 25 December 1852, with a surface rent of £250 per year and royalties of 8d. per ton for all ironstone extracted from under the Stapylton ground plus 1d. per ton for all ore won from under neighbouring properties. It was this that troubled the Trustees, who stated they owned one-third of the Moor and were therefore entitled to one-third of the royalties. The Trustees asked that the firm be restrained from mining under Eston Moor without licence or consent. The company maintained it had worked the mines and minerals continuously since the granting of that lease. Crucially, Bolckow Vaughan did not accept the Trustees' claim to minerals lying under Eston Moor, and declared that if the Trustees possessed freehold right there they should have said so long since. The case came to court in May 1878, when it was decided that, as Major Stapylton owned two-thirds of the Moor, he should be a co-defendant with the firm. The parties returned to court that November, when a compromise was reached. The Trustees' claim was accepted, including the 'Common Pasture' and the mines and minerals beneath. For their part, the Trustees waived their rights to royalties prior to the start of the case. The Court declared the Trustees entitled to one-third of the royalties since then and for the future so long as the lease remained in force.[367]

In 1889 a sub-lease was granted to another firm of ironmasters,

Messrs. Bernhard Samuelson & Co. of Middlesbrough, of a part of the area being worked by Gjers Mills and adjacent to a mine being worked by Samuelsons in another Royalty. Samuelsons would pay 5d. per ton (4d. to the Trustees and 1d. to Gjers Mills). In 1902 another sub-lease was executed, this time with Samuelsons paying 4d. per ton to the Trustees and a certain rent of £300 per year, to be worked out within five years.

From 1890 Samuelsons also had a wayleave licence to carry ironstone over the Hewley Trustees' ground at $\frac{1}{2}$d a ton, reduced in 1887 to $\frac{1}{4}$d. In 1890 a more complicated wayleave rate was negotiated, varying from $\frac{1}{4}$d. to $\frac{3}{4}$d. per ton according to the prevailing price of pig-iron. This was renewed in 1901. In 1906 the firm was given a short lease to work ironstone on Hewley property. The ironstone was, however, completely worked out by 1917, five years before Samuelsons were absorbed into the emerging giant Messrs. Dorman Long, by which time the wayleave was also time-expired.[368] (In 1876, in the midst of the bad times, two local ironmasters, Arthur Dorman and Albert Long, had joined forces to produce wrought iron bars and angles for shipbuilding. The two men increasingly developed a vigorous policy of buying up ailing ironworks, reducing the number of iron puddling furnaces and gradually replacing them with steel furnaces.)

By 1937 the Trust's Agent was reporting that the available ironstone in the 'Common Pasture' Royalty under Eston Moor was fast being worked out, although by the following year it was anticipated that the life of the mine might be extended to 1944; the number of miners working there was reduced to ten and additional shifts abandoned. Over the next few years, the number of miners employed, shifts worked and output in the Royalty fluctuated greatly. There were also problems encountered in working the stone, although the lessees stated that they wished to get as much out as possible 'as it is considered the best stone in Cleveland'. In 1941 the covenants of the original lease for 99 years of 1 January 1851 (renegotiated as from 23 December 1852) were varied.[369] However it was not until 1948 that Dorman Long gave six months' notice to the Hewley Trustees and the owners of the Stapylton Royalty of their intention to cease all mine workings at Eston, in both the 'Common Pasture' and 'Freehold' Royalties, as these were worked from the same shaft, on 30 June 1949. The Trust's Agent thought most of the available ironstone that could be worked economically had been won over the years – almost a century – apart from supporting pillars. Under the terms of the lease, the rent was due to be paid until at least 31 December 1950, so there need be no restriction if the firm decided to continue beyond its notice date, and so it proved, for when the Agent visited the mines on 22 August 1949 he discovered 14,808 tons had been won in the six months to 30 June and found ironstone still being worked at the 'Common Pasture Royalty' and likely to continue for a few more weeks; working at the 'Freehold Royalty' had stopped on 14 May (7276 tons from 1 January to May). The Trust owned one-third of the surface and any minerals, the Stapylton trustees the remainder, and any compensation for surface and other damage would be in the same ratio. There would be a need for the company to control water seepage in both mines and remove shale near the watercourse.[370] The last shift was on 16 September 1949, when a chapter of immense importance to Teesside and the British iron and steel industry virtually closed; in its 99 years of almost continuous activity, 63 million tons of iron ore were mined there and perhaps 360 million tons from the Cleveland hills as a whole.[371]

In 1944 the Trustees had authorised Dorman Long & Co. Ltd. to drive exploratory drifts for a short period into the north-east corner of the 'Freehold Royalty', under Eston Banks to ascertain if there was any workable ironstone remaining there, paying royalties of 6d. per ton. This area had previously been worked by Bolckow Vaughan and then Dorman Long (who took over the assets of Bolckow Vaughan in 1929), who had surrendered the lease at the end of 1933.[372] Work proved difficult and the miners were driven out by water for long periods that winter and over a six-month period won little more than 1100 tons of ore, necessitating an extension to the exploratory period.[373] However, matters improved and as late as 1948 it was reported that it had proved possible to recommence workings that May and up to the end of June some 2386 tons had been gained.[374]

That was not quite the end of the story. In 1913 the minerals under Ridge Farm and Stanghow Moor at Margrove Park had been leased to Messrs. Pease & Partners for 42 years and abandoned by them on 30 June 1934. In 1953 Lingdale Ironstone Mines Ltd, a subsidiary of Dorman Long, enquired about these and obtained a lease from the Trustees, with a view to working the underground pillars from a different direction. The lessees refused to pay a 'certain' rent but offered a small royalty of 2d. per ton extracted from an 88-acre tract of land, accepting liability for any surface damage. Work began on 1 September and by the end of the year

almost 9000 tons had been extracted, output gradually increasing over the next year or two, until technical difficulties were encountered and the lessees had to withdraw; work was resumed in 1956 and production in the last six months of that year reached 24,464 tons. However, the lessees withdrew two years later to concentrate on pillars in an adjoining Royalty and, with little prospect of winning the small amount of ironstone remaining, the Lingdale mine was finally abandoned by them in 1961.[375]

The cloth-capped (not safety-helmeted) Eston miners had a hard time of it, with long shifts underground working in pairs in galleries up to ten feet high, drilling holes (with hand not power tools) about five feet deep into the ironstone, packing with gunpowder and a fuse, withdrawing to a safe distance, and then after the explosion collecting the rough pieces of greenish ore into manageable sizes, perhaps averaging about 10 inches in diameter, and loading it into the ore trucks which had a capacity of two tons. The men were paid by the ton, and each pair needed to load about 20 tons each shift to earn sufficient wages to maintain themselves and their families. The wagons were weighed and the contents then conveyed to Bolckow Vaughan's works. It was dangerous work for both men and the horses pulling the wagons, and 'tapping' also frequently resulted in roof falls, injury and even death (around 400 miners were killed during the mines' existence). By the end of a shift a thin black mist pervaded the galleries. It was an unforgiving environment; some parts of the mines were dry but others were wet and cold. Later miners complained of their lunches being seized by rats. Until the 1930s when gas lights (and then safety lamps) were introduced, illumination was by candlelight. The system employed was 'Bord and Pillar', working outwards from the galleries on a grid system, leaving pillars of rock as supports and then gradually working back and demolishing the pillars to leave an entire hollowed-out underground area. By the 1880s there were about 1600 men working underground at the Eston mines, which stretched three miles to the Chaloner Royalty near Guisborough, with a ventilation house about one mile in. Their eight-hour shift began at about 6 a.m. with air purity and safety tests. The Eston seam varied from 8 to 14 feet, and exceptionally at one point 25 feet. Adjoining the mines was a blacksmith's forge (maintained by a Snowdon, whose family were Hewley tenants from at least the early eighteenth century), horse hospital and stables (the Eston Cottage Hospital for miners and steel workers was not built until 1884). The Trustees' drift was brick-lined. Water was pumped out at the rate of about 400 tons per minute.[376]

Eston was the 'jewel in the crown' of the new industry, although little has survived, like the iron and steel plants they supplied. A second and then a third rope-incline railway, on drums, were soon built, and the main exit from the mines was through the Trustees' drift, with the iron ore hauled down to the blast furnaces. A large saw mill was erected to make props for the mine galleries.[377]

Charitable Grants and their Distribution

In the seventeenth, eighteenth and even nineteenth centuries the incomes of Dissenting ministers were mostly low. The historian of 'the Great Ejection', Edmund Calamy, began his ministry on a stipend of £40, while the celebrated Oliver Heywood, perhaps the most famous northern Dissenting minister of his day, appears to have received only about £20 a year.[378] However, as early as July 1695, he describes a visit to York, attending worship at the chapel in St. Saviourgate, and then 'On taking my leave I received the Lady Hewley Charity'.[379]

It was not until 28 December 1711 that the Trustees felt confident enough to begin the formal distribution of charitable funds, agreeing to give a total of £64 to several 'necessitous persons'. However, in the two and a half year period between Dame Sarah's death and January 1713, Dr. Thomas Colton seems to have distributed £288.10s, presumably with the authority of his co-Trustees, probably for the most part to serving ministers. For many years the two Stewards periodically paid most of the rent monies they received direct to Thomas Colton, and it was he who supervised the bulk of the grants, perhaps because he was the one Trustee normally resident in York. The first Treasurer, James Wyndlow, seems to have been responsible for giving grants to ministers and their widows living outside the Northern Counties; indeed, by 1714 Wyndlow was distributing money to ministers, widows and those in hardship as far afield as Bicester, Brighthelmston [Brighton], Lewes, London, Ramsgate and Wisbech, suggesting there was already by this time a system of disseminating Dissenting news through the country.[380]

Originally, the Trustees agreed to 'take off' names according to circumstances, death or need, and add others: ministers moving to a new pastorate, or the 'necessitous' such as William Masterman 'a poor aged blind man of Nonmountain' [Nun Monkton, near York] in 1745. Most 'Poor Persons' were female, many of them ministers' widows or daughters. In 1739 the children of the Mr Joshua Hoyle, a deceased minister, were helped financially, as were Jane and Thomas, the children of the late Mr Roberts of Eastwood in 1782 and succeeding years.[381] In 1762 the Trustees allowed a Mrs Naylor 'on account of her extraordinary necessity' a generous grant of £10, 'until the time when she can regularly be put on the list of paupers', while in 1787 Ann Norton of Leeds 'she being now of

Mr Benjamin Bennet of Newcastle hath paid the following sumes of mony pursuant to the Trustees Order of Mar. 2d 1714 as appeares by Receipts in writing under the hands of sd persons next hereafter named. viz.

To Mr William Stoddart of South Shields	£ 3:0:0
To Mr John Horsley of Morpeth	£ 5:0:0
To Mr Alexander Shrighton of Seaworth Shore	£ 3:0:0
To Mr John Deans	£ 4:0:0
To Mr Jos. Tait of Birdhope Craig	£ 4:0:0
To Mr James Bain of Wooller	£ 3:0:0
To Mr Nicolas Story of Winlayton	£ 2:10:0
To Mr James Bell of Crow	£ 3:0:0
To Mr Mark & Gils of Starford	£ 5:0:0

£ 32:10:0

July. 14. 1715.

17/15 Distriburons &c to Mr Benj. Bennet paid to sd all persons as aforesaid . . £ 32:10:0

affluent circumstances' refunded the grant given to her.[382] In 1719, the Trustees seem to have given money to their first necessitous person outside the Northern Counties: Mrs Clemenson, a poor widow of Moseley in Warwickshire.[383]

As the eighteenth century progressed, the Trustees settled to a pattern of giving grants to 'Preachers' or 'Ministers' twice a year (May and September) and 'Beneficiaries' once a year (September). For many years, the latter category included the names of Mrs Eleanor Stretton and Mrs Sarah Tong, both widows of former ministers and Trustees, and Mary Brooks and Ann Thompson, respectively widows of the former ministers at St Saviourgate and Knaresbrough, all of whom received larger sums in appreciation. From 1725 to 1761 the list of 'poor widows and necessitous persons' included Mrs Penelope Woolrich of Leeds, perhaps a distant relative of Dame Sarah, and Hewley Moxon, possibly a godson whose name is mentioned in her will. After Mrs Woolrich's death, grants continued to be given to Edward and John Woolrich and a Mrs Walmsley (probably their sister).[384] In 1806 the Trustees decided that in future the list of Beneficiaries should be confined to the 'Widows and Daughters of Dissenting Ministers only' except in special circumstances.[385]

The names in each category tended to be repeated in each distribution, the ministers in particular effectively having their (mostly) low stipends regularly supplemented twice a year. In addition to ministers (and students) and beneficiaries, grants were given at various times 'for the use of the Protestant Dissenting Congregation at': Darlington, Doncaster, Malton, Pudsey, Scarborough, Selby, Topcliffe, Great Ayton, York and elsewhere, enabling them to have visiting ministers during vacancies, with Greenowhill being the one most frequently in need of assistance.[386]

Distributions were made to ministers in Yorkshire and the other five Northern Counties: Cumberland, Westmoreland, Lancashire, Northumberland and Durham. To start with distributions were made to around 40 ministers, including one in Derbyshire and, by 1720, the minister at 'Lin Regis' [King's Lynn].[387] As time went on and the number of ministers and meeting-houses grew, the total quantity of grants increased to preachers within the Northern Counties area. In the later eighteenth century, the Trustees began to extend distribution to selected individuals in the Midlands and East Anglia. By the nineteenth century some ministers in Cheshire, Derbyshire, Leicestershire, Lincolnshire, Nottinghamshire, Rutland, Shropshire and Staffordshire were regularly participating. In 1830 the total number of ministers benefiting at each distribution had (in 120 years) risen to around 250. By that date there are often instances of more than one minister per place, suggesting the presence of more than one denomination, and the possibility of some men becoming assistant pastors in the first instance, especially to larger congregations.[388] By the nineteenth century it is clear that, while the Unitarian Trustees may have shown some favouritism, the bulk of the grants were still being given to Independendents, Presbyterians and Baptists.[389]

By about 1720 receipt of grants was being checked through a numbered voucher system, ensuring that each person received the money earmarked for them. From 1785 the Trustees adopted a yet more thorough method: the accounts from that date down to 1830 record the number of 'Receipt Stamps', initially at 2d. each, sent out after the May and September meetings, presumably the equivalent of today's 'stamped addressed envelopes'. This was added expenditure, but clearly regarded as an essential check that the money was getting through *via* a distribution pyramid.[390] It would seem that for the 'ministers and widows in the North of England' district, for example, funds were forwarded to Close Gate (later Hanover Square) chapel, Newcastle upon Tyne, whose minister would then ensure that his colleagues in Northumberland, Durham and later Cumberland and Westmoreland, received their grants. To start with, from about 1715 money orders were sent to the minister there, the Revd. Benjamin Bennett (to 1726) and then his successor, Dr. Samuel Lawrence.

The system seems to have changed a little after Dr. Thomas Colton's death in 1731, although still channelled through Hanover Square. In 1740 the Trust Treasurer, Richard Wyndlow, personally rode to Newcastle to deliver these funds. In 1741 and for some years thereafter, a Hugh Boag was employed to ride north to Newcastle, as was his successor, John Hall. Later there was greater reliance on the developing postal system and receipt stamps for this as for other areas.[391] By the early nineteenth century, the method had become yet more sophisticated. The money was sent to William Turner, the Unitarian minister at Hanover Square, who then sent some of the funds on to 'G' (William Goldie, the minister at Alnwick), some to 'T' (Dr. Thompson, the minister at Carlisle) and the remainder to 'R' (at present unidentified).[392]

(Interestingly, amongst the archives of the Hanover Square chapel is a volume of statutes, minutes and accounts of an Association of Protestant Dissenting Ministers in the North of England, including resolutions and orders passed at meetings in Alnwick, Morpeth and Newcastle upon Tyne between 1778 and 1820, with a scheme of 1763 for raising and supporting a Widows' Fund, an organisation almost certainly enjoying links with the Hewley Trust).[393]

By 1720 Benjamin Bennet had received the first grant for a student in the Northern Counties, Thomas Lax, then studying at Sheffield.[394] The number of students fluctuated from this time on. At first, there were rarely more than one or two students mentioned at each distribution. Dame Sarah's wish that the total number of 'exhibitions' awarded (up to five) was honoured down to 1802 when this figure was suddenly increased to ten. From that date down to 1830, the number varied between five and ten. By 1775, students seem to have been given twice-yearly grants of £3 if in college and £7 10s. if attached to a particular meeting house. In 1791, grants were made to five students, two of them at Hackney and the other three at Manchester Dissenting Academies, both Unitarian colleges. By 1804 just five exhibitions were awarded, but all of these to students at York, where the Manchester Unitarian Academy had moved. From then on, until 1827, most student exhibitions awarded seem to have gone to Unitarian ministers in training at York or to students at academies with Unitarian sympathies; from 1827 to 1830, with legal proceedings increasingly rumoured, one smaller grant (£10) was also given to a student at Airedale College, an Independent institution, in addition to the four exhibitions given to York (£12.10s. each).[395]

Brought forward		£ 12.10	142
Sarah Hillary	York	2	
Julian Smith	do	3	
Isabel Wickham	do	2	
Sarah, Rebecca & Alice Wilbor	Hull	5	
Sarah Dawson	Leeds	2..10	
Mrs Walmsley	do	3..10	
John Wolrich	Morley	3.10	
Eliz Wilkinson	Newcastle	3	
Sarah Russel	Beverley	3	
Eliz Ambler	Morley	2	
Daniel Charlesworth	Swindon	2	
Esther Richie	Halifax	6	
Ellen Beaty	Hull	2	
Martha Clark	Bradford	2	
Isaac Clay	Sowerby	2	
Mrs Riddle	Kirkley	2	
Sarah & Mary Breary	Elland	3	£123..4
Joseph Wilkinson	Northowram	2	
Mrs Mary Naylor	Wakefield	15	
Francilina Gardiner	Swaledale	2	
Janet Baines	Wooler	2	
Sarah Copley	Wakefield	3	
Mrs Hebden	Leeds	2	
Dorothy Willans	Hunslet	3	
Susannah Smith	Alverthorpe	2	
Benjamin & Hannah Budded	Whitby	2	
Ann Norton	Leeds	2	
Mary Cozen	Wakefield	2	
John Fawcit	Leeds	2	
Mary Hackersley	do	2	
Hannah Elliot	Nottingham	2	
Mrs Denison	Leeds	2	
Miss Hotham	do	5	
Jes: Garnet	do	2	
Mr Cunningham	Knaresbrough	10	
And pursuant to a List settled & ordered 14th May 1778			
Mr Andrew Blackie of	Stockton	5	
— John Honeyman	Penrith	5	
— James Benn	Swaledale	5	
— Lowthian Pollock	Student N. 1	3	
— George Todd	Keithley	3	
— Richard Wilding	Knowsley & Prescot	6	
— Newcombe Cappe	York	30	
— John Coppeck	Pontefract	10	
— Jolley	Birdthorpe & c	3	
	Wooler		
— Adam Dean	Huddlescough	5	
— John Dunkley	Kirkstead	5	
— Joseph Dawson	Idle	10	
Carried over		£ 90	565

The petition of Isabella Hart of South Shields, school-mistress, and ministers widow, requesting that with advancing age and infirmity she might receive a supplement to her grant, 1818. Hewley MSS.

To the Gentlemen Trustees of Lady Hewley's Charity. —

The Humble Petition of Isabella Hart of South Shields in the County of Durham Widow. —

Sheweth

That your Petitioner is the Widow of James Hart late of South Shields aforesaid dissenting Minister of the Gospel who died in the Year 1782 — —

That since his Decease your Petitioner has maintained herself solely by keeping a School for the Education of Female Children, which she yet continues in the best manner she is able, but from Old Age and Infirmity (being in her Seventieth Year) she finds that the Means by which she has hitherto subsisted must shortly fail. —

That your Petitioner since the Year 1784 has received from your Charitable Fund the Sum of Five pounds per Year which has been of essential service, and which, after her own Efforts must cease will be her only means of Subsistence, excepting a small Annuity from the Independant Society. —

Your Petitioner therefore humbly prays that you will take those Circumstances into Consideration and make such Addition to her Annuity out of your most charitable Fund as to yourselves shall seem meet And your Petitioner as in duty bound shall ever pray

Isabella Hart

Signed ~~sealed & delivered~~ this eleventh day of August 1818 — In the presence of — }
Thos. F. Hindmarsh

One man to benefit from the Hewley Trust, first as a student and then as a minister, was the eminent Joseph Priestley (1734-1804), theologian, scientist and ardent republican, who entered the Dissenting Academy at Daventry around 1750 and became a Unitarian in 1755, about the same time as the Trust also changed. In 1762 he was appointed a tutor at Warrington Dissenting Academy and in 1767 became minister of the important Mill Hill chapel in Leeds, where he began to devote time to scientific experiments on air and chemistry, later moving to minister in Birmingham. When he celebrated the arrival of the French Revolution, the

The support document for Isabella Hart, signed by ministers and elders on her behalf. Inset, further signatures from the document. Hewley MSS.

mob destroyed both his chapel and manse, and he was compelled to leave the country for the United States.[396] Another ministerial recipient was the Revd. William Hazlitt (1738-1820) of Wem, Shropshire, an extreme Unitarian and, like Priestley, a republican. Hazlitt was the father of the writer, thinker and painter (who also attended the Unitarian Dissenting Academy at Hackney before deciding he was unsuited to the life of a pastor). After retiring from active ministry, William senior continued to receive generous grants twice a year from the Hewley Trustees as a 'beneficiary', first at Lower Swanswick near Bath, and then in the last year of his life, at Dawlish.[397] It would seem clear that the Trustees must have had a well-developed and constantly-updated intelligence system, no doubt aided by a network of local contacts, to keep abreast of ministers' stationings, removals and deaths as well as the circumstances of their widows, daughters and young sons.

The minister of St. Saviourgate chapel in York was, as previously noted, always in a privileged position, the Trustees allowing him a much larger grant than anyone else, down to 1830. As early as 1713, John Hotham was receiving £20 each half year, and by 1810 Charles Wellbeloved had £40 twice a year. This practice appears to have been started by Lady Hewley during her lifetime, suggesting the Trustees were faithful to her expressed wishes. Indeed, when Mr John Brooke of Norwich accepted the invitation to become the pastor of the St. Saviourgate congregation, the Trustees gave him £50 towards his removal expenses.[398] In addition, while the Trustees, calculating the sum available for distribution each half-year, appear to have taken individual cases on their merits, presumably differentiating according to some criteria of need, down to 1830 they tended to be especially generous to a few ministers and places in particular.[399] Notable amongst these was Knaresborough, where a Presbyterian society was founded in the late seventeenth century; its first meeting-house was a barn in Windsor Lane registered in 1697. It is said this society enjoyed the support of Dame Sarah, perhaps on account of her nearby estate at Haya Park.[400] The first mention of a Knaresborough minister, one Ralph Hill, receiving a grant is recorded in 1717 and by 1721 his successor, Caius Thompson, received the first of many half-yearly grants of £10 till his death in 1745 (most grants at this time were from £3 to £5).[401] It is said that meetings ceased at Knaresborough about 1730.[402] However, the records do not support this statement for the first account book of the Charity mentions substantial repairs to the meeting house at Knaresborough in both 1729 and 1731.[403] According to one authority, the chapel was rebuilt on or near its original site in 1779 and then became a Congregational cause in 1782.[404] In 1762 it was reported to the Trustees that another Mr Thompson was now in possession of both the chapel and the manse and was willing to deliver them up into the possession of the Trustees, but was threatened with eviction by a person with no right to either property; the Trustees replied that they would indemnify him if ejected.[405] By 1774 the minister at Knaresborough was a Mr Cunningham, and in 1780 (the year he retired) he stated to the Trustees that the house belonging to the chapel at Knaresborough was a borough tenement possessing two votes for Parliamentary elections and two Toll cards, entitling the owner to a proportion of all tolls collected at the town's markets and fairs for life. Caius Thompson had informed him that this right was still being exercised 30 years before, but many of the burgages had been sold off and an 'arbitrary person' had acquired management of the tolls and payment had long been discontinued. The minister in Knaresborough in receipt of grants from the Hewley Trust in 1781 (and through to 1829) was a William Howell, who was also consistently given one of the highest grants (£12).[406] There evidently was a connection with the Trust, for in 1820 the Steward, John Matthews, was paid for preparing the new Trust Deed for the Knaresborough chapel 'as ordered by the Trustees'.[407]

In 1779, following complaints from members of the 'Protestant Dissenting Congregation' at Howden, near Goole, the minister, Jotham Foljambe, told the Trustees (from whom he had regularly received generous grants of £10 since about 1752) that he had not undertaken any duty at the chapel there for over a year, fearing violence during divine service. The Trustees insisted Foljambe lead worship regularly, and that they would prosecute any persons committing acts of violence during services. The following year, nine members of Foljambe's congregation attended the Trustees' meeting and stated they were willing to repay their minister the money recently laid out on account of enclosure and allotted to the chapel estate, and also expressed their willingness to keep the chapel in good repair, provided Foljambe conveyed the chapel and lands allocated to proper trustees for the benefit of the Dissenting congregation. The Trustees approved the proposal, and added that if Foljambe did not comply or failed to conduct services they would cease to award grants to him. The Trustees were instrumental in ending the disagreement between

Foljambe and his congregation, the latter agreeing to keep the chapel in good repair and their minister undertaking to do his duty diligently, preach there 'twice on every other Lord's Days ... and on such other Lord's Days as he shall be at Howden, if not unwell', administering the Sacraments of Baptism as required and the Lord's Supper four times each year, although no-one else was to preach there without Foljambe's permission. However, in 1790, the Trustees tackled Foljambe again for not conducting services, despite enjoying the benefit of a dwelling house, barn and stable, half an acre of land, together with a further two houses, an orchard and garden in Howden and 14 acres of land in Market Weighton; the Trustees again declared Foljambe should regularly perform his duty in the chapel otherwise the grants to him would cease.[408]

In 1818 the annual amount available for distribution was said to be around £4000, but this gross figure does not allow for certain constant outgoings.[409]

At the final minuted meeting of the old Trustees, on 9 September 1830, and having received legal advice following the 'Information' laid against them in the Chancery Court, they decided not to award any student exhibitions at that time.[410] Soon after the end of the prolonged period of litigation, and the appointment of new Trustees, grants and exhibitions were again being made, the first such awards being on 18 June and 19 September 1850 (196 ministers: £1882; 34 widows: £305; 20 poor persons £165; 18 poor places: £170; 5 students £200). That year one grant intended for a 'Decimus Dolomore' was returned from Bedale as he had gone to Australia.[411] At the September meeting, at Scarborough, a memorial was received from former beneficiaries requesting that grant arrears (unpaid between 1830 and 1849) now be paid to them. The Trustees felt unable to accede but promised to give these individuals first consideration in any future application they might wish to make.[412]

The new Trustees reaffirmed that distributions would be made primarily to the six Northern Counties, but decided to include Cheshire and Derbyshire as well 'according to the practice of the former Trustees' and Lincolnshire, Nottinghamshire, Shropshire and Staffordshire were accorded supplemental eligibility status at the same time. In 1861, what came to be regarded as 'Additional Counties' applications were to be considered after the Northern Counties had been dealt with, reaffirmed in 1881 following the Charity Commission instrument of that year.

Counsel's opinion was obtained, as a result of which the Trustees

Date	Name	Residence	County	Denomination		
	Ministers		Disbursements			
1856			Brought Forward	£	650	
May 5	Hillyard James	Thorne	Yorkshire	Independent	√	10
√	Auld Thomas	Workington	Cumberland	do	√	10
√	Inman William	Doyley Lane near Huddersfield 3	Yorkshire	do	√	10
	Jowett Thomas	Guisborough	do	do	√	10
√	Jones Robert	Staindrop Darlington	Durham	do	√	10
√	Jones Pierce	Sedbergh	Yorkshire	do	√	10
√	Knox William	Berwick on Tweed	Northumberland	do	√	10
√	Kenworthy Abraham	Hill Cliffs or Warrington	Lancashire	Baptist	√	10
√	Kay James	Millwood Todmorden	Yorkshire	do	√	10
√	Kightley Joseph	Mills Hill Oldham	Lancashire	do	√	10
√	Kirkbride Daniel	Maryport	Cumberland	do	√	10
√	Kelsey William	Dent or Sedbergh	Yorkshire	Independent	√	10
√	Leitch Alexander	Wigton	Cumberland	Presbyterian	√	10
√	Lowndes Charles	Gatley Manchester	Lancashire	Independent	√	10
√	Lothean William	Coatham Redcar	Yorkshire	do	√	10
√	Leng William	Stockton upon Tees	Durham	Baptist	√	10
√	Lee Job	Slack Lane Keighley	Yorkshire	do	√	10
√	Miller John	Penruddock, Penrith	Cumberland	Presbyterian	√	10
√	Morris John	Tattenhall	Chester	Independent	√	10
√	Mitchell William	Staithes Whitby	Yorkshire	do	√	10
√	Maden James	Cambleside or Rawtenstall	Lancashire	Baptist	√	10
√	Marshall John	Hunmanby or 3 Scarbro'	Yorkshire	do	√	10
√	Needham George	Audlam or Nantwich	Cheshire	do	√	10
√	Pywell Joseph	Stockport	do	do	√	10
√	Phillips Thomas	Robin Hoods Bay, Whitby	Yorkshire	Independent	√	10
√	Prout Peter	Nuttall Lane 3 Ramsbottom	Lancashire	Baptist	√	10
√	Robinson Thomas	Etue Coldstream	Northumberland	Presbyterian	√	10
√	Ross William	Embleton Alnwick	do	do	√	10
√	Reed John	Blyth	do	do	√	10
√	Rolls John William	Queenshead Halifax	Yorkshire	Independent	√	10
√	Roe James	Batley	do	do	√	10
√	Ryan George Fredk.	Bridlington Quay	do	do	√	10
			Carried forward	√	970	

agreed to give five exhibitions per meeting (or ten a year) to approved students, although there was some doubt whether students studying outside the Northern Counties would be eligible. In 1851, it was reported that college tutors had stated that their students were all making satisfactory progress, and it was agreed to continue their grants. In 1859 the Trustees agreed to increase the number of student grants to eight per half year, increasing this to 16 in 1873 and 18 in 1875.[413] In 1927 the amount permitted to be given each year to students was increased to £2500. In 1956, after an accidental overspend, the Charity Commission agreed to vary the 1881 scheme again and raise the figure to £3250.[414]

In 1875, the Trustees received a memorial from the solicitor, George Hadfield, who played a prominent part in the legal proceedings against the former Trustees, appealing on behalf of the Misses Ann and Sarah Blower, the daughters of the late Mr Blower, 'a former Secretary to the Trustees', for an annual grant to them of £50 for life. Joseph Blower was not in fact a previous Secretary but the Receiver appointed by the Court of Chancery to manage the Trust estates from 1830 until his death in 1845. The Trustees agreed to Hadfield's request.[415]

However, by 1849, the Hewley estates were said to produce an annual income of around £3000 a year.[416] By 1938 this figure had risen to over £10,000 gross, and after expenses (such as the maintenance of buildings, including the Almshouses) there was a net sum of about £8000 available to distribute amongst serving ministers, retired ministers, ministers' widows and daughters, students for the ministry, and 'poor places of worship' especially where there was no resident minister.[417]

After 1850, the Trustees regularly made annual grants (ranging from £2 to £10) to Day and Sunday Schools at Eston and West Ayton, and in the latter case not only paid for the building of the Day School and two cottages (£195 in 1857) but later contributed to its extension also and then gave a further £30 towards the school's continued progress. From the 1860s a donation was also given to Eston Clothing Club, and to a variety of other good causes, related in some way to the Charity. Sometimes the issues were clear cut, and applications could be rejected; at other times it proved more problematical. Contributions were made in 1854 and again in 1865 'to meet the needs of the increased population' towards the erection of the Primitive Methodist chapel (£20) at Eston and towards the stipend of an Independent missionary agent at Eston, a grant of £40 being paid for several years. The Trustees took the view that the building of chapels and expansion of church work had come about mostly from the working of the ironstone 'from which the Charity derives great benefit'. In 1854 the Trustees also agreed a 70-year lease for a site for a Wesleyan Methodist chapel at Eston, at a nominal rent, but refused to contribute towards the cost of its construction. However, when the incumbent of Escomb, Bishop Auckland, applied for a grant towards the building of infant schools, and the vicar of Hutton Buscel asked for a grant towards the repair of his parish church, the Trustees declined both as outside the scope of the charity. When requests for books were received in 1858 from the recently-established Eston Mechanics' Institution and in 1863 from the Guisborough Mechanics' Institution, the Trustees asked Vizard to select and supply books to the value of £10 in each case. When the incumbent of Eston church appealed to the Trustees for a subscription or donation towards the National (Church of England) Schools there, because numbers had greatly increased with the iron mining, the Trustees contributed £5 but only after satisfying themselves that the pupils were not required to learn the Church Catechism and were permitted to attend any place of worship their parents might wish. When Bolckow Vaughan applied to the Trust in 1858 for a grant towards the erection of a new church and parsonage at Eston, and for a contribution towards the support of the school they had established there run on the British & Foreign School Society (Nonconformist) educational system, the Trustees refused the first as outside the Charity's objects and gave £10 towards the school. In 1856 the Trustees gave £100 towards the building of an Independent chapel at Eston. Later on (1862) the chapel trustees appealed for a grant towards paying off debt which had quickly reached £400; the Hewley Trustees agreed to donate £100 towards this. In 1859 an application was received for a grant towards building the Independent chapel at Redcar; this was refused as being outside the objects of the charity, as was the request by the vicar of Knaresborough in 1862 for contributions towards a memorial window to Prince Albert and to building a church tower, and also the request for a grant for the new Temperance Society in Eston, and building a chapel in Sheffield, in 1863.[418]

In September 1862 'the Trustees taking into consideration the great distress existing in the Cotton Districts of Lancashire and Yorkshire, and the probability that many Ministers labouring in those Districts could be seriously affected by such distress, resolved that £500 be placed in the hands of a Sub-Committee to distribute among such Ministers as occasion may require'. A further £250 was voted for this purpose in May 1864.[419]

By the 1880s, the Trustees were using sophisticated forms of application, which when completed, were to be forwarded to the Clerk by mid-March or mid-July. The form for ministers ('Poor and Godly Preachers') and for 'Poor and Godly Persons' (interpreted at this time to be 'Preachers of the Gospel having no Charge' or 'Retired through Infirmity') was exceedingly detailed, asking for full name and address, denomination, age, number and ages of children and whether these were dependent or contributing to the family's income, applicant's place and length of university or college education, when ordained, where ministered and for how long in their present chapel, the population of the town or village where the chapel was situated, its capacity and average congregation exclusive of Sunday School, the number of church members, from what 'class of society' the congregation was chiefly derived and their occupations. In addition, questions were asked: are the efforts of the congregation to provide for its minister proportionate to its ability to pay? What weekday or Sabbath schools are connected with the congregation, and what are the average attendances? Were there any debts outstanding on the chapel and what efforts are being made to pay these off? What was the minister's average annual income over the previous three years and what sources of income are received other than from the Hewley Trust (congregational, endowment, other charities, private sources)? Is the applicant occupying a free manse or dwelling house, and does he follow a secular occupation as well? Applicants were also requested to supply any supporting information that might carry additional weight. Each application was to be signed by two referees (two ministers or a minister and a layman not connected with the congregation) able to testify to the applicant's character and circumstances.[420]

In 1910, because of some uncertainty and confusion on the subject, the Trustees resolved to redefine the nature of a 'Poor Place'. Henceforth this would be understood to be 'a place of worship with no settled minister'.[421]

At the end of the Second World War, the Trustees expressed their thankfulness for the end of hostilities in Europe and the Far East, and as a consequence, in both September 1945 and May 1946, gave an additional Victory Thankfulness sum of £1 to each almswoman and £2 to each recipient of a Hewley grant (excluding students with an ex-Serviceman's grant, and those Presbyterian ministers in receipt of 'Driving Grants').[422]

It was at about this time (1946) that the question arose as to whether 'Women Preachers of the Gospel' were eligible 'to participate in the benefits of the Lady Hewley Trust'. The first application from a woman was however refused as she lived outside the Northern Counties. The Trustees were quite explicit in their resolve that future applications from women living in the North, or training at any of the Northern Colleges (then interpreted as Bradford, Paton and Lancashire), would be sympathetically treated and that there should be no discrimination between male and female ministers and missionaries. The matter surfaced again the following year, and it was then indicated that the Congregationalists had been making grants to women since the time their first female minister, Constance Coltman, was ordained in 1917, that they underwent precisely the same training as their male counterparts and were equally entitled to be regarded as 'Preachers in Charge'. No distinction was therefore to be made provided that women underwent the same course of ministerial training; the first woman to receive a Hewley 'exhibition' for ministerial training was a Sunderland Congregationalist, Cynthia Joyce Brook, in 1948. This discussion took place some years before the Presbyterians felt able to ordain their first female minister, Ella Gordon. However, it was not until 1982 that the Trust formally applied to the Charity Commission for authority to give grants to women wishing to enter the ministry; the Scheme was amended the following year and at the same time the number of annual student exhibitions permitted was increased from 50 to 75; this enabled students attending Mansfield College, Oxford, to be added to the list of recipients.[423]

In 1944 the Trustees were pleasantly surprised to discover that Emily (the elderly daughter of a Congregational minister, the Revd. W. Rowe) had bequeathed one third of her residuary estate to 'The Lady Hewley Charity for the assistance of Ministers' daughters' (single or married) to supplement grants made by the Trust. The bequest was to be known as 'The Emily Rowe Gift and acknowledged by the charity in my name'. Although it was unclear why Miss Rowe had selected the Hewley Trust, other than that she was herself a minister's daughter, the Trustees accepted her generous gift, investing the capital sum involved (almost £800), and then sought to offer grants to ministers' daughters from the net annual interest. The Trustees took the view that this bequest might help in those cases where they were inhibited from giving direct assistance.[424] In 1983 the Trustees acknowledged a legacy from the estate of a Mrs E J Duguid of £332; after some consideration as to whether to add this to the Emily Rowe Gift, it was decided to use it to supplement general funds instead.[425]

The question of student National Insurance arrears surfaced during a Trustees' meeting in 1956. It was realised that these could impose real hardship on students just completing their studies and entering into active, full-time ministry. The Trustees determined to write to the theological colleges saying they would consider grant-aiding students if funds allowed. These National Insurance grants were paid for a few years only.[426]

When the United Reformed Church came into being, formed from those Presbyterian and Independent congregations that wished to merge (and since joined by the Churches of Christ and the Scottish Congregational Church), an Act of Parliament was necessary to give force to the union. This received the Royal assent on 29 June, and was agreed by a United Assembly of the two denominations on 5 October, 1972. The Trustees consulted the Charity Commission on the implications for the Hewley Trust. In addition, one Trustee would take on responsibility for those Independent congregations who preferred to maintain the previous federal arrangement, which endured through a new body, the Congregational Federation. The Baptist situation was largely unaffected by the changes, with the future ratio of distribution being seven-ninths URC & Congregational and two-ninths Baptist. To give effect to the alterations, the Charity Commission issued a new Scheme in 1976, incorporating recommendations from the Trustees and Sub-Trustees for the governance of the Almshouses.[427]

Over the years we see the Trustees have from time to time changed the emphasis of their grant-giving. Today, the charity income, thanks to wise investment and other sources of revenue, is substantial, and the size of the grants reflects this. In just under 300 years the Trustees have distributed rather more than £3,000,000 in total, but this is a net figure and fails to allow for inflation (and occasional deflation) as a consequence of which the actual value of the money distributed must be many times greater than this at today's prices. In addition, the Trustees have from time to time, within the strict confines of Charity Commission schemes, made occasional grants not recorded within the table (*see* Appendix 6).

Appendix 1: The Will of Dame Sarah Hewley, proved 1710 [*very faint*]

... Lady Sarah Hewley of the city of York widow ... my Body to be disposed of with as little cost and ceremony as may be. I give all my capital messuage with the appurtenances called Bell Hall and all lands, tenements in Bell Hall and Naburn to Mrs Barbara Ward, wife of Mr William Ward advocate ... during the minority of Hewley Baines (son and heir of John Baines late of the city of York esq., deceased) ... until Hewley Baines is 21. Barbara Ward and her heirs to maintain the Bell Hall buildings with all needful repairs without committing waste upon any of the said premises. When Hewley Baines is 21 then I give and devise all my lands ... at Bell Hall and Naburn to him and his lawful heirs. If Hewley Baines does not survive 21 or have heirs, then [I give] them to ... of his mother Elizabeth. All the copyhold estate ... I have surrendered into the hands of the Lord of Knaresborough Forest's Steward Marmaduke Prickett ... [for] Hewley Baines. I give to the children of the aforesaid Elizabeth £500 to be improved towards the maintenance and preferment of them, equally divided as they reach 21. I give to Hatton Woolrich (son of late Sir Toby Woolrich) £300. I give my house in St. Saviourgate which I lately purchased of Mr Hugh Carter to Thomas Woolrich (whom I put apprentice to Alderman Forster) and his heirs forever. I give to Mrs Barbara Ward £400 which Montague Giles brickmaker oweth me upon a mortgage, with the mortgage deeds. I give my house where I now live in St. Saviourgate with all its appurtenances to Mrs Mercy Mott and her heirs forever. I give Mrs Mott £1000 that James Bradshaw oweth on a mortgage, together with the mortgage deeds. I give to Mrs Mott, daughter to Mrs Mary Manton, £100. I give to Richard Wynne sergeant at law £50. I give to Mary, wife of Joseph Walker of Hutton Conyers, Yorks. £50. I give the cottage, barn ... and tithes of Boulton in Bishop Wilton, Yorks. to Timothy Hodgson for his life, then to Thomas Woolrich and his heirs forever. I give the tenements with the kiln in Walmgate, York, to Hewley Moxon upholsterer of York. I give to the Lord Mayor and Aldermen of York £500 to be improved and laid out in lands for providing coals for poor necessitous persons as the Lord Mayor and Aldermen judge proper, with 30 shillings out of this to a person to distribute it. I give to the Lord Mayor and Aldermen £100 towards maintaining a school or hospital for poor boys lately erected. I give £100 towards the erection and maintaining of a school or hospital for poor girls in the city of York. I give to Hatton Woolrich's two sisters £100 each if living, if not to Hatton Woolrich. And I make and appoint Dame Ursula Rokeby of New Building in York widow with Thomas Colton of St. Saviourgate gent. my executors.

Sarah Hewley

Witnessed: S Williams; Sam Smith;
          Drewry Peake; Robert Rhodes

Codicil made 21 August 1710 (two days before her death):

I give to Mr Ward the mortgage ... house in Black Street ... if Colton for £800. I give £200 to Mrs Dorothy Mott, and £200 to Mr Mott her younger brother, and to Mrs [Green?] £100. My two messuages ... house in ... London to Thomas Woolrich.

In the presence of: Timothy Hodgson; Drewry Peake
     (*also* Thomas Colton *but he did not sign in my Ladyship's lifetime*)

Private instructions given to her surviving Executor the day before she died:

Forgive Harrison the £50 money he owes, and give £50 more – he has a great family. Forgive Mr Scarlet £100 he owes, if he pays the £50 he took without my knowledge. Let Mrs Mercy Mott have my £200 in the lottery tickets ... Give Mrs Brooks £20 and her son £100. I give to John Hotham £100. You may give the six Trustees [*named, and excluding Colton as Executor*] 10 broads [black cloth] each. You may give Mrs Barbara Ward £100. Give Mr Hutton £50. Give Mrs Hill (formerly her Ladyship's servant) £10 and to Hannah Smith £10. To each of my present servants (except Mrs Green and Mr Hodgson) as many times 40 shillings as they have served me years, over and above their wages. Dispose of my books to scholars as you think fit. I leave to 10 bearers two sceptres each. I allow £20 for keeping house some decent time after my death.[428]

Appendix 2: The Foundation Deeds: First and Second Charities (Abstract)

Declaring the trusts of the General Charity

Indenture of 13 January 1705, between (i) Dame Sarah Hewley of York, widow and executrix of Sir John Hewley, and daughter and executrix of Robert Woolrich, and (ii) Richard Stretton senior of Hatton Garden, Middlesex, gentleman; Nathaniel Gould of St. Mary Newington, Middlesex, esquire; Thomas Marriott of Lincoln's Inn, Middlesex, esquire; John Bridges of Hatton Garden, merchant; Thomas Nesbitt of London, merchant; Thomas Colton of York, gentleman; James Wyndlow of Yarm, gentleman [her Trustees].

Whereas by deeds of lease and release of 12 & 13 January 1705, (i) [Dame Sarah] has conveyed to (ii) [her Trustees] the manors of Killinghall and Braycroft, and the enclosed ground known as Haya Park, together with lands, tenements, meadows, pastures, woods etc. in Killinghall, Ripley, Sussacres [or Southacres], Brearton and Knaresborough, for her to use for the rest of her life and thereafter for the use of her Trustees; and whereas by deed of bargain and sale, dated 13 January 1705, (i) has granted to (ii) all those three of four parts of the manor of West Ayton: -

Now this indenture witnesses that this property of which (i) is possessed, shall be used after her death by (ii) for the following special purposes: an annuity of £100 payable out of Haya Park to Lady Brownley; each Trustee (or Manager) to receive £5 per year plus their expenses; the Trustees to distribute such sums as they see fit to (1) poor and godly preachers of Christ's Holy Gospel (2) their widows (3) poor places to encourage and promote the preaching of Christ's Holy Gospel (4) provide exhibitions to assist in the education, for as long as they wish, of young men designed for the ministry of Christ's Holy Gospel, the grants not to exceed five at any one time (5) the remainder and any surplus to be used for the relief of godly persons in distress who are fit objects of Dame Sarah's charity.

In disposing of these sums for charitable purposes, the Trustees are to give preference to those living in York, Yorkshire and other Northern Counties, but not necessarily to the exclusion of those living elsewhere; charitable contributions previously made by (i) in York and Yorkshire to be continued to be paid out of the income of the charity property, until such time as the Trustees feel justified in ceasing to pay them.

After (i)'s death, the Trustees are to elect from amongst their number a

Treasurer, who shall be allowed a clerk to keep the account books, within which are to be kept 'a true and perfect account' of the rents, issues and profits of the Trust estates, and of all monies paid out to fulfil the objects of the Trust, together with such other transactions as occur; the Treasurer's clerk to receive a 'reasonable and moderate income' out of Trust income. And, after (i)'s death, the Trustees are to hold an annual meeting at which the accounts are inspected and audited; if approved by the other Trustees, this shall be the Treasurer's sufficient discharge.

As and when any Trustee dies, the remaining Trustees are to choose and elect a successor, to become a Manager for the Trust; such elections are to be recorded in the Trust's books. When two, or at most three, Trustees have died, their replacements shall be made full Trustees to bring the number up to seven again, with the execution of a new Trust deed. Reasonable notice of the dates to be given, and where Trustees live at a distance, they are to be consulted by post. Trustees are not to be chargeable for more than the actual monies received by them, nor liable for any losses unless by wilful default; nor for the acts or neglect of any other Trustee. Finally, it is agreed that (i) may at any time during the remainder of her life or by her will, revoke, alter or void any of the Trust arrangements, charities and orders.[429]

Declaring the Trusts of the Almshouses

Indenture made 26 April 1707, between (i) & (ii) [as above].

Whereas by deeds of lease and release dated 25 & 26 April 1707, Dame Sarah has conveyed to her Trustees 'all that new erected house, messuage or building, used for an Hospital, Almshouse, or habitation for some poor people', with the buildings, curtillages, outhouse, courts, easements and boundaries with all the fruit trees and other trees therein and all other appurtenances, situate within and near unto the walls of the city of York … ', and also her farms, lands and tenements at Eston, Yorkshire, leased to James Mewburne, Asculph Snowdon, Alice & Thomas Gill, and also her one-third part of the manor of Eston, for the use of Dame Sarah during her lifetime and thereafter for her Trustees.

Now this indenture witnesses that after the death of (i), (ii) will permit the newly-erected house or Almshouse, with its courts, garths and appurtenances, to be used for ever as a Hospital for poor people in the same way as now, subject to the following orders: (ii) are to pay, out of the income from the lands at Eston, all costs, charges, and expenses for the maintenance and repair of the Almshouse, the provision of catechisms, and £60 each year for ever for the support of ten poor people as shall be elected, put or placed in the almshouse, in accordance with (i)'s intentions as already declared or will in future indicate in writing or in a book of rules and orders for the better selection and government of the poor people in the Almshouse. When there are vacancies, (ii) are to restore the number of inmates to ten, nine of whom are always to be poor widows or unmarried women, aged 55 or over, and the tenth person to be a 'sober, discreet and pious' old man; if such a man cannot easily be found, the tenth place is to be filled by another poor woman, similarly qualified to the other nine. (ii) are to pay each poor person in the Almshouse ten shillings on the first day of every calendar month for ever. (ii) are to observe (i)'s directions as carefully and exactly as possible. (ii), or a majority of them, are to be the only special visitors and governors of the Almshouse and the poor people there, with full power to admit and expel. If for any reason (ii) are unable to carry out their responsibilities, they are to redeploy the annual sum of £60 for the almspeople for such other purposes as (i) may signify or towards the same charitable objectives [*as indicated in the deed of 1705, save that the number of exhibitions to be given is not stated*].

[*The remaining provisions (such as the deaths of (ii) and the election of replacements, notice of (ii) meetings, their financial and other liabilities, and the power of (i) to change these arrangements) are couched in the same words and terms as the deed of 1705*].[430]

Lady Hewley's Endorsement to the 1707 deed, appointing Managers [Sub-Trustees]

Memorandum. It is Dame Sarah's will and pleasure that the management of the Hospital [and] the filling of vacancies shall be in the hands of Thomas Colton, Timothy Hodgson gentleman, Matthew Baycock gentleman, Samuel Smith grocer, Robert Rhodes upholsterer, Martin & William Hotham mercers, all of the city of York, and such as shall succeed them when they die. And the Grand Trustees are at the beginning of each year to give funds to them to provide the monthly allowance [of the almspeople] and also to pay sufficient monies for repairing and rebuilding the Almshouse as and when needed, and their receipts shall be a sufficient discharge for this. In testimony whereof I set my hand and seal the 10 May 1709.[431]

Appendix 3: Rules and Orders for the Almshouses (Abstract)

Rules, Orders, and Directions, to be observed by the Trustees of the newly-erected Hospital, Almshouse, or habitation for ten poor people, built and settled upon them by Dame Sarah Hewley, of the City of York, widow, for its better government, and also by the poor persons placed, or to be placed, there.

Rules and Orders to be kept by the Sub-Trustees:

1. That they, when their number shall be reduced to three, or sooner, upon the death of any one or two of them, shall within three months after a vacancy, elect some other fit person or persons, and transfer and assign their interests in the Almshouse, as directed in the Deed of Settlement, so that the number of six Sub-Trustees at least is where possible preserved.

2. The Sub-Trustees, upon every vacancy, by death or otherwise, of any of the ten poor persons in the Almshouse, shall, before they proceed to an election, have the rules and orders for the qualifications of suitable candidates clearly read and perused, so they may be better informed in their choice. And when a person is selected to fill a vacancy, one of the Sub-Trustees shall read, or have read, to all the almsfolk, the respective duties and requirements expected.

3. The Sub-Trustees are each year to choose one of their number as a Treasurer to handle all the income and expenditure of the Almshouse, and to distribute ten shillings of English money on the first day of each month (or thirty shillings each quarter) to each of the almsfolk. And each recipient shall promise to account for this money faithfully to the Trustees.

4. In all elections, either of new Sub-Trustees, or of poor people, and in all other matters relating to the visitation and good government of the Almshouse, if all the Trustees cannot agree unanimously, then the majority view shall prevail and be of equal force.

5. All the poor people to be elected into the Almshouse shall be either widows or unmarried women, aged 55 years or more, up to ten persons – except when the Sub-Trustees can find a fit, married man (with a sober, pious wife) whom they judge capable and willing to read God's Holy Word or any other pious discourse to the

Hospitallers, and to pray with them daily, each morning and evening – the husband and wife together to be regarded as the tenth person.

Rules and Orders about the qualities or qualifications of the poor people elected:

1. No-one to be elected into a vacancy who has a clear personal estate of more than £60 or real estate of more than £3 annual income, or near relations with sufficient wealth to look after them, as the laws of God maintain.
2. All persons elected shall prove their age, by good testimonials if required.
3. No-one is to be admitted into the Almshouse who cannot be easily separated from their children, who must not be allowed to live with their parents there (save in cases of infirmity and sickness when they are bound by duty and charity to minister to their parents' needs).
4. No-one of bad reputation or evil fame is to be admitted to the Almshouse, but only those who are poor and pious, and of the Protestant faith. Specifically, none given to strong drink, gossip, or with misspent youth, or those justly known for immoral conduct; but if any such are elected, they must provide sufficient evidence of their repentance and improved ways.
5. The persons chosen are to bring settlement certificates from their home parishes, so that if they forfeit their right to live in the Almshouse, they will be received back.
6. Each almsperson shall be able to recite by heart the Lord's Prayer, the Creed, the Ten Commandments, and Mr Edward Bowles's *Catechism.*
7. All the almspeople, unless prevented by illness or infirmity, shall attend a Protestant church each Sunday morning and afternoon.
8. The almsfolk shall be ready to help their alms-sisters when sick, and assist them in turns.
9. No-one is to receive visitors on a Sunday, except when unwell.
10. No-one is to receive servants into the Almshouse, bringing gossip or bad reports of the families where they are or were servants.
11. No-one is ever to be overcome by strong drink, nor behave uncharitably or rowdily with another, by scolding or using bad language; nor should they be busybodies, talebearers or wander about from house to house; they should be content to stay at home, not swear, curse or

tell lies.

12. Each person is to keep their own rooms clean, and all are to share responsibility for keeping the communal areas clean.

13. No almsperson is go begging from door to door, either in the Almshouse or beyond, on pain of expulsion. But they should accept with gratitude such gifts as are given to them by any person.

14. No-one admitted to the Almshouse shall then go out selling bread, eggs, cakes or anything else, except what they have made themselves. And what they have by their own labour honestly acquired they may enjoy.

15. Let every almsperson commend themselves to God in prayer both morning and evening, and in their prayers remember Sarah Lady Hewley during her lifetime, and after her death pray for her Trustees.

16. If any of the almspeople disobeys any of these rules, they are to be warned by one of the Sub-Trustees. If that fails, then they are to be warned a second time. If there is a third transgression, the Sub-Trustees shall have the power to remove such persons with all their effects and to choose another almsperson in their place.

17. No-one is to be admitted to the Hospital without making this declaration:

    'I, A B, being chosen for admission into the Hospital founded by Sarah Lady Hewley, do solemnly promise that I will do my utmost sincerely to observe and keep all these rules and orders (and any others that Sarah Lady Hewley shall add during her lifetime) which shall concern me here; and I do hereby covenant and agree with the said Sub-Trustees that if I fail to keep these rules it shall be lawful for them to withhold my salary and turn me out of the Almshouse. Witness my hand' (and seal, if required)

These Rules and Orders above written I appoint to be observed. Witness my hand:

Sarah Hewley

Witnesses: Mercy Mott, Stephen Wilson[432]

Appendix 4: The Revd. Edward Bowles' *A PLAIN AND SHORT CATECHISM* (Sample)

Q. Who made you? A. God, the creator of heaven and earth. (Acts 17, 24-26; Genesis 1, 1)

Q. To what end did he make you? A. He made me and all things for his glory. (Prov. 16,4)

Q. In what condition did he make man? A. Righteous and happy. (Ecclesiastes 7, 29; Genesis 1, 27)

Q. Did man continue in that state? A. No: he fell from it by sin. (Genesis 3)

Q. What is sin? A. A transgression of the law of God. (1 John 3, 4)

Q. What was the sin of our first parents? A. Eating the forbidden fruit. (Genesis 3, 6)

Q. What was the fruit of that first eating? A. It filled the world with sin and sorrow. (Genesis 3, 14, 16-17; Romans 6, 12)

Q. Hath thy life been better than thy birth? A. No: I have added sin to sin, and made myself above measure sinful. (Romans 3, 10; Colossians 1, 21)

Q. Is there no way to get out of this sinful and miserable state? A. Yes. (2 Timothy 1, 9-10)

Q. What way hath God appointed? A. Only by Jesus Christ. (John 14, 6; Acts 4, 12)

Q. What is Jesus Christ? A. The Son of God manifest in the flesh. (Galatians 4, 4; 1 Timothy 3, 16)

Q. What hath Jesus Christ done for man? A. He hath laid down his life for our Redemption. (Matthew 20, 28; Colossians 1, 14)

Q. What further benefit have we by him? A. Life and salvation. (John 6, 27, 48; Hebrews 5, 9)

Q. By what means may a sinner obtain a part in this redemption? A. By faith in Christ. (Ephesians 2, 8; John 3, 16)

Q. What is it to believe? A. To rely on Jesus Christ, and him alone, for pardon and salvation according to the Gospel. (John 3, 36; Acts 16, 36; Isaiah 1, 10; John 5, 44)

Q. How doth the Gospel teach us to rely on Jesus Christ? A. So as to cast our burden upon him as to take his yoke upon us. (Matthew 11, 28-29)

Q. How is faith wrought in the soul? A. By the Word and Spirit of God.

(Romans 10, 14, 17; 2 Corinthians 3, 6; John 16, 7, 9-10)

Q. What call you the Word of God? A. The Holy Scriptures of the Old and New Testament. (2 Timothy 3. 16)

Q. Doth God work faith by the Word read or preached? A. Ordinarily, by the Word preached. (Romans 10, 14; Ephesians 1, 13; Corinthians 1, 18)

Q. In what order doth God work faith by the Word? A. First he shews men their sins, and then their Saviour. (Acts 2, 37; John 16, 9)

Q. What is repentance? A. It is a sorrowful sense of sin, with a turning from it unto God. (Acts 26, 20; 2 Corinthians 7, 10; 1 Thessalonians 1, 6)

Q. How is true faith further discerned? A. By its fruits. (Galatians 5, 6; Romans 5, 1; James 2, 18; Hebrews 11, 39)

Q. What are the fruits of faith? A. Love in the heart, peace in the conscience, holiness in the life. (Galatians 5, 6; Romans 5, 1; Acts 15, 9; 1 Peter 1, 2)

Q. How must we express our love to Christ? A. By our love to Christians, and keeping his commandments. (John 14, 15; 1 John 5, 1-2)

Q. What doth God look for from his redeemed people? A. That they should walk before him in holiness and righteousness. (Luke 1, 74-75; Titus 2, 12, 14)

Q. Have we strength of ourselves so to walk? A. No: without Christ we can do nothing. (John 15, 5)

Q. What are the ordinances of Christ to this purpose? A. The word preached, the administration of the sacraments, and prayer. (Romans 10, 14-15; 1 Corinthians. 11, 23; Matthew 28, 19-20; 1 Thessalonians 5, 17)

Q. What are the sacraments which Christ hath left to his church? A. Two: baptism and the supper of the Lord.

Q. What is prayer? A. It is a making our request unto God according to his will, in the name of Christ. (Philippians 4, 6; 1 John 5, 14; John 16, 23)

Q. Wherein lieth the strength of prayer? A. In faith and fervency. (Matthew 21, 22; James 1, 6; 5, 16)

Q. What other duties are especially required in a holy life? A. Watchfulness and Christian communion. (Matthew 26, 41; 1 Corinthians 16, 13; Hebrews 10, 24; Colossians 3, 16)[433]

Appendix 5: Grand Trustees, Sub-Trustees and Officers

The first Grand Trustees included Richard Stretton, one of the ministers ejected in 1662. He was for a time chaplain to Thomas, Lord Fairfax, at Nun Appleton in Yorkshire, where he probably made the acquaintance of the Hewleys. When Fairfax died in 1671 he left £100 to Stretton to be distributed amongst 20 poor ministers of his choosing. Stretton was an enthusiastic promoter of co-operation between Presbyterians and Independents, and worked hard to provide for Dissenting ministers and their widows not only in England and Wales but also in Scotland, and was indefatigable in his efforts to raise funds for the training of ministers in 'all three countries'. He was appointed a Trustee of the Presbyterian Common Fund in 1690 and was also a Trustee of the Fund created by the devout Lady Mary Armine, who had her own household chaplain and had consulted no less a person than Richard Baxter about her charitable work. Lady Mary's charitable objectives bear some resemblance to those of Dame Sarah Hewley: distributing money among necessitous ministers and their families, providing books, advice and finance to encourage people to a religious life, making money available to be distributed to poor elderly widows and widowers; and founding three almshouses, including one in Yorkshire. It seems likely that Richard Stretton had some influence on the Trust created by Dame Sarah.[434]

Another Trustee, Thomas Colton, a doctor, was Lady Sarah Hewley's chaplain, and seems to have been held in high regard by her and was certainly heavily involved in the years after her death in ensuring that the Trust started well. Both Colton and Stretton are described as 'gentlemen' in the first years of the Trust, it not being particularly safe to identify them as 'ministers' until after Queen Anne's death in 1714. An important member of that first group of Trustees was the London lawyer, Thomas Marriott, who seems to have provided Dame Sarah with professional advice during her lifetime, perhaps drawing up the Trust deeds, and certainly the man entrusted with the two major lawsuits that arose almost immediately after her death. Another of the first Trustees, probably an Independent by persuasion, was Nathaniel Gould, a wealthy London merchant supplying materials to the Royal Navy after the 1688 Revolution. He invested £2000 in the newly-founded Bank of England, and was one of its directors from 1697 until his death in 1728, serving as Deputy-Governor

1709-1711 and Governor 1711-13. He negotiated trade rights with Russia and was a director of the East India Company. In 1701 he was elected to Parliament and, apart from a two-year gap, served in the Commons for the rest of his life. He was knighted in 1721.[435] Another of the first Trustees, Thomas Nesbitt, was also a London merchant, and may have been related to John Nesbitt, a leading Independent minister in London, who was appointed manager of the denomination's Common Fund in 1692.[436]

Many of the Trustees have somehow found the time to serve the Lady Hewley Trust despite important church, professional and business commitments. Quite a few have been distinguished Members of Parliament (all of them in the Whig or Liberal interest) and councillors, often becoming mayors or aldermen, and many have served as magistrates. Several have been eminent in their chosen professions, such as the Unitarian benefactor, John Lee, from Leeds (a close friend of leading Unitarians, like Joseph Priestley and Theophilus Lindsey), who became Solicitor and then Attorney-General in the later eighteenth century: 'a rare case of a committed dissenter who held office in the eighteenth century'[437] Industrialists have included Sir Samuel Morton Peto, the first Baptist to be elected to Parliament 'and perhaps the most distinguished Nonconformist of his day' and 'a man of uniform urbanity kindliness and consideration' (the sponsor of the 'Peto Act' of 1850 governing the appointment of Nonconformist trustees).[438] Peto was an eminent railway and civil engineering contractor (notably, the London to Norwich Railway, Nelson's Column, part of the Houses of Parliament structure) and was knighted for his heavy involvement with the Great Exhibition of 1851. The list of businessmen who were Trustees also features John and Edward Crossley, the carpet manufacturers, and Samuel Morley, at the forefront of the textile industry; these and others like them were notable for their enlightened concern for their employees, providing educational and welfare facilities, promoting good labour relations, paying above average wages, arranging better accommodation, and fostering a degree of loyalty envied by competitors. The Sub-Trustees have also had many significant members over the years, eminent in a number of fields. The perceptive Professor Hugh Campbell was at the forefront of English Presbyterianism, while Sir James Hamilton was a noted businessman and YMCA leader.[439]

In the list of Grand Trustees from 1705 to 1830, the data on the left-hand side refers to the dates of Trust deeds, usually drawn up for every three new Trustees. Where possible, an attempt has been made to indicate when Trustees died or resigned during this period, and when their successors became 'Managers'. Similarly, with the list of Sub-Trustees from 1709 to 1830, the dates given on the left-hand side are those of Trust deeds, where known.

In a few cases some names are not recorded in Trust deeds (such as the two London Presbyterian divines John Shower, apparently invited to succeed Richard Stretton in 1713, and William Tong, who not only preached Shower's funeral sermon but then succeeded him as a Trustee in 1715. We only know of their service to the Trust through the first Account Book although biographies indicate that both men were outstanding ministers, and experienced trustees of other Dissenting charities. Shower succeeded Dr. Daniel Williams at one stage during his ministry and twice moved his own congregation to larger premises, while Tong was a vigorous Trinitarian exponent involved in the controversial national meeting held at his chapel, Salters' Hall, in 1719.

For the period from 1849 to the present time, the year in which Grand Trustees were chosen is shown, together with denominational adherence so that the lineal sequence can be traced. Dates are also given to show when Trustees ceased to continue because of resignation or death. Again, a similar process has been used for the list of Sub-Trustees. In October 1972, most Presbyterian and many Congregational churches and congregations came together to be known henceforth as the United Reformed Church. Where previously, under the 1849 court settlement, the Congregationalists (Independents) and the Presbyterians were to have three members each and the Baptists one member on both the Grand Trust and the Sub-Trust, from 1976 (as a result of a new Charity Commission Order amending the previous scheme), the URC was to have five members (seven-ninths representation, subject to there being Congregationalists remaining outside the new denomination), and the Baptists and Congregationalists one (one ninth) each on both the Grand Trust and the Sub-Trust.[440]

It is remarkable how long some Grand Trustees and Sub-Trustees have served, and in particular the sequence of Baptist representatives since 1849; to date there have been just five Baptist Grand Trustees from 1849 to the present time. But the officers have just as good a record; from 1711-1830, two Harrisons and three Matthews, all related, served as Stewards. And in the modern period, the legal practice now known as Vizard, Tweedie has provided a continuous service since 1849 (and was involved in the affairs of the Trust during the succession of legal cases between 1830 and that date).

1848-1976: B Baptist; I Independent or Congregational; P Presbyterian. 1976 on: B Baptist; CF Congregational Federation; URC United Reformed Church.

Grand Trustees

13 Jan. 1705 [*Revd.*] Richard Stretton, Hatton Garden, London, gent [*d. 1712,*
& seemingly succeeded by Revd. John Shower [*d. 1715*] and followed by
26 April 1707 Revd. William Tong (*d. 1727*); Nathaniel Gould [*knighted 1721*], St. Mary Newington, Middlesex, esq. [*d. 1728*]; Thomas Marriott, Lincoln's Inn, Middlesex, esq; John Bridges, Hatton Garden, merchant [*d. 1729*]; Thomas Nesbitt, London, merchant; [*Revd.*] Dr. Thomas Colton, York, gent; James Wyndlow, Yarm, gent. [*d. 1729*].

8 August 1729 Thomas Nesbitt; Thomas Colton [*d. 1731*]; James Wyndlow; Gilbert Horsman & Isaac Ewer, both of Lincoln's Inn; Matthew Tanner, Fishmongers' Hall, London; Richard Wyndlow, London and later York, embroiderer.

24 October 1735 Thomas Nesbitt, James Wyndlow, York; Matthew Tanner [*d. 1742*]; Richard Wyndlow; John Witter, Hull; Ambrose Rudsdell, Gainsborough; James Paice, London, merchant.

3 April 1744 James Wyndlow; Richard Wyndlow; John Witter; Ambrose Rudsdell; Robert Moody, London, later Handsworth, Yorkshire, later York, merchant; Richard Gilpin Sawrey, Little Horton, Yorkshire; Richard Milnes, Wakefield.

20 June 1755 James Wyndlow, John Witter; Robert Moody; Richard Gilpin Sawrey; Samuel Shore I, Sheffield, later Norton, Derbys; Aymor Rich, Bullhouse; Thomas Lee I, Leeds.

17 October 1760 Robert Moody [*d. 1767*]; Samuel Shore I; Aymor Rich [*d. 1770*]; Thomas Lee I; John Dawson, Morley [*d. 1770*]; John Milnes I, Wakefield; Richard Markham, Leeds.

12 July 1770 Samuel Shore I; Thomas Lee I [*d. 1773*]; John Milnes I [*d. 1773*]; Richard Markham; Robert Milnes, Wakefield [*1767, d. 1771*]; Samuel Shore II, Norton, Derbys; John Lee, Lincoln's Inn.

10 May 1774 Samuel Shore I [*d. 1787*]; Richard Markham [*d. 1778*]; Samuel Shore II; John Lee; Pemberton Milnes, Wakefield [*1771*]; James Milnes I, Wakefield [*1773, d. 1793*]; Richard Lee [*1773*].

9 May 1793 Samuel Shore II; John Lee MP [*d. 1793*]; Pemberton Milnes [*d. 1796*]; Richard Lee; James Milnes II [*alias* Rich], Thornes House [*1778, d. 1805*]; Samuel Shore III, Norton Hall, near Sheffield, and Lincoln's Inn [*1787*]; Richard Slater Milnes [*alias* Rich] MP, Frystone, Yorks. [*d. 1805*].

12 Sept. 1805   Samuel Shore II, Richard Lee [*resigned 1810*]; Samuel Shore III; William Walker I, Killingbeck, near Leeds [*1793, d. 1817*]; Benjamin Heywood, Wakefield [*1796, d. 1823*]; John Pemberton Heywood, Wakefield and Lincoln's Inn; Thomas Walker, Killingbeck.

13 May 1824   Samuel Shore II, Mearsbrook, Derbys. [*d. 1829*]; Samuel Shore III; John Pemberton Heywood; Thomas Walker; Thomas Lee II, Leeds [*1810, resigned 1828*]; Daniel Gaskell, Lupsett House, near Wakefield [*1817*]; William Walker II, Middleton Lodge, near Leeds [*1823, d. 1830*].

3 October 1830   Samuel Shore III; John Pemberton Heywood; Thomas Walker; Daniel Gaskell; Offley Shore, Richmond Hall, Handsworth, Yorks. [*1829*]; Peter Heywood, Inner Temple [*1829*]; John Wood, Inner Temple, chairman, Board of Stamps & Taxes.

1849 **P** Robert Barbour, Manchester and Bolesworth Castle, Chester [*resigned 1879*]

1849 **P** William Hamilton, Woburn Square, London [*d. 1851*]

1849 **I** Joseph Hodgson, Bakewell, Derbyshire [*resigned 1854*]

1849 **I** John Remington Mills, Englefield Green, Surrey [*resigned 1875*]

1849 **B** Sir Samuel Morton Peto MP, Westminster & Pinner, Middlesex [*d. 1889*]

1849 **P** James Ross, Tynemouth (later Carlisle) [*d. 1875*]

1849 **I** Joshua Wilson, Highbury Place, Islington, London [*resigned 1860*]

1851 **P** Thomas Lonsdale, Stanwick, Carlisle [*d. 1856*]

1855 **I** Thomas Barnes MP, Farnworth, near Bolton [*resigned 1887*]

1857 **P** Alexander Gillespie, London [*resigned 1863*]

1860 **I** John Crossley MP, Halifax [*d. 1879*]

1863 **P** Samuel Stitt, The Grange, Claughton, Birkenhead [*d. 1898*]

1875 **I** Samuel Morley MP, Grosvenor St, London & Hall Place, Tonbridge [*d. 1886*]

1875 **P** James Cochran Stevenson MP, London & South Shields [*resigned 1904*]

1879 **P** Sir George Barclay Bruce, Westminster Chambers, London [*d. 1908*]

1879 **I** Edward Crossley MP, Halifax [*resigned 1891*]

1887 **I** John W Willans, Woodlands, Kirkstall, Leeds [*d. 1910*]

1888 **I** William Crosfield, Aigburth, Liverpool [*d.1909*]

1890 **B** Richard Watson, Rochdale [*resigned 1932*]

1891 **I** Mark Oldroyd MP [*knighted 1909*], Hyrstlands, Dewsbury [*d.1927*]

1898 **P** John James Evans, Higher Bebington, Cheshire [*d.1917*]

1904 **P** Alexander Taylor, West Hartford Grange, Cramlington, North'd [*d.1906*]

1906 **P** Thomas Carter, Ravensdowne, Berwick upon Tweed [*resigned 1925*]

1908 **P** William Sutton, Jesmond, Newcastle upon Tyne [*resigned 1918*]

1909 I George Henry Baines, Bradgate, West Hartlepool [*d. 1913*]

1910 I Herbert Knott, Wilmslow, Cheshire [*resigned 1938*]

1913 I Thompson Gradon, Hanover Square, Newcastle upon Tyne [*resigned 1918*]

1914 P Stephen Moriarty Swan, Sunderland (later Harrogate) [*resigned 1949*]

1917 P George Downie, Waterloo, Liverpool [*d. 1933*]

1918 I Frederic William Buck, Newcastle upon Tyne (later Carlisle) [*resigned 1935*]

1926 P William John Storrow Scott, Ponteland, Northumberland [*d. 1935*]

1927 I William Mercer Wade, Ilkley, Yorkshire [*d. 1937*]

1933 B John Stanley Holmes, Bycullah, Cundall Way, Harrogate [*resigned 1954*]

1933 P Richard Hall Gardner, Waterloo, Liverpool [*resigned 1950*]

1935 P John Crown Graham, Gosforth, Newcastle upon Tyne [*d. 1938*]

1936 I Frederick Fox, Muggleswick, Shotley Bridge, Co. Durham [*d. 1943*]

1938 I Ronald Fitzjohn Walker [*knighted 1853*], Mirfield, Yorks. [*resigned 1970*]

1938 P George Thomas Hall, Newcastle upon Tyne (later Leith) [*resigned 1957*]

1938 I Edward Mansergh Hodgkinson, Alderley Edge, Cheshire [*resigned 1954*]

1944 I Albert Darnley Raine, Gosforth, Newcastle upon Tyne [*resigned 1955*]

1949 P Stephen Hedley Swan, Sunderland [*resigned 1962*]

1950 P John Palmer Moffat, Meols, Wirral, Cheshire [*resigned 1964*]

1954 I J Beveridge Chirnside, Lancaster [*resigned 1961*]

1954 B George Neil Glover, Leeds [*resigned 1996*]

1955 I Clarence Henry Renney, Sunderland [*resigned 1980*]

1957 P John Matthewson Dodds, Harrogate [*d. 1978*]

1962 I Edgar Bradley, Oldham (later Grange over Sands) [*d. 1973*]

1963 P John Moonie, Clifton, York [*resigned 1995*]

1965 P William Douglas Cairney Goldie, Sale, Greater Manchester [*d. 1981*]

1970 I Harold Savage [*resigned 1973*]

1973 I Walter Thomas Foggin Johnson, Newcastle upon Tyne [*d. 1992*]

1977 CF Dennis Brierley Berry, Oldham [*resigned 2002*]

1979 URC Kenneth Alexander McKinlay [*resigned 1996*]

1982 URC Dr. Leslie Murray McKenzie, Southport [*d. 1993*]

1982 URC Dr. Raymond John Morda Evans [*d. 1992*]

1992 URC Bryan Teasdale Herbert, Leeds

1993 URC John Burnett Lumsden, Ponteland, Northumberland

1995 URC Anne Muir [Muriel] Proven, Liverpool

1995 URC Philip Arthur Thake, York

1996 B Edward Stephen Gorton, Redcar, Teesside

1996 URC Dr. James Porteous, Harrogate

2002 CF Gordon Allan Mart Simmonds, Stockport, Greater Manchester

Treasurers

1710 James Wyndlow

1726 John Bridges

1729 Richard Wyndlow

1752 James Wyndlow

1760 Thomas Lee

1773 Richard Lee

1810 Benjamin Heywood

1823 Daniel Gaskell

1830-1849 *In Chancery*

1849 Joseph Hodgson

1854 James Ross

1862 John Crossley

1877 Samuel Stitt

1897 William Crosfield

1909 John James Evans

1917 George Downie

1933 Richard Hall Gardner

1951 John Palmer Moffat

1965 William Goldie

1978 John Moonie

1995 Bryan Teasdale Herbert

Sub-Trustees of the York Almshouses

10 May 1709 [*Revd.*] Dr. Thomas Colton; [*Revd.*] Timothy Hodgson gent [chaplain to Dame Sarah]; Matthew Baycock gent; Samuel Smith grocer; Robert Rhodes upholsterer; Martin & William Hotham mercers, all of York.

1 March 1722 Thomas Colton, Samuel Smith, [*Revd.*] John Hotham [Thomas Colton's assistant]; William Hotham; Thomas Mell; Thomas Beverley; Thomas Wilcock, all of York.

1746 John Hotham; Thomas Beverley; [*Revd.*] John Root; Laurence Hill; Joseph Hawkesworth; Lawrence Jobson; Alexander Harrison, all York.

c.1759 Alexander Harrison; Thomas Beverley; Laurence Jobson; [*Revd.*] Newcome Cappe; Thomas Ellis; James Marshall; Josiah Hotham.

13 July 1769 [*Revd.*] Newcome Cappe; Alexander Harrison; Josiah Hotham; Lawrence Jobson; William Jackson grocer; Robert Driffield linendraper, all of York; Joshua Hainsworth, Leeds, woolstapler.

17 Sept 1807 [*Revd.*] Charles Wellbeloved; Robert Driffield [*d. 1816*]; Robert Sinclair [d. by 1830]; John Rawdon [d. by 1823]; Thomas Smith [*d. by 1830*], all of York; George Palmes, Naburn near York [*C. of E.*]; William Walker, Wilsick, Doncaster (later Middleton, near Leeds) [*Grand Trustee, 1823*]

17 Sept 1817 [*Revd.*] Charles Wellbeloved; Robert Sinclair, Thomas Smith, all of York; George Palmes; William Walker; Thomas Bischoff & Henry Oates, both of Leeds.

[13 May]1830 [*Revd.*] Charles Wellbeloved; Varley Beilby [Bealby]; [*Revd.*] John Kenrick, all of York; John Wood, Scarby, York; Thomas Bischoff; Henry Oates; George Palmes.

1849 **B** Revd. Dr. Benjamin Godwin, Bradford [*resigned 1867*]

1849 **I** Dr. Henry Brown, Bloomsbury, Manchester [*resigned 1865*]

1849 **P** Revd. Professor Hugh Campbell, Torrington Square, London [*d. 1855*]

1849 **P** Revd. Richard Hunter, Carlisle [*d. 1853*]

1849 **I** James Pigott Pritchett, York [*d. 1868*]

1849 **I** Revd. James Parsons, York [*resigned 1877*]

1849 **P** Revd. James Pringle, Newcastle upon Tyne [*d. 1866*]

1853 **P** Revd. George Wilson Adam, Leeds [*later Dumfries, then to Australia 1866*]

1855 **P** Revd. James Towers, Birkenhead [*d. 1891*]

1866 **P** Revd. Dr. William McCaw, Manchester [*resigned 1888*]

1866 **I** James Oldham, Hull [*resigned 1888*]

1867 **B** Revd. Dr. Acworth, Scarborough [*resigned 1880*]

1868 **I** John Bellerby, York (later Northallerton) [*d. 1903*]

1877 **I** Revd. Eustace Conder, Leeds [*d. 1893*]

1880 **P** Revd. J H Collie, York [*resigned 1893*]

1880 **B** Revd. T E Cozens Cooke, York [*resigned 1885*]

1886 **B** Revd. William Turner, York [*resigned 1889*]

1888 **P** Revd. Alexander Stirling, York [*resigned 1906*]

1889 **I** Henry Empson, York [*d. 1911*]

1889 **B** Revd. George Hill, Leeds [*resigned 1891*]

1891 **P** Revd. John G Train, Hull [*resigned 1893, resumed 1910, resigned 1914*]

1891 **B** Revd. Arthur Fayers, Yeadon, Leeds [*resigned 1904*]

1893 **P** Revd. J Scott Cockburn, Harrogate [*resigned 1910*]

1893 **P** Patrick Munro, Harrogate [*resigned 1902*]

1894 **I** Joshua Watkinson, York [*d. 1935*]

1902 **P** William Scollay Eassom, Harrogate [*resigned 1909*]

1904 **I** Arthur Bellerby, York [*d. 1912*]

1904 **B** Revd. T Graham Tarn, Harrogate [*d. 1906*]

1906 **P** James Hamilton [*knighted 1929*], Benningbrough, York [*d. 1935*]

1907 **B** John Holmes, Harrogate [*d. 1929*]

1909 **P** Revd. J A McIlvride, York [*resigned 1915*]

1910 **P** Revd. John G Train, Hull [*resigned 1914*]

1912 **I** C E Robinson, York [*d. 1944*]

1912 **I** Thomas Allan [*resigned 1927*]

1914 **P** A M Wisely, York [*d. 1939*]

1915 **P** Revd. Herbert H Stephenson, Dringhouses, York [*resigned 1921*]

1921 **P** Revd. W McNaught, York [*resigned 1928*]

1927 **I** Martha Cattle, York [*resigned 1940*]

1928 **P** Revd. Roy Drummond Whitehorn, York [*resigned 1935*]

1929 **B** John Stanley Holmes, Harrogate [*resigned 1933, on becoming Grand Trustee*]

1933 **B** George W Glover, Leeds [*d. 1951*]

1935 **P** Revd. Malcolm William Wilson, York [*resigned 1938*]

1936 **I** Lewis Leadley, York [*resigned 1940*]

1936 **P** Thomas Gray, York [*resigned 1956*]

1938 **P** J M Melville, York [*resigned 1957*]

1939 **P** Revd. W Y S Colquhoun, York [*resigned 1965*]

1940 **I** J W Saunders, York [*d. 1961*]

1940 **I** Revd. W West, York [*resigned 1943*]

1944 **I** F Carter, York [*resigned 1956*]

1944 **I** H R Worth, York [*d. 1950*]

1950 **I** Arthur Dixon, York [*resigned 1962*]

1951 **B** Revd. Dr. D J Davies, York [*resigned 1964*]

1956 **P** Charles Benjamin Mein, York [*d. 1967*]

1957 **I** Roy Selby, York [*resigned 1961*]

1958 **P** James Hourston Henderson, York [*resigned 1976*]

1962 **I** Revd. N B Pace, York [*resigned 1969*]

1962 **I** John Frederick Allinson [*resigned 1983*]

1962 **I** Mrs Harriet Emily Louise Gatenby, York [*resigned 1979*]

1964 **B** John C Dawson [*resigned 1965*]

1965 **B** Revd. M W Powell, York [*resigned 1971*]

1966 **P** Revd. Alisdair J G Walker, York [*resigned 1976*]

1968 **P** Robert Alexander Smith [*d. 1979*]

1969 **I** Revd. James Henderson [*resigned 1972*]

1971 **B** Revd. Robert Hammond Neill Robb, York [*resigned 1982*]

1972 **I** Cecil James Mee, York [*resigned 1996*]

1976 **URC** Revd. Alan Gerald Burroughs [*resigned 1983*]

1976 **URC** Mrs Gertrude Laing Moonie, York [*resigned 1995*]

1979 **URC** Mrs Agnes Burnet MacLeod [*resigned 1986*]

1979 **URC** Robert Hume Kerr [*resigned 1980*]

1980 **URC** Thomas William Burton [*resigned 1985*]

1982 **B** Revd. Edgar W Wright [*resigned 1984*]

1983 **URC** Revd. John Hamilton Fraser [*resigned1987*]

1983 **URC** George S Pritchard [*resigned 1999*]

1985 **B** Revd. David Iain Wilson Collins [*resigned 1995*]

1985 **URC** Thomas Macfarlane [*resigned 1992*]

1986 **URC** Gerald Miller [*d. 1988*]

1988 **URC** Revd. Ambrose David Wright [*resigned 1994*]

1989 **URC** Leonard Peter Wade Hall, York

1992 **URC** Alan John Goldfinch [*resigned 2001*]

1995 **URC** Mrs Barbara Mary Skelton, York

1996 **B** Revd. John Richard Hennings [*resigned 2000*]

1996 **URC** Revd. Thomas Owen Williams, York

1996 **URC** Alan William Marr [*resigned 2001*]

1999 **URC** William James, York [*resigned 2005*]

2001 **URC** Mrs Catherine E Halliday, York

2003 **B** Revd. Gary Patchen, York

2004 **URC** Revd. G Maskery, York

2005 **URC** Mrs Janet Ponsford, York

Almshouses

Secretaries/Clerks	*Treasurers*
1849 Revd. Dr Benjamin Godwin	1849 James Pigott Pritchett
1865 James Pigott Pritchett	1868 James Oldham
1868 Revd. Dr. Acworth	1869 John Bellerby
1880 Revd. J H Collie	1891 Henry Empson
1893 Revd. J Scott Cockburn	1912 Joshua Watkinson
1910 Joshua Watkinson	1936 Lewis Leadley
1911 Revd. J A MacIlvride	1940 J W Saunders
1912 Joshua Watkinson	1961 J H Henderson
1918 Revd. H H Stephenson	1976 Mrs G L Moonie
1921 A M Wisely	1986 Gerald Miller
1922 Revd. W McNaught	1989 Peter Hall
1929 Revd. R D Whitehorn	
1935 Revd. M W Wilson	
1939 J M Melville	
1957 C B Mein	
1968 R A Smith	
1979 R H Kerr	
1980 Thomas Burton	
1985 Thomas Macfarlane	
1992 Alan Goldfinch	
2001 Mrs Catherine Halliday	

Officers

Stewards (1710-1830)

1710   Alexander Harrison I (York, Hayapark, Brearton, Sussacres, Coneythorpe & West Ayton) & George Matthews (Eston & Skelton [Margrove Park])

1723   Alexander Harrison II & George Matthews

1733   Alexander Harrison II & John Preston of Stokesley, attorney at law

1734   Alexander Harrison II & John Matthews I, attorney at law

1769   John Harrison & John Matthews I, attorney at law

1779   John Matthews I, attorney at law, Stokesley (all properties)

1790   Zachariah [or Zachary] Hubbersty, attorney at law [Matthews' son in law]

1793   John Matthews II, Dockwray Square, North Shields, attorney at law

1830-1849 *Administered by the Court of Chancery*

Secretaries

1849   William Vizard II, Lincoln's Inn Fields, London

1876   George Augustus Crowder, Lincoln's Inn Fields

Clerks

1880   George Augustus Crowder

1886   William Henry Crowder

1887   Robert Calder, 17 Water Street, Liverpool [formerly Clerk to the Treasurer]

1892   Alexander Armour, Liverpool

1908   William Grisewood, 2 Exchange Street East, Liverpool

1915   William Harold Grisewood CA, 2 Exchange Street East, Liverpool

1923   W R MacGregor, 5 Fenwick Street, Liverpool

1954   John Cochrane MacGregor, 5 Fenwick Street, Liverpool

1981   David R Wharrie FCA, Chester

Legal Advisors

[Firm founded 1797 by William Vizard senior, involved with the Hewley Trust since 1830; now known as Vizard, Tweedie]

1830   Joseph Blower (Receiver for the Court of Chancery)

1845   William Vizard II (Receiver for the Court of Chancery)

1849   William Vizard II & Mr Capes

1850   William Vizard II

1876   George Augustus Crowder   1914   George Bertram Crowder

1886   William Henry Crowder   1942   Alfred S Cash

1900   Ernest Fitzjohn Oldham   1973   Ronald E Perry

Investment Advisors
1966 Duncan C Fraser & Co.
1979 Ashton Tod McLaren & Co.
(later Morgan Stanley Quilter Co. Ltd.)
2003 Tilney Investment Management,
Liverpool (Duncan Brooke)

Auditors
1876 John Lankester, London
1894 William Grisewood & Son, Liverpool
1909 Thomas A Hanmer, Liverpool
1912 T A Hanmer & Son, Liverpool
merged with Grant Thornton & Co.,
2005 Voisey & Co., Warrington

Land Agents
1852- c.1860 Mr John Parrington
1877 Mr Prior (& Mr Dewes)
1880 R W F Mills, York
1886 Charles Mansfeldt Forbes, York
[Mills' nephew]
1925 Edward Samuel Cox, York
1934 John Allison, Gainford, Darlington
1976 Brian Wilkinson, Boulton & Cooper Stephenson's, of York

Mining Agents
1849 Mr John Parrington
1851 G B Forster, Newcastle upon Tyne
1893 G B & T E Forster, Newcastle
1934 F W Allison, Guisboro
1934 John Allison JP, Gainford, Darlington

Clerks to the Treasurer
1712-1717 Thomas Burrell
1718-1760 *Not named*
1761-1770 John Banks
1771-1776 Samuel Banks
1777-1780 William Stead
1781-1786 John Scurr
1787-1811 Dominick Forster
1812-1830 John Gotthardt
1830-1849 *In Chancery*
1849-1886 *Not named*

(Since 1887 this post has been combined with
that of the Clerk to the Trustees)

Property Manager (Almshouses)
1999 Richard Brown (York Conservation Trust)

[*Compiled from Minutes; Accounts; Sub-Trustees minutes, 1849- to date; Memoranda Book,
1840-1959; CC1829; FDD1849 & Sub-Trustees MS addition; Short Account 1877; Tottie;
Lords' Hearing, 1839; Charity Commission Order, 1976; N Glover, Sir Morton Peto; notes by
J B Lumsden, 2003*].

Appendix 6: Hewley Estate rental fluctuations (1710-1854)[441]

Date	West Ayton	Haya Park &	B/S*	York**	& Margrove Park
1710/11	£308.03.08	£411.06.02	£24	£33.05.06	£183.05.02
1711/12	£283.17.08	£468.11.08		£33.05.06	"
1714/15	"	£452.03.08		£32.03s.	"
1715/16	£284.00.11	£452.17s.		£31.08s	"
1716/17	£284.10.11	£472.09.08		£31.18s.	"
1717/18	£284.06.11	£472.10.08		£33.15s.	"
1718/19	£308.13.11	"		£33.16s.	"
1719/20	£310.13.11	"		"	£248.05.02
1720/21	"	"		£34.16s.	"
1721/22	"	£482.12.04		"	"
1725/26	"	£488.12.04		£36.06s.	£262.05.02
1726/27	"	"		£37.16s.	"
1727/28	£312.17.11	"		"	"
1729/30	£336.17.11	£500.13.04		£38.11s.	"
1731/32	£318.01.03	£464.12.04	£24	£38.01s.	£274.00.02
1735/36	"	£445.08.04	"	"	"
1741/42	"	£469.08.04	"	"	£254.00.02
1743/44	"	£510.05.04	"	"	"
1744/45	"	£511.03.04	"	£39.19s.	£255.10.02
1746/47	"	£469.08.04	£26.16s	£39.09.06	"
1748/49	£358.01.03	£397.09.08	"	£39.07s.	"
1750/51	£319.06.06	£396.19.08	"	"	"
1754/55	£312.02.03	£410.09.08	"	"	£256.05.06
1756/57	"	"	"	"	£261.00.00
1758/59	"	£689.14s.	"	"	£261.14s.
1780/81	£570.01s.	£870.10s	£35	£40.05s.	£293.14.06
1781/82	£570.01s.	£920.10s.	"	£40	"
1783/84	£571.13.04	"	"	"	"
1787/88	£575.07.06	"	"	"	"
1790/91	£577.09.11³/₄	"	"	"	"
1792/93	£577.08.03	£1104.16s.	£42	"	"
1793/94	£575.07.06	£1102.16s.	"	"	£336.04.06
1796/97	£577.01.06	"	"	"	£508.04.06
1797/98	£761.06.011/4	"	"	"	£524.04.06
1798/99	£821.06.041/4	"	"	"	"
1799/1800	£831.05.033/4	"	£42.15s. "		£491.04.06
1800/01	£850.17.11¹/₄	£1122.14s.	£42.17s. "		£500.17s.
1801/02	£863.11.02	£1142.12s.	£43.14s. "		£510.09.06

Date	West Ayton	Haya Park &	B/S*	York**	Eston & Margrove Park	
1802/03	£1011.18.06	£1186.6s. (incl. B/S)		"	£423.12.06	£120.06s.
1806/07	£1011.14.02$^{1/2}$	£1929.11s.	"	"	"	"
1807/08	£1011.04.07$^{3/4}$	"	"	"	£611.05.06	"
1808/09	£1031.07.02	£1849.11s.	£80	"	"	"
1810/11	£1031.09.08	£1854.10s.	"	"	"	"
1811/12	£1031.04.01$^{1/2}$	£1849.11s.	"	"	"	"
1812/13	£1031.04.07$^{1/2}$	"	"	£70	"	"
1820/21	£1030.05.00$^{1/2}$	£1575.00	£73	"	"	"
1822/23	£1029.16.11$^{3/4}$	£1564.00	"	"	"	"
1825/26	£1029.18.11$^{3/4}$	"	"	£90	"	"
				Whixley		
1849/50	£954.18.07	£1574.15.04		£94	£558.7s.	£96.05.06
1851/52	£966.17s.	£1721.02.06		"	£580.14.06	"
1853/54	£1030.10.05	£1818.17.04		"	£698.05.02	£124.15s.

Note: Only years included where significant changes took place.

*Brearton and Sussacres   ** York Hospital lands

Appendix 7: Grants made, by decade[442]

Decade	Preachers/Students	Widows/Necessitous Persons/Poor Places	Total
1711-20			£5253.00
1721-30			£6707.10s.
1731-40			£6950.00
1741-50			£6127.00
1751-60			£6576.00
	Ministers (& Students)	*'Beneficiaries'*	
1761-70	£8353	£1443	£9796.00
1771-80	£8576	£1350	£9926.00
1781-90	£12421	£1562. 10s.	£13983.10s.
1791-1800	£16604.10s.	£2717.10s.	£19321.00
1801-10	£20040	£3477.10s.	£23517.10s.
1811-20	£24931.10s.	£4244	£29175.10s.
1821-30 (May)	£21547	£2683	£24230.00
1830-1849	*In Chancery and other Courts*		

	Preachers	Widows	Poor Places	Poor Persons	Students	Total
1849-60	£25266*	£4935*	£2335*	£2935*	£4180*	£39651.00
1861-70	£26496	£8694	£3235	£6285	£5040	£49750.00
1871-80	£30987	£12533	£2844	£8636	£6080	£61080.00
1881-90	£21428	£11329	£3309	£6927	£7200	£50193.00

	Ministers	RM	Widows	Daughters	P. Pl.	Students	Total
1891-1900	£16357	£3834	£10239	£2507	£3106	£7140	£43183.00
1901-10	£18761	£4970	£9775	£3712	£3455	£7720	£48393.00
1911-20	£19657	£6778	£10809	£6233	£2168	£8235	£53880.00
1921-30	£19945	£13103	£1991	£11260	£1602	£17510	£83330.00

	Ministers	SDG**	NI***	RM	Widows	Daughters	P. Pl	Students	Total
1931-40	£9596	£286		£14900	£25825	£11215	£1645	£20740	£84207
1941-50	£6975	£1482		£15100	£36125	£10324	£1105	£11149	£82260
1951-60	£5695	£2162	£215	£18041	£37923	£9232.	£1360	£21679	£96306
1961-70	£4995	£9520	£408	£26920	£54378	£8800	£3870	£23575	£132466
1971-80	£39725	£16970		£53540	£97950	£11255	£3175	£41910	£264525

	Ministers	RM	Widows	Daughters	P. Pl.	Students	Total
1981-90	£86315	£163350	£187090	£19320	£940	£90210	£547225.00
1991-2000	£66465	£287275	£396165	£29565		£201090	£980560.00
2001-05	£18740	£109370	£171715	£14500		£102050	£416375.00

(to June 2005)

Key:

RM: Retired Ministers; P. Pl: Poor Places

* Includes applicants from outside Northern Counties from this date

** Special Driving Grant paid to Presbyterian Ministers in rural areas from September 1939 to September 1976

*** National Insurance contributions paid from September 1959 to June 1964 to assist ministers just completing their training and faced with possible hardship.

Appendix 8: Almshouse Residents 1841-1891 (Census)[443]

1841
1. Ralph Davison, Dissenting Minister, aged 66
2. Ann Barker, 70
3. Elizabeth Ridsdale, independent, 73
   Mary Ridsdale, independent, 45
4. Elizabeth Fearby, independent, 60
5. Hannah Coates, independent, 70
   Hannah Coates, dressmaker, 25
6. Isabella Silversides, independent, 74
7. Mary Brown, independent, 67
8. Elizabeth Pennoak, independent, 65
9. Elizabeth Steel, independent, 65.

[Note: census enumerators were supposed to round ages up or down to the nearest five years]

1851
1. Peter Appleton, retired dry salter's clerk, 72
   Fanny Appleton, wife, 76
2. Eleanor Wilson, widow, almswoman, 66, born Richmond, Yorks.
3. Grace Horsfall, widow, almswoman, 69, Halifax
4. Ann Rheader, widow, almswoman, 81, Rufforth, Yorks.
   Margaret Potter, her unmarried sister, almswoman, 75, Muxley
5. Hannah Middleton, widow, almswoman, 62, York
6. Rebecca Edward, widow, almswoman, 68, York
7. Elizabeth Pennoak, unmarried, almswoman, 75, York
8. Mary Ann Stubbs, widow, almswoman, 64, Ireland
9. Elizabeth Steele, widow, almswoman, 70, York
10. Jane Robinson, widow, annuitant, 75, York
    Frances Robinson, unmarried daughter, asst. Ragged School mistress, 54, York
    Sarah Gamble, married daughter, tin-plate worker, 38, York.

1861
1. George Beckitt, chaplain & agent, 62, born Batley Carr, Yorks.
   Hannah Beckitt, wife, 60, Lumby, Yorks.
2. Eleanor Wilson, Baptist Minister's widow, 76, Richmond, Yorks.
3. Grace Horsfall, watchmaker's widow, 79, Halifax
4. Eleanor Harris, unmarried, former governess of boarding schools, 64, Essex
   Eleanor Carley, niece, domestic servant, 22, Westminster
5. Hannah Middleton, shoemaker's widow, 71, York
6. *Uninhabited*

7. *Visiting friends*

8. Mary May, former schoolmistress in Scotland, 66, Scotland

9. Elizabeth Steel, waterman's widow, 80, Holtby

    Anne Fraser, grand-daughter, scholar, 11

10. Jane Turner, widow, former nurse, 64, Wakehall

    Annie Kenyon, grand-daughter, 9 months, York.

1871 1. George Beckitt, house agent, 74, born Batley Carr, Yorks.

    Hannah Beckitt, wife, 72

2. Ann Duncan, widow, 65, Holywell, Wales

3. *Uninhabited*

4. Ann Leeming, unmarried, formerly dressmaker, 65, Nottingham

5. Frances Rayward, widow, 74, Skipton

6. Frances Smith, unmarried, 74,Selby

7. Mary Willdon, widow, annuitant, 66, Apperley Bridge, Yorks.

8. Mary May, widow, no occupation, 78, Edinburgh

9. Margaret Clark, widow, laundress, 66, York

    Mary Ann Clark, laundress, 39, York

10. *Tenant absent*

1881 1. Henry Bland, chaplain to Lady Hewley's Hospital, 62, York

    Margaret Bland, wife, 66, York

    Emma Bland, daughter, 32

2. Ann Barrett, unmarried, 78, Holderness

3. Frances Noble, unmarried, 64, York

4. *Uninhabited*

5. Eliza Stave, widow, 66, York

    Annie E Stave, daughter, dressmaker, 34, Barton on Humber

6. *Uninhabited*

7. Mary Willdon, widow, annuitant, 76, Apperley Bridge, Yorks.

8. Sarah Davison, unmarried, 63, Hull

9. Margaret Clark, widow, 76, York

    Margaret A Clark, laundress, 49, York

10. Jane Turner, widow, 84, Bedale.

1891 1. Henry Bland, caretaker, 72, born York

    Margaret Bland, wife, 74, York

2. Jane Wandby, unmarried, 66, Hull

3. Frances Noble, unmarried, 74, York

4. Mary Anne Clark, unmarried 59, York

5. Eliza Stave, widow, 76, York

   Ann Eliza Stave, daughter, dressmaker, 46, Barton on Humber

6. Sarah Lazenby, widow, 76 York

7. Anne Pawson, unmarried, 74, York

8. Sarah Davison, unmarried, 74, Hull

9. Mary Oates, unmarried, 63, Halifax

10. Elizabeth Render, unmarried, retired dressmaker, 60, York.

1901 1. Henry Bland, widower, 82, Chaplain, Lady Hewley's Hospital, born Heworth, York

   Jessie Bland, single, 42, daughter and housekeeper to father, St. Peter's, York

2. Emma Panketh, single, 61, almswoman, Berlin, Prussia

3. Mary Freeman, widow, 71, almswoman, Croydon, Surrey

4. Mary A Clark, single, 69, almswoman, York

5. Mary Webb, widow, 82, almswoman, West Haddon, Northamptonshire

6. Sarah Lazenby, widow, 86, almswoman, York

7. Anne Pawson, single, 84, almswoman, York

8. Clare McGillivray, widow, 79, almswoman, Scotland

9. Mary Oates, single, 71, almswoman, York

10. *Not indicated.*

Time Chart 1517-2003

Date	Hewley	Church affairs	Major occurrences
1517		Luther's *95 Theses*	
1533		English Reformation begins	
1536		Calvin starts Presbyterian revolution, Geneva	
1545-1563		Roman Catholic Council of Trent	
1563		Elizabethan settlement for Church of England	
1570		Cartwright's 'presbyterian' lectures	
1580		'Separatist' movement develops	
1588			Spanish Armada
c.1590			Shakespeare's first plays
1593		John Penry executed; Henry Barrow & John Greenwood hanged	
1605			Gunpowder plot
1607		Puritanism first evident in York	
1611		*King James Bible*	
1619	**John Hewley born**		
1620		*Mayflower* pilgrims sail to America	
1627	**Sarah Woolrich born**		
1639	**John Hewley admitted to Gray's Inn**		
1641-1646			English Civil War
1642-1644			Royalists occupy York
1642-60		Puritan social repression	
1643		Westminster Assembly	
1644			Battle of Marston Moor
1645		Presbyterianism established in York	
1649	**John Hewley & Sarah Woolrich marry** [*circa*]		Charles I beheaded
1650	**John Hewley starts to buy estates**		
1654	**John & Sarah Hewley buy land at Naburn near York**		
1658-1660	**John Hewley MP for Pontefract**		
1660			Monarchy restored
1660-62		'The Great Ejectment'	

Date	Hewley	Church affairs	Major occurrences
1661	**Robert Woolrich dies**	Corporation Act	
1662	**Edward Bowles dies**	Act of Uniformity	
1663	**John Hewley knighted**		
1664		Conventicle Act	
1665		Five-Mile Act	Great Plague, London
1666			Great Fire of London
1667			Milton's *Paradise Lost*
1672		Declaration of Indulgence	
1673		Test Act	
1675			Wren starts to rebuild St. Paul's
1679-1681	**John Hewley MP for York**	Exclusion crisis	
1680	**Bell Hall built**		
1684			Bunyan's *Pilgrim's Progress*
1685		Huguenots flee France	Charles II dies
1688		'The Glorious Revolution': James II replaced by William & Mary	
1689		Toleration Act	
1690		Presbyterianism established in Scotland	Battle of the Boyne
1691	**Ralph Ward dies**	Attempted 'Happy Union' between Dissenters	
1692	**Dr. Thomas Colton becomes pastor of Ward's congregation**		Massacre of Glencoe
1693	**(Lady Hewley's) St Saviourgate chapel licensed for worship**		National Debt commenced
1694			Bank of England founded
1695	**Hewley charity monies already being distributed to ministers**		
1697	**Sir John Hewley dies**		
1698			London Stock Exchange founded
1699	**Dame Sarah Hewley purchases land in Tanner Row**		
1700	**Hewley Almshouses open**		
1702			Queen Anne
1704			Battle of Blenheim
1705	**First Hewley Trust created**		
1707	**Second Hewley Trust created**		Act of Union with Scotland
1709	**Almshouse rules and Sub-Trustees appointed**		Abraham Darby first smelts iron
1710	**Dame Sarah Hewley dies**	Dr. Sacheverell impeached	

Date	Hewley	Church affairs	Major occurrences
1711	**Mott family dispute Lady Hewley's will; Trustees at law against Hewley Baines**		
1712			Newcomen steam engine
1714			George I
1715			First Jacobite rebellion
1719		Salters' Hall Conference	
1720			South Sea Company bubble' bursts
1738		John Wesley 'strangely moved'	
1739	**Trustees purchase Mauleverer interest in West Ayton estate**		
c.1740			Industrial Revolution starts
1745			Second Jacobite rebellion
1755	**Hewley Trust influenced by Unitarians**	Lisbon earthquake	Dr. Johnson's Dictionary
1760	**Robert Moody ceases to participate in financial aspects of Trust**		
1761-1830	**Hewley Trustees meet at Wakefield**		
1767			Hargreaves' Spinning Jenny
1771			Arkwright's spinning frame
1774			Dr Joseph Priestley discovers oxygen
1776			US Declaration of Independence
1777			James Watts' steam engine
1778		Lady Huntingdon's chapels declared illegal	
1779			Ironbridge built over River Severn
1789			Storming of Bastille; French Revolution
1791		John Wesley dies	
1792		Baptist Missionary Society formed	
1795		London Missionary Society founded	
1796			Jenner's smallpox vaccine
1803		Manchester Unitarian College moves to York	Trevithick's steam locomotive
1805	**Almspeople's stipend raised**		Battle of Trafalgar
1807			First Anti-Slavery Act
1813		Unitarians given legal status	
1815			Battle of Waterloo
1817		Wolverhampton chapel case commences	

Date	Hewley	Church affairs	Major occurrences
1819			Factory Act limits children's work
1824		Start of 'Socinian' controversy	
1825			Stockton-Darlington Railway opened
1826	Complaint to Parliamentary Commission re Unitarians		First known photograph
1828		Test and Corporation Acts repealed	
1829		Catholic Emancipation Act	Metropolitan Police
1830	Unitarian Trustees in Chancery court: *Attorney-General v. Shore & others*		
1831			Faraday's electric dynamo
1832			The Great Reform Act passed
1833	Vice-Chancellor's verdict	Congregational Union founded	Slavery banned in British Empire
1834			Tolpuddle martyrs convicted; Poor Law Act
1836	Lord Chancellor's confirmation	United Presbyterian Church formed	
1837	Master's report re new Trustees		
1838	York railway station plan announced		Brunel's Great Britain; Peoples' Charter (Chartists)
1839	Site procured for new Almshouses in St. Saviourgate, York		
1840	New Almshouses opened in St. Saviourgate; Whixley estate bought		Penny Post
1841	York's first railway station opens		Thomas Cook's first excursion
1842	Lords' decision in Hewley case	Churches of Christ extant in UK	
1843	Master's revised report		
1844		Dissenters' Chapels Act	
1846		Irish potato famine; Corn Laws repealed; Anaesthetics first used 1848	
1848	*Attorney-General v. Wilson & others*		California Gold Rush
1849	Hewley litigation finally resolved and new Trustees appointed		
1850	Eston iron first mined		
1851	Eston iron mines officially opened		The Great Exhibition
1853		Charity Commissioners first appointed	
1853-1856		The Crimean War; Florence Nightingale	
1856		Bessemer converts iron into steel; Pasteur finds germs spread disease	
1859			Darwin's *Origin of Species*
1860-1865			Lister pioneers antiseptic surgery
1861-1865			American Civil War
1864			Red Cross founded
1865		Salvation Army founded	

Date	Hewley	Church affairs	Major occurrences
1867			Marx's *Das Kapital*
1870			Forster's Education Act
1871			Stanley finds Livingstone
1873	Peak year for Cleveland iron production		
1876		Presbyterian Church of England formed	Bell invents telephone
1878	Hewley Trust Estates vested in Official Trustee		Swan's incandescent electric light bulb
1879	Gilchrist & Thomas process of converting Cleveland iron into steel successful		
1879-1881	Hewley Charity more precisely regulated by Charity Commissioners		
1881	New Charity Commission scheme for Hewley Trust; Almspeople's stipend raised		
1882	Eliza Taylor's bequest for the Almshouses		'Movies' pioneered
1885			Benz petrol-driven car
1895			X-Ray process invented
1898			Curies discover radium
1899-1902			The Boer Wars
1901			Marconi's wireless signal across the Atlantic
1902			Balfour's Education Act
1903			Wright brothers' powered flight
1904	New rules for Almshouse determined	Welsh Revival	
1908			Baden Powell founds Boy Scouts
1910		Missionary Conference, Edinburgh	
1911			Rutherford discovers nucleus of atom
1912			Scott's expedition to South Pole; sinking of Titanic
1913		Schweitzer founds African hospital	Suffragette Emily Davison dies
1914-1919			First World War
1917		Ordination of Constance Coltman to Congregational ministry	Russian Revolution
1918 & 1928			British women given vote
1920		Welsh Church disestablished	League of Nations created
1922			BBC begins regular broadcasts
1926			General Strike; Baird invents television
1927			Fleming discovers penicillin
1929			Wall Street crash
1930			Whittle invents jet engine

Date	Hewley	Church affairs	Major occurrences
1932		Methodist Church Union	
1935			Radar developed
1936			The Jarrow March
1938		World Council of Churches formed	
1939-1945			Second World War
1940		Free Church Federal Council created	
1942			Beveridge Report; first electronic computer
1943	**Incendiary bomb damage to Almshouses**		
1944			Butler Education Act
1945			United Nations established
1946			National Health Service founded
1947		Dead Sea Scrolls discovered	
1949	**Last shift at Eston iron mines**		
1953			DNA structure discovered
1962	**Subsidence at Almshouses first apparent**		
1963	**Lady Hewley Charity registered by Charity Commission**		
1969			Apollo 11 lands on moon
1970		*New English Bible*	
1972		United Reformed Church & Congregational Federation formed	
1973			EEC enlarged to include UK
1976	**Revised Scheme for Lady Hewley Charity**		
1978	**Increased concern about Almshouses subsidence**		First test-tube baby
1981		Churches of Christ unite with URC	
1983	**Revised Scheme for Lady Hewley Charity**		
1988-1989	**Major underpinning and structural repair work to Almshouses**		
1992	**Amended Scheme for Hewley Charity**	Church of England admits women priests	
1999	**York Conservation trust assumes responsibility for Almshouses structure**		
2000	**Amended Scheme for Lady Hewley Charity**; Congregational Church of Scotland unites with URC		
2003			Invasion of Iraq

[Compiled from Cornick, Carter, and other sources][444]

Notes

'Hewley MSS' and 'Hewley MSS (addnl.)' refer to the Hewley collections held at the North Yorkshire County Council Record Office, Malpas Road, Northallerton. 'BIHR' refers to the Borthwick Institute of Historical Research, University of York, whose holdings include probate records and documentary material relating to St. Saviourgate Chapel, York. 'WCC' refers to the Reformed Studies Centre, Westminster College, Cambridge, which holds mainly Presbyterian manuscript material and a significant quantity of nonconformist printed history and literature.

For full bibliographic details see 'Bibliography and Archive Sources'.

BACKGROUND

1 David Thompson, *Nonconformity in the Nineteenth Century*, pp. 1-2

2 H S Skeats & C S Miall, *History of the Free Churches of England, 1688-1891*, p. 102; Westminster College, Cambridge [WCC], York envelope: *St. Columba's Presbyterian church, York, Jubilee Book*, 1935, p. 7.

3 G Burnet, *History of His Own Times*, p. 79.

4 Ibid.

5 Skeats & Miall, *op. cit.*, p. 147.

6 Skeats & Miall, *op. cit.*, p. 157.

7 Skeats & Miall, *op. cit.*, pp. 74, 239-240, 243, 361, 714; I P Pressley, *A York Miscellany*, p. 91; M R Watts, *The Dissenters*, vol. II, p. 96; G F Nuttall, 'Methodism and the Old Dissent', *Journal of the United Reformed History Society* [*JURCHS*], vol. 2, no. 8, 1981, pp. 272-273.

8 Thompson, *op. cit.*, pp. 2-3; Watts, *op. cit.*, vol. II, p. 96.

9 G D H Cole, *Persons and Periods*, p. 51.

10 Ibid.

11 J Hunter, *An Historical Defence of the Trustees of Lady Hewley's Foundation*, p. 78-80

12 Thompson, *op. cit.*, p. 3.

13 Thompson, *op. cit.*, p. 4.

14 Thompson, *op. cit.*, p. 84; Cowherd, *The Politics of English Dissent*, p. 85.

15 Thompson, *op. cit.*, p. 147; C G Bolam, 'J R Beard and the New Function of Unitarianism in the 1850s', *Transactions of the Unitarian Historical Society* [*TUHS*], vol. III, no. 4, 1962, p. 157.

16 *York: Official Guide*, 1951.

17 *International Dictionary of Historical Places*, vol. II, pp. 813-815

18 *York: Official Guide*, 1951, *op. cit.*

19 P M Tillott (ed.), *Victoria History of the County of York: the City of York* [*VCH York*], pp. 193-194, 205.

20 *A Short Account of the Hewley Charities*, 1935 [Short Account, 1935], p. 5.

21 Borthwick Institute of Historical Research [BIHR], University of York: Unitarian chapel, St. Saviourgate, York, records [ref. UCSS 5/10 (renewal of lease to Snowden family, 1730); North Yorkshire County Council Record Office, Hewley MSS (additional material): Declarations of Trusts, 1729 & 1774.

22 *VCH York*, *op. cit.*, p. 199; Nikolaus Pevsner & David Neave, *The Buildings of England: York and the East Riding*, p. 65, notes the superbly-carved overmantel attributed to John Etty of York (1634-1709) at the Hewleys' country house, Bell Hall, Naburn.

23 Daniel Defoe, *A Tour Through the Whole Island of Great Britain*, pp. 520-523.

24 Asa Briggs, *Victorian Cities*, pp. 70, 377.

25 *International Dictionary of Historical Places*, *op. cit.*, p. 816; York: Official Guide, 1951, *op. cit.*

26 *York: Official Guide*, 1975.

SIR JOHN AND LADY SARAH HEWLEY

27 WCC, John Peddie's volume of portraits and notes; G Hadfield, (ed.), *The Report of His Majesty's Commissioners concerning Dame Sarah Hewley's Charity*. 1829 [CC1829], p. 58.

28 C V Wedgwood, 'Sir John Hewley, 1619-1697', *TUHS, op. cit.*, vol. VI, no. 1, 1935, p. 4; *VCH Yorkshire* [*VCH* Yorks.]: General Volume III, p. 53; *Dictionary of National Biography* [*DNB*], vol. L, p. 283; *Oxford Dictionary of National Biography* [*ODNB*], vol. 48 pp 914-922.

29 Wedgwood, *op. cit.*, p. 4; WCC, Peddie.

30 *DNB, op. cit.*, vol. XXVI, p. 310; *ODNB, op. cit.*, vol. 26 pp 933-934.

31 *ODNB, op. cit.*, vol. 26; Wedgwood, *op. cit.*, p. 4.

32 Pressley, *op. cit.*, p. 84.

33 Wedgwood, *op. cit.*, p. 5; CC1829, *op. cit.*, p. 58; Pressley, *op. cit.*, p. 84; *ODNB, op. cit.*, vol. 26; Hewley MSS, account book, 1711-1760.

34 *DNB, op. cit.*, vol. XXVI, p. 310; CC1829, *op. cit.*, p. 58.

35 *DNB, op. cit.*, vol. XXVI, p. 310; Pressley, *op. cit.*, pp. 84-85; E Brunskill, 'Some York Almshouses', York Georgian Society occasional paper no. 7, p. 24.

36 Wedgwood, *op. cit.*, p. 5; *DNB, op. cit.*, vol. XXVI, p. 310.

37 Wedgwood, *op. cit.*, p. 5; CC 1829, *op. cit.*, p. 2; J Horsfall Turner, *The Rev. Oliver Heywood, B.A., 1630-1702: His Autobiography, Anecdote and Event Books,* vol. I, p. 298, vol. II, pp. 44, 104, vol. IV, pp. 92, 117, 148, 156.

38 Brunskill, *op. cit.*, p. 24; Wedgwood, *op. cit.*, p. 3; *ODNB, op. cit.*, vol. 26.

39 Pressley, p. 86; *York Official Guide*, 1975, *op. cit.*

40 *ODNB, op. cit.*, vol. 26.

41 Wedgwood, *op. cit.*, pp. 5-6.

42 Wedgwood, *op. cit.*, p. 12.

43 *ODNB, op. cit.*, vols. 18, 26; Hunter, *op. cit.*, pp. 78-84.

44 Wedgwood, *op. cit.*, pp. 12-13.

45 *ODNB, op. cit.*, vol. 26.

46 *DNB. op. cit.*, vol. XXVI, p. 310; Wedgwood, *op. cit.*, p. 7.

47 Wedgwood, *op. cit.*, p. 7; *ODNB. op. cit.*, vol. 26

48 *ODNB, op. cit.*, vol. 26.

49 *Ibid.*

50 York City Archives, Corporation House Book, 30 November 1659.

51 Wedgwood, *op. cit.*, p. 3.

52 VCH Yorks., *op. cit.*, vol. III, p. 82.

53 Alberic Stacpoole, *The Noble City of York*, p. 383.

54 J & J A Venn, *Alumni Cantabrigiensis*, part 1, vol. II, p. 63, mentions a Thomas Hewley, born at Wistow, proceeding to Cambridge in 1648, aged 18, the son of George Hewley attorney. George may have been John Hewley's uncle.

55 Wedgwood, *op. cit.*, p. 6; CC 1829, *op. cit.*, p. 58.

56 Wedgwood, *op. cit.*, p. 6.

57 K J Allison, *Victoria History of the County of York*: vol. III, East Riding [*VCH.ER*], p.78; Pressley, *op. cit.*, p. 87; *ODNB, op. cit.*, vol. 26.

58 Hewley MSS, accounts, 1711-1760 (George Hadfield's subsequent notes).

59 *VCH.ER, op. cit.*, vol. III, p. 78; Pevsner & Neave, *op. cit.*, p. 65; Pressley, *op. cit.*, p. 87.

60 Watts, *op. cit.*, vol. I, pp. 358-359.

61 Wedgwood, *op. cit.*, pp. 11-12.

62 Wedgwood, *op. cit.*, pp. 12-13; Pressley, *op. cit.*, p. 88; Skeats & Miall, *op. cit.*, pp. 148, 200.

63 Watts, *op. cit.*, vol. I, pp. 358-359.

64 A H Drysdale, *History of the Presbyterians in England: their Rise, Decline and Revival*, p. 445.

65 *ODNB, op. cit.*, vol. 26.

66 *Ibid.*

67 Brunskill, *op. cit.*, p. 24.

68 Skeats & Miall, *op. cit.*, p. 200.

69 Hunter, *op. cit.*, pp. 78-84; *ODNB*, *op. cit.*, vol. 26.

70 *CC 1829*, *op. cit.*, pp. 15-16.

71 WCC, York envelope: *St. Columba's Presbyterian church, York, Centenary* brochure, 1973, p.4.

72 Wedgwood, *op. cit.*, pp. 12-13; CC1829, *op. cit.*, p. 59; Pressley, *op. cit.*, p. 88; Hunter, *op. cit.*, pp. 78-84.

73 Wedgwood, *op. cit.*, p.13; BIHR, will of Sir John Hewley, proved 1697.

74 Wedgwood, *op. cit.*, p. 13.

75 Wedgwood, *op. cit.*, p.13; Edward Royle (ed.), *A History of the Nonconformist Churches of York*, p. 14.

76 Francis Drake, *Eboracum or the History and Antiquities of the City of York*, p. 312.

77 Pressley, *op. cit.*, p. 88.

78 *DNB*, *op. cit*, vol. XXVI p. 311; *VCH* York, *op. cit.*, pp. 253, 438, 447; Pressley, *op. cit.*, p. 88; Stacpoole, *op. cit.*, pp. 819-820; BIHR, will of Dame Sarah Hewley, proved 1710.

79 Wedgwood, *op. cit.*, p. 13; *ODNB*, *op. cit.*, vol. 26.

80 Pressley, *op. cit.*, p. 91.

81 VCH York, *op. cit.*, p. 403.

82 Wedgwood, *op. cit.*, p. 13; St. Saviour's is now deconsecrated and in the care of the York Archaeological Research Centre [ARC], from whom permission to view can be obtained.

83 *VCH* York, *op. cit.*, p. 75; Brynmor Jones Library, University of Hull, Baines of Bell Hall MSS, introduction.

84 Hewley Mortimer Baines, MS Reminiscences of the Baines family of Bell Hall.

85 Short Account 1935, *op. cit.*, pp. 5-6.

86 Brunskill, *op. cit.*, p. 24.

87 Pressley, *op. cit.*, p. 85; newspaper report of the discovery of the remains of Lady Hewley, 1850. It was Rawdon who presented the Corporation of York with the gold chain worn by successive Lady Mayoresses, and the gold loving cup, the most valuable piece of the city's plate.

88 Pressley, *op. cit.*, pp. 88-89; BIHR, will of Dame Sarah Hewley, proved 1710.

ST. SAVIOURGATE CHAPEL

89 *VCH* York, *op. cit.*, p. 151.

90 *VCH* Yorks., *op. cit.*, vol. III, p. 63; *VCH* York, *op. cit.*, pp. 201-202 passim.

91 *VCH* Yorks., *op. cit.*, vol. III, pp. 61-62; *VCH* York, *op. cit.*, pp. 203-204

92 *VCH* York, *op. cit.*, p. 205.

93 G Lyon Turner, *Original Records of Early Nonconformity under Persecution and Indulgence*, vol. I p. 177.

94 *CC 1829*, *op. cit.*, p. 58; *VCH* York, *op. cit.*, p. 404; Lyon Turner, *op. cit.*, vol. I, pp. 622, 658; Ronald Willis, 'Nonconformist Chapels of York, 1693-1840', *York Georgian Society occasional paper no. 8*, p. 3; Horsfall Turner, *op. cit.*, vol. I, p. 298; WCC, York envelope: R S Robson's printed and MS notes on Presbyterianism in York, pp. 1, 3-4.

95 WCC, Robson's York notes, pp. 4-5.

96 WCC, York envelope: *St. Columba's Presbyterian church, York, Centenary* brochure, 1973, p.4.

97 Watts, *op. cit.*, vol. I, p. 238; Pressley, *op. cit.*, p. 238.

98 *VCH* York, *op. cit.*, p. 404; *CC 1829*, *op. cit.*, p. 58.

99 *VCH* York, *op. cit.*, p. 404; CC1829, *op. cit.*, p. 60; Skeats & Miall, *op. cit*, p. 147.

100 *VCH* York, *op. cit.*, p. 404; CC1829, *op. cit.*, p. 60; Willis, *op. cit.*, p. 3; *ODNB*, *op. cit.*, vol. 9 pp. 490-495.

101 WCC, Robson's York notes, p. 5.

102 Wedgwood, *op. cit.*, p. 13; WCC, Robson's York notes, p. 1.

103 *VCH* York, *op. cit.*, pp. 160, 404; Willis, *op. cit.*, p. 2; *Royal Commission on Historic Monuments: City of York* [RCHM York], p. 55.

104 WCC, Robson's York notes, p. 5.

105 *CC 1829*, *op. cit.*, pp. 404-405.

106 Christopher Stell, *An Inventory of Nonconformist Chapels and Meeting Houses in the North of England*, p.185.

107 Willis, *op. cit.*, p. 3; WCC, York envelope, notes on Presbyterianism in York.

108 *CC 1829*, *op. cit.*, p. 61; WCC, Robson's York notes, p. 5.

109 *CC 1829*, *op. cit.*, pp. 24n., 61; Robson's York notes, p. 5.

110 *CC 1829*, *op. cit.*, p. 60.

111 CC1829, *op. cit.*, p. 61; Robson's York notes, p. 5.

112 E Axon, 'Yorkshire Nonconformity in 1743', *TUHS*, *op. cit.*, vol. V, no. 3, 1933, pp. 253-254.

113 Drake, *op. cit.*, p. 312.

114 William Hargrove, *History and Description of the Ancient City of York*, vol. II, part 2, p. 336.

115 Hewley MSS, accounts, 1761-1809.

116 *VCH* York, *op. cit.*, p. 404; Willis, *op. cit.*, pp. 3-6, 34; Hargrove, *op. cit.*, vol. II, part 2, pp. 334-336; *RCHM* York, *op. cit.*, pp. 55-56; Hewley MSS, accounts, 1761-1809.

ESTABLISHING DAME SARAH'S CHARITIES

117 Kenneth Wadsworth, 'Philip, Lord Wharton - Revolutionary Aristocrat', *JURCHS*, *op. cit.*, vol. 4, no. 8, 1991, pp. 472-473.

118 Lyon Turner, op.cit., vol. II, p. 647; A G Matthews, *Calamy Revised, being a Revision of Edmund Calamy's Account of the Minister's and others Ejected and Silenced*, 1660-1662, p.466-467; Hewley MSS, accounts, 1711-1760 (George Hadfield's subsequent notes).

119 Lyon Turner, *op. cit.*, vol. III.

120 *Short Account of the Hewley Charities, 1881-1913 [Short Account, 1913]*, pp. 5-6; *DNB* XXVI, p. 311, adds that determining documents included her will of 9 July 1707 and codicil of 21 August 1710. See Appendices 1 & 2.

121 *Short Account 1913*, *op. cit.*, pp. 27, 41; *ODNB*, *op. cit.*, vol. 26

122 Skeats & Miall, *op. cit.*, p. 201; Hunter, *op. cit.*, pp. 78-84.

123 *Hargrove*, *op. cit.*, vol. II, part 2, p. 335.

124 Hewley MSS, accounts 1711-1760 (Hadfield's subsequent notes); WCC, Robson's York notes, p. 2. In her will (at BIHR), Dame Sarah named two executors: Dr. Thomas Colton and Dame Sarah's close friend and fellow Dissenter, Dame Ursula Rokeby, who predeceased her (the widow of the Queen's Bench judge, Sir Thomas Rokeby). *See* Appendix 1.

125 Short Account, 1913, *op. cit.*, p. 6; WCC, Robson, p. 2; Hewley MS, accounts, 1711-1760 (Hadfield's subsequent notes).

126 Hewley MSS, accounts, 1711-1760; BIHR, Dame Sarah Hewley's will, proved 1710.

LADY HEWLEY'S ALMSHOUSES: TANNER ROW

127 *VCH* York, *op. cit.*, p. 425.

128 Hewley MSS, title deeds, Tanner Row, York, 1664-1699, 1818 (ZTP I 13. 2-3).

129 *CC 1829*, *op. cit.*, p. 43; *VCH* York, *op. cit.*, p. 425; Hargrove, *op. cit.*, vol. II, part 1, p. 182; Stacpoole, *op. cit.*, pp. 493-494; Hewley MSS, title deed, Tanner Row, York, 1818 (ZTP I 13. 3).

130 Pressley, *op. cit.*, pp. 88-89.

131 *Short Account,* 1913, *op. cit.* p. 35.

132 Drake, *op. cit.*, p. 274.

133 Hargrove, *op. cit.*, vol. 2, part 1, pp. 182-183.

134 *DNB*, *op. cit.*, vol. VI, p. 67.

135 WCC, York envelope: Yorkshire Gazette, 1 January 1932.

136 *DNB*, *op. cit.*, vol. VI, p. 67; *ODNB*, *op. cit.*, vol. 6.

137 WCC, York envelope: *St. Columba's Presbyterian church, York: Centenary* brochure, 1973.

138 WCC, York envelope: *St. Columba's Presbyterian church, York, Jubilee Book 1935*, p. 6; and notes on Edward Bowles.

139 *VCH* Yorks., *op. cit.*, vol. III, p. 62n; WCC, York envelope: *York Presbyterian church, Jubilee Book* 1935, p. 6; *Centenary* brochure, 1973.

140 *DNB*, *op. cit.*, vol. VI, p. 67.

141 WCC, York envelope: notes on Edward Bowles.

142 *DNB*, *op. cit.*, vol. VI, p. 67; *CC 1829*, *op. cit.*, pp. 44-45; Pressley, *op. cit.*, p. 73.

143 *VCH* Yorks., *op. cit.*, vol. III, p. 68; *DNB, op. cit.*, vol. LIV, p. 375; *DNB, op. cit.*, vol. LVI, p. 392; *ODNB, op. cit.*, vol. 6, pp. 959-960.

144 *CC 1829, op. cit.*, p. 45

145 *VCH* Yorks., *op. cit.*, vol. III, p, 68; RDW, 'Mr Edward Bowles' Catechism', *Journal of the Presbyterian History Society*, vol. 7, no. 2, 1941, p. 93.

146 *JPHS, op. cit.*, vol. 7, no. 2, p. 93.

147 Hewley MSS, accounts, 1711-1760.

148 Hewley MSS, memorandum book, 1730-1751.

149 Hewley MSS, accounts, 1761-1809.

150 Hewley MSS, minutes, 14 September 1769

151 Hewley MSS, minutes, 13 May 1813; accounts, 1711-1760, 1761-1809, 1810-1830.

152 Hewley MSS, minutes, 1 September 1805; 19 September 1811; 14 May 1818; accounts, 1711-1760, 1761-1809, 1810-1830.

153 Hewley MSS, minutes, 16 September 1824.

154 Hewley MSS, minutes, 21 September 1826; accounts, 1810-1830.

155 Stacpoole, *op. cit.*, p. 326

156 Pressley, *op. cit.*, p. 90; Hewley MSS, title deed, Whixley, 1840 (ZTP I 10. 1).

157 Hewley MSS, title deeds, 1834-1839 (ZTP I 13. 4); Hewley MSS (addnl.), minutes, 18 September 1946.

158 Hewley MSS, title deed, Whixley, 1840 (ZTP I 10. 1).

159 *VCH* York, *op. cit.*, p. 480; Stacpoole, *op. cit.*, p.362; W W Tomlinson, *The North Eastern Railway: its Rise and Development*, pp. 321, 323, 350. The present railway station in York did not open until 1877.

ADMINISTERING THE CHARITY: THE ANCIEN REGIME

160 *DNB, op. cit.*, vol. XXVI, p. 311; CC1829, *op. cit.*, p. describes Lady Hewley and her first Trustees only as 'Protestant Dissenters'; Hewley MSS, accounts, 1711-1760; 1761-1809, 1810-1830.

161 WCC, Robson notes on York, p.2.

162 *Short Account*, 1913, *op. cit.*, p. 29.

163 Charity Commission Order, 1976.

164 Hewley MSS, accounts, 1711-1760.

165 Cole, *op. cit.*, p. 78.

166 Hewley MSS, minutes and memoranda, 1730-1751, 1762-1730; accounts, 1711-1760, 1761-1809, 1810-1830.

167 *Short Account*, 1913, *op. cit.*

168 *CC 1829, op. cit.*, p. 61; *DNB, op. cit.*, vol. IX, p. 24.

169 *VCH* York, *op. cit.*, pp. 404-405; *CC 1829, op. cit.*, p. 62; *Short Account*, 1913, *op. cit.*, p. 8; *ODNB, op. cit.*, vol. 10, pp. 1-2; Pressley, *op. cit.*, p. 91.

170 *VCH* York, *op. cit.*, p. 405; *CC 1829, op. cit.*, p. 62; *DNB, op. cit.*, vol. IX; *ODNB, op. cit.*, vol. 10; Pressley, *op. cit.*, p. 91; Hewley MSS, accounts, 1711-1760.

171 *CC 1829, op. cit.*, pp. 20-22; *Short Account*, 1913, *op. cit.*, p. 8; Hewley MSS, accounts, 1711-1760 (Hadfield's subsequent notes).

172 G M Ditchfield, 'Two Unpublished Letters of Theophilus Lindsey', *TUHS, op. cit.*, vol. XX, no. 2, 1992, pp. 137f; Hewley MSS, accounts, 1711-1760 (Hadfield's notes).

173 Hewley MSS, accounts, 1711-1760 (Hadfield's notes).

174 *Ibid.*

175 Hewley MSS, minutes, 1762-1830; accounts, 1761-1809, 1810-1830.

176 Hewley MSS, accounts, 1711-1760, 1761-1809.

177 Hewley MSS, minutes, 1762-1830; accounts 1810-1830.

THE TRUST IN CHANCERY, 1830 - 1849

178 Skeats & Miall, *op. cit.*, pp. 146, 361.

179 *Short Account*, 1913, *op. cit.*, p. 9; Drysdale, *op. cit.*, p. 617; *ODNB, op. cit.*, vol. 24, pp. 421-422; WCC, pamphlet: *Two Hundred and Fifty Years of the Church of the Divine Unity*, Newcastle upon Tyne, 1672-1922.

180 *Short Account*, 1913, *op. cit.*, p.; Drysdale, *op. cit.*, p. 617.

181 *Encyclopaedia Britannica*, 1958 edn., vol. V, p. 253; Neil Glover, typescript notes on 'Sir Morton Peto MP and the Lady Hewley Trust', 1996.

182 *Short Account*, 1913, *op. cit.*, p. 10.

183 *Ibid.*

184 *CC 1829*, *op. cit.*, pp. 54-57; Watts, *op. cit*, vol. II, p. 94.

185 *ODNB*, *op. cit.*, vol. 24; WCC, George Hadfield's MS notes, 1861, p. 22.

186 Peter B Godfrey, 'Joseph Hunter, 1763-1861', *TUHS*, *op. cit.*, vol. XVIII, no. 2, 1984, p. 17f; WCC, Lady Hewley papers.

187 Drysdale, *op. cit.*, p. 618.

188 *Short Account*, 1913, *op. cit.*, p. 11; Drysdale, *op. cit.*, p. 619; T S James, *The History and Legislation respecting Presbyterian Chapels and Charities in England and Ireland between 1816 and 1849*, p. 243

189 Brunskill, *op. cit.* p. 23-24; Ian Sellers, 'The Risley Case', *TUHS*, *op. cit.*, vol. XVI, no. 4, 1978, p. 180.

190 Drysdale, *op. cit.*, p. 619.

191 *DNB*, *op. cit.*, vols., XXXI p. 15 and LX p. 166; *VCH* York, *op. cit.*, pp. 405, 449; CC1829, *op. cit.*, p. 19; *Short Account*, 1913, *op. cit.*, p. 9; H McLachlan, 'More Letters of Theophilus Lindsey', *TUHS*, *op. cit.*, vol. III, no. 4, 1926, p. 361-377; Hewley MSS, accounts, 1810-1830.

192 *CC 1829*, *op. cit.*, p. 31.

193 *DNB*, *op. cit.*, vol. LX, p. 166.

194 Thompson, *op. cit.*, pp. 85-87; Pressley, *op. cit.*, p. 92

195 *Short Account*, 1913, *op. cit.*, p. 12.

196 Watts, *op. cit.*, vol. II, p. 95.

197 Tyne and Wear Archives Service [TWAS]: records of the Church of the Divine Unity, Newcastle upon Tyne (TWAS 1787/113: newspaper cutting, 13 February 1836, from a report in the Leeds Gazette).

198 *Short Account*, 1913, *op. cit.*, pp. 12-15.

199 *Ibid.*

200 Sir Thomas Erskine May, *The Constitutional History of England since the Accession of George the Third*, vol. 3, cap. 14: 'Dissenters Chapels', p. 199; *VCH* York, *op. cit.*, p. 405; Skeats & Miall, *op. cit.*, pp. 726-727; Drysdale, *op. cit.*, p. 618; Watts, *op. cit.*, vol. II, p. 95; Bolam, *op. cit*, p.157; Arthur Long, 'The Dissenters' Chapels Act after 150 Years, some concluding reflections', *TUHS*, *op. cit.*, vol. XXI, no. 1, 1995, p. 43; K G Jones, 'The Authority of the Trust Deed', *Baptist Quarterly*, vol. XXXIII, no. 3, 1989, p. 108.

201 Foundation Deeds and Other Documents relating to Dame Sarah Hewley's Charity, 1849 [FDD 1849], pp. 34-41; Glover, typescript notes, 1996.

202 A *Short Account* of the Hewley Charities, 1877 [*Short Account*, 1877], p. 15; Pressley, *op. cit.*, p. 93.

203 *Short Account*, 1913, p. 19; Hewley MSS, minutes, 1849-1883.

204 Hewley MSS, Trust deed, 1840 (ZTP II 3. 2).

THE NEW DISPENSATION

205 Hewley MSS, minutes, 1849-1883.

206 Hewley MSS, minutes, 1849-1883, 1884-1905, 1906-1923, 1923-1937; Hewley MSS (addnl.,), minutes 1938-1958.

207 Hewley MSS, accounts, 1849-1861.

208 *Short Account*, 1913, *op. cit.*, p. 66.

209 *Short Account*, 1913, *op. cit.*, pp. 66-67.

210 *Short Account*, 1913, *op. cit.*, p. 67.

211 *Short Account*, 1913, *op. cit.*, pp. 67-68.

212 *Short Account*, 1913, *op. cit.*, p.68.

213 Hewley MSS, minutes, 1923-1937.

214 Hewley MSS (addnl.), minutes, 16 September 1953; 19 May 1954; 7 June & 14 September 1955.

215 Hewley MSS (addnl.), minutes, 1938-1988, specifically, 28 October 1958.

216 Hewley MSS (addnl.), minutes, 27 September 1967.

LADY HEWLEY'S ALMSHOUSES: ST. SAVOURGATE

217 Hewley MSS (addnl.), minutes, 18 September 1946.

218 Brunskill, *op. cit.*, p. 23; Hargrove, *op. cit.*, vol II, part 2, p. 332.

219 *ODNB*, *op. cit.*, p. 45; *RCHM* York, *op. cit.*, p.15; Willis, *op. cit.*, p. 9.

220 Hewley MSS, memoranda book, 1840-1959; Hewley MSS (addnl.), minutes, 18 September 1946.

221 *RCHM* York, *op. cit.*, p. 15.

222 *VCH* York, *op. cit.*, p. 425; Brunskill, *op. cit.*, p. 24; *RCHM* York, p. 15 & plates 153, 182.

223 Hewley MSS, accounts of William Vizard junior as Receiver for the Hewley Trust estates whilst in the Court of Chancery, 1845-1849.

224 Hewley MSS, minutes, 1849-1883.

225 Hewley MSS, accounts, 1849-1861.

226 Hewley MSS, minutes, 1849-1883, 1906-1923.

227 *VCH* York, *op. cit.*, p. 425.

228 Hewley MSS, minutes, 1849-1883, 1906-1923.

229 Hewley MSS (addnl.), minutes. 16 September 1943.

230 Hewley MSS (addnl.), minutes, 19 May 1943.

231 Hewley MSS (addnl.), minutes, 23 May & 18 September 1946, 14 May & 24/25 September 1947.

232 Hewley MSS (addnl.), minutes, 28 May 1952.

233 Hewley MSS (addnl.), minutes, 16 September 1953; 15 September 1954; 7 June & 14 September 1955; 6 June & 18 September 1956; 28 May & 28 October 1957.

234 Hewley MSS (addnl.), minutes, 20 May 1958.

235 Hewley MSS (addnl.), minutes, 8 June 1976.

236 Hewley MSS (addnl.), minutes, 3 October 1973.

237 Hewley MSS (addnl.), minutes, 3 October 1972.

238 Hewley MSS (addnl.), minutes, 3 June 1975.

239 Hewley MSS (addnl.), minutes, 29 September 1975.

240 Hewley MSS (addnl.), minutes, 5 June 1979.

241 Hewley MSS (addnl.), minutes, 7 October 1980.

242 Hewley MSS (addnl.), minutes, 6 October 1981; 8 June 1982.

243 Hewley MSS (addnl.), minutes, 5 June 1984.

244 Hargrove, *op. cit.*, vol. II, part 2, p. 330; York Official Guide, 1975, *op. cit.*

245 Hewley MSS (addnl.), minutes, 5 June & 2 October 1984.

246 Hewley MSS (addnl.), minutes, 4 June & 1 October 1985.

247 Hewley MSS (addnl.), minutes, 3 June & 7 October 1986.

248 Hewley MSS (addnl.), minutes, 2 June & 6 October 1987.

249 *VCH* York, *op. cit.*, p. 425; Hewley MSS, minutes, 1849-1883.

250 Unless otherwise stated, the details in this section are from Sub-Trustees' minutes, 1923-1988 and 1988-2001.

THE CHARITY ESTATES AND THEIR MANAGEMENT

251 Cole, *op. cit.*, p. 55.

252 Hewley MSS, accounts, 1711-1760.

253 *Short Account*, 1877, *op. cit*, pp. 17-18.

254 Cole, *op. cit.*, p. 85

255 Hewley MSS, title deed, 1670 (ZTP I 4. 2).

256 *Short Account*, 1877, *op. cit.*, pp. 23-24.

257 *Short Account*, 1877, *op. cit.*, pp. 18-21.

258 Hewley MSS, title deeds, 1657-1699 (ZTP I: 1. 1; 4. 2; 5. 1; 6. 1; 8. 1; 13. 2; 14. 1).

259 Hewley MSS, title deed, 1840 (ZTP I 10).

260 *Short Account*, 1877, *op. cit.*, pp. 24-25.

261 Hewley MSS, minutes and memoranda, 1730-1751.

262 Hewley MSS, accounts, 1711-1760.

263 Hewley MSS, minutes, 1906-1923; accounts, 1711-1861.

264 Hewley MSS, accounts, 1711-1760, 1761-1809, 1810-1830. One of the Cayleys, Sir George (1773-1857), was a famous aeronautical pioneer who designed and built several successful manned gliders.

265 Hewley MSS, accounts, 1711-1760.

266 Hewley MSS, minutes and memoranda, 1730-1751.

267 Hewley MSS, minutes 18 November 1795.

268 Hewley MSS, minutes, 9 September 1802.

269 Hewley MSS, minutes, 21 September 1815.

270 Hewley MSS, minutes, 19 September 1816; 8 May 1817; 14 May 1818; 11 May 1820; 9 May 1822; 22 May 1823; ZTP VIII 1. 3.

271 Hewley MSS, minutes, 13 May & 16 September 1824; 26 May 1825; 13 September 1827; 9 September 1830.

272 Hewley MSS, accounts, 1711-1760. See, for example, 1717 and 1724.

273 Hewley MSS, accounts, 1711-1760.

274 Hewley MSS, accounts, 1711-1760.

275 Hewley MSS, minutes, 1762-1830.

276 Hewley MSS, accounts, 1711-1760.

277 Hewley MSS, minutes, 1849-1883.

278 Hewley MSS, minutes, 1762-1830: 24 September 1778; 11 May 1780; accounts, 1761-1809.

279 Hewley MSS, minutes, 1762-1830: 10 May 1803.

280 Hewley MSS, accounts, 1711-1760, 1761-1809, 1810-1830.

281 Hewley MSS, minutes, 1906-1923.

282 Hewley MSS, accounts, 1810-1830.

283 Hewley MSS, accounts, 1711-1760.

284 Hewley MSS, minutes, 1762-1830: 8 May 1766; accounts, 1761-1809.

285 Hewley MSS, minutes, 1762-1830: 20 September 1792; accounts, 1761-1809.

286 Hewley MSS, minutes, 1762-1830: 9 May 1799.

287 Hewley MSS, minutes, 1762-1830; accounts, 1761-1809, 1810-1830.

288 Hewley MSS, minutes: 1762-1830: 8 May 1817; accounts, 1810-1830.

289 Hewley MSS, minutes, 1762-1830; accounts, 1711-1760, 1761-1809, 1810-1830 etc.

290 Hewley MSS, accounts, 1711-1760.

291 Hewley MSS, minutes and memoranda, 1730-1751.

292 Hewley MSS, accounts, 1711-1760.

293 Hewley MSS, accounts, 1761-1809.

294 Hewley MSS, minutes, 1762-1830.

295 Hewley MSS, accounts, 1810-1830.

296 Hewley MSS, minutes, 1762-1830; accounts, 1810-1830; letters re work at Haya Park, 1818-1822 (ZTP IX 2).

297 Cole, *op. cit.*, p. 89. Hewley MSS, minutes, 1762-1830. The first of the great road engineers, John Metcalfe - 'Blind Jack of Knaresborough', probably knew Haya Park; he was the pioneer of road drainage, making side ditches and giving roads a convex surface off which water could run freely - he also insisted on firm foundations.

298 Hewley MSS, minutes, 1762-1830; accounts, 1761-1809.

299 Hewley MSS, minutes, 1762-1830.

300 Hewley MSS, minutes, 1762-1830; accounts, 1761-1809.

301 Hewley MSS, minutes, 1762-1830: 9 May 1805; accounts, 1761-1809.

302 Hewley MSS, Wm. Vizard's account book as Receiver, 1845-1849 (ZTP VIII 1. 9).

303 Hewley MSS, accounts, 1849-1861.

304 Hewley MSS (addnl.), minutes, 27 May 1938; 14 May 1947.

305 Hewley MSS (addnl.), minutes, 24 May 1950; 17 September 1952; 6 June 1956.

306 Hewley MSS, accounts, 1849-1861.

307 Hewley MSS, accounts, 1849-1861.

308 Hewley MSS, minutes, 1849-1883.

309 Hewley MSS, minutes, 1884-1905.

310 Hewley MSS, minutes, 1849-1883.

311 Hewley MSS, minutes, 1884-1905.

312 Hewley MSS (addnl.), minutes, 23 May 1946; 21/22 September 1948.

313 Hewley MSS, minutes, 1849-1883.

314 Hewley MSS, accounts, 1849-1861.

315 *Short Account*, 1913, *op. cit.*, pp. 73-74.

316 Hewley MSS, minutes, 1906-1923; Hewley (addnl.), minutes, 26 May 1948.

317 Hewley MSS, minutes, 1923-1937.

318 Hewley MSS (addnl.), minutes, 21 September 1939, 19 May 1943, 24 May 1944, 14 May 1947, 24 & 25 September 1947, 26 May 1948, 18 May 1949, 30 May 1951.

319 Hewley MSS, minutes, 1849-1883.

320 Hewley MSS, minutes, 1884-1905.

321 Hewley MSS (addnl.), minutes, 16 May 1949.

322 Hewley MSS, ledger, 1938-1951 (ZTP VIII 2. 3); Hewley MSS (addnl.), minutes, 18 May & 21 September 1949, 21 May, 20 September & 29 November 1950, 30 May & 27 September 1951, 28 May 1952.

323 Hewley MSS, minutes, 1849-1883.

324 Hewley MSS, minutes, 1849-1883.

325 Hewley MSS, minutes, 1849-1883.

326 Hewley MSS, minutes, 1849-1883.

327 Hewley MSS, minutes, 1906-1923.

328 Hewley MSS, minutes, 1849-1883.

329 Hewley MSS, minutes, 1849-1883, 1884-1905.

330 Hewley MSS, minutes, 1849-1883; Hornby video: *A Century in Stone, the Eston and California Story*.

331 Hewley MSS, minutes, 1849-1883.

332 Hewley MSS, minutes, 1849-1883.

333 Hewley MSS (addnl.), minutes, 21 May 1941.

334 Hewley MSS (addnl.), minutes, 12 September 1945; 23 May 1946.

335 Hewley MSS (addnl.), minutes, 23 May 1946; 14 May 1947; 5 October 1965.

336 *Short Account*, 1935, *op. cit.*, p. 42; Hewley MSS (addnl.), minutes, 18 May 1949.

337 Hewley MSS (addnl.), minutes, 7 June 1966; 23 May 1967.

338 Charity Commission Scheme, 1976; *Short Account*, 1935, *op. cit.*, pp. 34-50; Hewley MSS (addnl.), minutes, 21 September 1949; 28 May 1952; 20 May 1953; 28 May 1963.

339 Hewley MSS, minutes, 1849-1883; accounts, 1849-1861.

340 Hewley MSS, minutes, 1849-1883.

341 Hewley MSS (addnl.), minutes, 19 May 1943.

342 Hewley MSS, cash journal, 1911-1952 (ZTP VIII 2. 1); Hewley MSS (addnl.), minutes, 27 September 1967.

343 Charity Commission schedule, 1976.

344 Hewley MSS, minutes, 1849-1883.

345 Hewley MSS, minutes, 1884-1905, 1906-1923.

346 Hewley MSS, minutes, 1923-1937; memorandum book, 1840-1959 (ZTP VIII 6).

347 Hewley MSS, minutes, 1762-1830, especially 1802, 1805.

348 Hewley MSS, minutes, 1884-1905, 1906-1923, 1923-1937. ZTP VII 3-6.

349 Hewley MSS (addnl.), minutes, 23 May 1940 & 24/25 May 1947.

THE IRON AGE

350 *DNB*, *op. cit.*, vol. V, p. 316; *ODNB*, *op. cit.*, vols. 6 pp. 461-462, 56 pp. 189-190; John K Harrison, 'The

Impact of Industry', *Historic Reflections across the Tees,* p. 45; William Lillie, *The History of Middlesbrough: An Illustration of the Evolution of English Industry* [Lillie, 1968], p. 70.

351 Harrison, *op. cit.,* p. 42f.

352 William Lillie, Middlesbrough, 1853-1953 [Lillie, 1853], p. 11; Lillie, 1968, *op. cit.,* p.70; Robert Carson, *A Short History of Middlesbrough,* pp. 19-21; Hornby, *op. cit.*

353 Lillie 1968, *op. cit.,* p. 70; Briggs, *op. cit.,* p. 254.

354 *ODNB, op. cit.,* vols. 6, 56; Lillie 1968, *op. cit.,* p.96; Carson, *op. cit.,* pp. 19-20.

355 Briggs, *op. cit.,* p. 255.

356 Lillie 1968, *op. cit.,* p. 97; *DNB, op. cit,* vol. V, p. 316; Harrison, *op. cit.,* pp. 45-46; Lady Hugh Bell, *At the Works,* p. 20; Charles Postgate, *Middlesbrough, its History, Environs and Trade,* pp. 44-45; Hornby, *op. cit.*

357 Hewley MSS, minutes, 1849-1883.

358 Lillie 1968, *op. cit.,* p.

359 Hewley MSS (addnl.), Eston mining leases. Messrs. Bolckow Vaughan, 30 August 1852 & 18 May 1853.

360 *DNB, op. cit.,* vol. V, p. 316; *ODNB, op. cit.,* vols. 6 pp. 461-462, 56 pp. 189-190; Lillie 1953, *op. cit.,* pp.11-12; Lillie 1968, *op. cit.,* p. 25, 96-100; Carson, *op. cit.,* p.; Postgate, *op. cit.,* p. 46; Bell, *op. cit.,* p. 1f; Harrison, *op. cit.,* pp. 42-45; Hornby, *op. cit.*

361 Hewley MSS, quantities of ironstone vended from the Lady Hewley Royalty, 1853-1867 (ZTP VI 2); minutes, 1849-1883, 1884-1905, 1906-1923, 1923-1937; accounts, 1849-1861; Hewley MSS (addnl.), minutes, 1938-1958.

362 Hewley MSS, minutes, 1849-1883, 1884-1905.

363 Hewley MSS, minutes, 1849-1883.

364 Hewley MSS, minutes, 1884-1905.

365 Lillie 1968, *op. cit.,* pp. 100-101.

366 Carson, *op. cit.,* p. ?; Lillie 1968, *op. cit.,* pp. 26-27, 101-102; Bell, *op. cit.* (introduction to the 1969 edition, pp. 36-38 ; Harrison, *op. cit.,* pp. 42, 46; Hornby, *op. cit.*

367 *Short Account,* 1913, *op. cit.,* pp. 7-73; Hewley MSS, minutes, 1884-1905; memoranda book, 1840-1959 (ZTP VIII 6).

368 *Short Account,* 1935, *op. cit.,* p.70; Hewley MSS, minutes, 1906-1923; memoranda book, 1840-1959.

369 Hewley MSS (addnl.), minutes, 27 May & 23 September 1938; 19 May & 21 September 1939; 20 May & 25 September 1940; 20 May 1942, 18 May 1949.

370 Hewley MSS (addnl.), minutes, 18 May & 21 September 1949.

371 Lillie, 1953, *op. cit.,* p. 11; Lillie, 1968, *op. cit.,* pp. 27, 52-53; Hornby, *op. cit.*

372 Hewley MSS (addnl.), minutes, 20 September 1944.

373 Hewley MSS (addnl.), minutes, 12 September 1945; 23 May 1946.

374 Hewley MSS (addnl.), minutes, 22 September 1948; 21 September 1949.

375 *Short Account,* 1935, *op. cit.,* p. 70; Hewley MSS (addnl.), minutes, 20 May & 16 September 1953; 19 May & 15 September 1954; 7 May & 14 September 1955; 18 September 1956; 28 May 1957; 28 October 1958; 3 October 1961.

376 Bell, *op. cit.,* p. 21; Harrison, *op. cit.,* p. 49; Hornby, *op. cit.*

377 Harrison, *op. cit.,* p. 49; Hornby, *op. cit.*

CHARITABLE GRANTS AND THEIR DISTRIBUTION

378 Skeats & Miall, *op. cit.,* p. 127.

379 WCC, Robson's notes on York, p. 5.

380 Hewley MSS, accounts, 1711-1760.

381 Hewley MSS, accounts, 1711-1760, 1761-1809; minutes and memoranda, 1730-51.

382 Hewley MSS, minutes, 1762-1830: 14 May 1787: accounts. 1761-1809.

383 Hewley MSS, accounts, 1711-1760.

384 Hewley MSS, accounts, 1711-1760, 1761-1809.

385 Hewley MSS, minutes, 18 September 1806.

386 Hewley MSS, accounts, 1711-1760, 1761-1809, 1810-1830.

387 Hewley MSS, accounts, 1711-1760.

388 Hewley MSS, accounts, 1810-1830.

389 Hewley MSS, accounts, 1761-1809, 1810-1830.

390 Hewley MSS, accounts, 1711-1760, 1761-1809.

391 E Mackenzie, *A Descriptive and Historical Account of the Town and County of Newcastle upon Tyne*, p. 370f.; *ODNB, op. cit.*, 5; WCC, Black papers, vol. II, p.53 ; TWAS: Church of the Divine Unity, Newcastle upon Tyne, manuscripts (Accession 1787); Hewley MSS, accounts, 1711-1760, 1761-1809.

392 Hewley MSS, beneficiaries and distribution correspondence, 1790-1829 (ZTP VIII 4. 1-2).

393 TWAS 1787/172.

394 Hewley MSS, accounts, 1711-1760.

395 Hewley MSS, accounts, 1711-1760, 1761-1809, 1810-1830.

396 *DNB, op. cit.*, vol. XLVI pp. 376-396; Hewley MSS, accounts, 1711-1760.

397 *ODNB, op. cit.*, vol. 26; Hewley MSS, accounts, 1761-1809, 1810-1830.

398 Hewley MSS, accounts, 1711-1760.

399 Hewley MSS, accounts, 1711-1760, 1761-1809.

400 Stell, *op. cit.*, pp. 283-284.

401 Hewley MSS, 1711-1760.

402 Stell, *op. cit.*, p. 284.

403 Hewley MSS, accounts, 1711-1760.

404 Stell, *op. cit.*, pp. 283-284.

405 Hewley MSS, minutes, 1762-1830: 16 September 1762.

406 Hewley MSS, minutes, 1762-1830: 11 May 1780; accounts, 1761-1809, 1810-1830.

407 Hewley MSS, minutes, 1762-1830: 21 September 1820; accounts, 1810-1830.

408 Hewley MSS, minutes, 1762-1830: 9 September 1779, 11 May & 21 September 1780, 9 September 1790.

409 Hargrove, *op. cit.*, part II, part 2, p. 335; Hewley MSS, accounts, 1810-1830.

410 Hewley MSS, minutes, 1762-1830.

411 Hewley MSS, accounts, 1849-1861.

412 Hewley MSS, minutes, 1849-1883.

413 *Ibid.*

414 Hewley MSS (addnl.), minutes, 6 June & 18 September 1956.

415 Hewley MSS, minutes, 1849-1883.

416 WCC, Lady Hewley Trust envelope, newspaper cutting, 1849.

417 Pressley, *op. cit.*, p. 93.

418 Hewley MSS, minutes, 1849-1883; accounts, 1849-1861.

419 Hewley MSS, minutes, 1849-1883.

420 WCC, Lady Hewley Trust envelope, specimen application form, c. 1880.

421 Hewley MSS, minutes, 1906-1923.

422 Hewley MSS (addnl.), minutes, 16 May & 12 September 1945, 23 May 1946.

423 Hewley MSS (addnl.), minutes, 18 September 1946, 25 September 1947, 26 May 1948; 5 October 1982; 8 June 1983; 5 June 1984.

424 Hewley MSS (addnl.), minutes, 24 May & 20 September 1944; 16 May 1945; 23 May 1946; 18 May 1949.

425 Hewley MSS (addnl.), minutes, 4 October 1983; 5 June 1984.

426 Hewley MSS (addnl.), 18 September 1956.

427 Hewley MSS (addnl.), minutes, 6 June & 3 October 1972; 28 September 1976; Sub-Trustees' minutes, 1923-1988.

APPENDIX 1
428 BIHR, will, codicil etc., of Dame Sarah Hewley, proved 1710.

APPENDIX 2
429 *CC 1829*, pp. 1-8; FDD 1849, pp. 3-14.

430 *CC 1829*, pp. 8-14; FDD 1849, pp. 15-26; Hewley MSS (addnl.).
431 FDD 1849, p. 27; *Short Account*, 1913, p. 45.

APPENDIX 3
432 *Short Account*, 1913, pp. 46-51.

APPENDIX 4
433 *Short Account*, 1913, pp. 60-65.

APPENDIX 5
434 *ODNB*, *op. cit*, vol. 2.
435 *ODNB*, *op. cit.*, vol. 23; Hewley MSS: Reports of Cases in the High Court of Chancery, 1840-1843 (ZTPX 7).
436 *ODNB*, *op. cit.*, vol. 40.
437 *ODNB*, *op. cit.*, vol. 33; Ditchfield, pp. 137f.
438 *ODNB*, *op. cit.*, vol. 43 pp. 897-900; *Baptist Quarterly*, vol. XXIX, no. 2, p. 53..
439 David Cornick, *Under God's Good Hand; A History of the Traditions which have come together in the United Reformed Church in the United Kingdom*, pp. 33, 70, 107, 141.
440 Neil Glover's typescript notes on 'Sir Morton Peto MP and the Lady Hewley Trust', 1996. Compiled from *DNB*, *op. cit*; *ODNB*, *op. cit*; CC1829, *op. cit*; FDD1849, *op. cit*; *Short Account*, 1877, *op. cit*; *Short Account*, 1913, *op. cit*; *Short Account*, 1935, *op. cit*; Hewley MSS, minutes, accounts etc.; Sub-Trustees, minutes; Charity Commission Order, 1976; Neil Glover's notes; notes by John Lumsden.

APPENDIX 6
441 Hewley MSS, accounts, 1711-1760, 1761-1809, 1810-1830, 1849-1861.

APPENDIX 7
442 Hewley MSS, minutes, 1762-1830, 1849-1883, 1884-1905, 1906-1923, 1923-1937; accounts, 1711-1760, 1761-1809, 1810-1830, 1849-1861; Hewley MSS (addnl.), minutes, 1938-1958, 1958-1981, 1981-1988, 1988-1992, 1993-1998, 1999-2005.]

APPENDIX 8
443 Census returns for the Hewley Almshouses, 1841-1901 (from microfilm and fiche copies in York Reference Library; the originals are at the National Archives)

TIME CHART
444 Compiled from Cornick, *op. cit*; G Carter, *Outlines of English History*, and other sources.

Bibliography and Archive sources

Printed material

International Directory of Historic Places, vol. 2 (Northern Europe), London, 1995.

Leslie Stephen & Sidney Lee (eds.), *Dictionary of National Biography*, 1886?-1896? [*DNB*, followed by vol. no.].

H C G Matthew & Brian Harrison (eds.), *Oxford Dictionary of National Biography*, Oxford, 2004 [*ODNB*, followed by vol. no.]

David J. Jeremy (ed.) *Dictionary of Business Biography*, vol. 4: P L Cottrell, 'Sir Samuel Morton Peto', London, 1985, pp. 645-653.

Michael Stenton (ed.), *Who's Who of British Members of Parliament*, Hassocks, Sussex, vol. I, 1976; vol. II (with Stephen Lees), 1978.

J & JA Venn, *Alumni Cantabrigiensis*, part I (to 1751), vol. II, Cambridge, 1922.

Encyclopaedia Britannica, 1958 edn., vol. V (Charity Commission).

Basil Duke Henning, *The House of Commons, 1660-1690*, History of Parliament Trust, London, 1983.

Sir Thomas Erskine May, *The Constitutional History of England since the Accession of George the Third*, vol. 3, cap. 14 'Dissenters' Chapels', 11th edn., 1882

G Carter, *Outlines of English History*, London, revised edition, 1984.

G D H Cole, *Persons and Periods*, London, 1937.

John & Emanuel Bowen, *Britannia Depicta or Ogilby Improved: being a Direct Coppy of Mr Ogilby's Actual Survey of all ye Direct & Principal Cross Roads in England and Wales ...* , London, 1720.

Pat Rogers (ed.), Daniel Defoe: *A Tour Through the Whole Island of Great Britain* [1724-1726], London, 1971.

John Black, *Presbyterianism in England in the Eighteenth and Nineteenth Centuries*, London, 1887.

David Bogue & James Bennet, *The History of Dissenters*, 2 vols., London, 1833.

David Cornick, *Under God's Good Hand; A History of the Traditions which have come together in the United Reformed Church in the United Kingdom*, London, 1998.

Raymond Cowherd, *The Politics of English Dissent*, London, 1959.

G R Cragg, *The Church and the Age of Reason*, 1648-1789, London, revised edn., 1970.

A H Drysdale, *History of the Presbyterians in England: their Rise, Decline and Revival*, London, 1889.

A G Matthews (ed.), *Calamy Revised, being a Revision of Edmund Calamy's Account of the Ministers and Others Ejected and Silenced*, 1660-1662, Oxford, 1934.

James G Miall, *Congregationalism in Yorkshire*, London, 1868.

H S Skeats & C S Miall, *History of the Free Churches of England*, 1688-1891, London, 1891.

Thomas Stackhouse (ed.), *An Abridgement of Bishop [Gilbert of Salisbury] Burnet's History of His Own Times*, London, 1906.

David Thompson, *Nonconformity in the Nineteenth Century*, London, 1972.

J Horsfall Turner, *The Rev. Oliver Heywood BA, 1630-1702: His Autobiography, Diaries, Anecdote and Event Books*, 4 vols., Brighouse, 1881-1885.

G Lyon Turner, *Original Records of Early Nonconformity under Persecution and Indulgence*, 3 vols., London, 1911 (2) & 1914.

M R Watts, *The Dissenters: vol. I: The Restoration to the French Revolution*, Oxford, 1978; vol. II: *The Expansion of Evangelical Nonconformity*, Oxford, 1995.

D W Bebbington, 'Baptist Members of Parliament, 1847-1914', *Baptist Quarterly* [Journal of the Baptist Historical Society], vol. XXIX, no. 2, 1981.

K G Jones, 'The Authority of the Trust Deed', *Baptist Quarterly*, vol. XXXIII, no. 3, 1989.

'RDW', 'Mr Edward Bowles' Catechism', *Journal of the Presbyterian Historical Society of England*, vol. VII, no. 2, 1941.

G F Nuttall, 'Methodism and the Older Dissent: Some Perspectives', *Journal of the United Reformed History Society* [JURCHS], vol. 2, no. 8, 1981.

Kenneth Wadsworth, 'Philip, Lord Wharton – Revolutionary Aristocrat?', *JURCHS*, vol. 4, no. 8, 1991.

H McLachan, 'More Letters of Theophilus Lindsey', *Transactions of the Unitarian Historical Society* [*TUHS*], vol. III, no. 4, 1926.

Ernest Axon, 'Yorkshire Nonconformity in 1743' (The Archbishop of York, Thomas Herring's, Visitation), *TUHS*, vol. V, no. 3, 1933.

C V Wedgwood, 'Sir John Hewley, 1619-1697', *TUHS*, vol. VI, no. 1, 1935.

C G Bolam, 'J R Beard and the New Function of Unitarianism in the 1850s', *TUHS*, vol. XII, no.4, 1962.

Ian Sellers, 'The Risley Case', *TUHS*, vol. XVI, no. 4, 1978.

Peter B Godfrey, 'Joseph Hunter, 1783-1861', *TUHS*, vol. XVIII, no. 2, 1984.

G M Ditchfield, 'Two Unpublished Letters of Theophilus Lindsey', *TUHS*, vol. XX, no. 2, 1992.

Arthur Long, 'The Dissenters' Chapels Act after 150 years: some concluding reflections', *TUHS*, vol. XXI, no. 1, 1995.

G Hadfield (ed.), *The Report of His Majesty's Commissioners concerning Dame Sarah Hewley's Charity, published and circulated by the Independent churches of the County of Lancaster*, Manchester, 1829.

Foundation Deeds and other Documents relating to Dame Sarah Hewley's Charity, London, 1849.

A Short Account of the Hewley Charities, Vizards, London, 1877.

A Short Account of the Hewley Charities, 1881-1913, Vizard, Oldham & Co., London, 1913.

A Short Account of the Hewley Charities, 1913-1935, Vizards, London, 1935.

Joseph Hunter, *An Historical Defence of the Trustees of Lady Hewley's Foundations, and of the Claims upon them of the Presbyterian Ministry of England*, London, 1834.

T S James, *The History and Legislation respecting Presbyterian Chapels and Charities in England and Ireland between 1816 and 1849*, London, 1867.

Judy Slinn, *The History of Vizards, 1797-1997*, Cambridge, 1997.

Thomas William Tottie, *Hewley Charities: Reports and Arguments: A Plain Statement of the Trusts and Recent Arguments of Lady Hewley's Charities*, London, 1834.

William Page (ed.), *Victoria History of the County of York*, vols. II (London, 1912, reprinted 1974) & III (London, 1913).

P M Tillott (ed.), *Victoria History of the County of York: the City of York*, London 1961.

K J Allison (ed.), *Victoria History of the County of York: Yorkshire East Riding*, vol. III, London, 1976.

Francis Drake, *Eboracum or the History and Antiquities of the City of York*, London, 1736.

William Hargrove, *History and Description of the Ancient City of York*, 2 vols., York, 1818.

I P Pressley, *A York Miscellany*, London, n.d. [1938].

Alberic Stacpoole (ed.), *The Noble City of York*, York, 1972.

Edward Royle (ed.), William Ellerby & James Pigott Pritchett, *A History of the Nonconformist Churches of York*, York, 1993.

W W Tomlinson, *The North Eastern Railway: its Rise and Development*, Newcastle upon Tyne, 1914.

Royal Commission on Historical Monuments, *York: Central Area*, London, 1981.

Christopher Stell, *An Inventory of Nonconformist Chapels and Meeting Houses in the North of England*, London, 1994.

Nikolaus Pevsner & David Neave, *The Buildings of England: York and the East Riding*, 2nd. edn., London, 1995.

Elizabeth Brunskill, 'Some York Almshouses', *York Georgian Society occasional paper no. 7*, 1960.

Ronald Willis, 'Nonconformist Chapels of York, 1693-1840', *York Georgian Society occasional paper no. 8*, 1964.

York: Official Guides, York, c.1951, c.1975.

Lady Hugh Bell, *At the Works*, 3rd. impression, London, 1907 [David & Charles reprint, 1969].

Asa Briggs, *Victorian Cities*, London, 1963 (with section on Middlesbrough).

W H Burnett (*et al.*), *Middlesbrough and District*, Middlesbrough, 1881.

Robert Carson, *A Short History of Middlesbrough*, Middlesbrough, 1977.

John K Harrison, 'The Impact of Industry', *Historic Reflections across the Tees*, Cleveland & Teesside Local History Society, 2001.

William Lillie, *Middlesbrough, 1853-1953*, Middlesbrough, 1953.

William Lillie, *The History of Middlesbrough: An Illustration of the Evolution of English Industry*, Middlesbrough, 1968.

Norman Moorson, *Vintage Middlesbrough*, Nelson., Lancs., 1978.

Charles Postgate, *Middlesbrough, its History, Environs and Trade*, Middlesbrough, 1899.

H G Reid (ed.), *Middlesbrough and its Jubilee*, 1881.

D M Tomlin & M Williams, *Who Was Who in Nineteenth-Century Middlesbrough*, 1997.

E MacKenzie, *A Descriptive and Historical Account of the Town and County of Newcastle upon Tyne*, 1827.

Manuscript etc. material

Records of the Hewley Trust: minutes, accounts, deeds and trust deeds, leases, maps and plans, reports, correspondence etc, at North Yorkshire County Council Record Office, Northallerton [NYC-CRO ZTP]; minutes, reports, correspondence, maps and plans, sale particulars, etc. including additional manuscript and printed material transferred over the last year or so from the Trust's Clerk and Legal Advisor, to the North Yorkshire County Record Office [NYRO ZTP additional],

Wills of Sir John & Lady Sarah Hewley, proved 1697 & 1710 [BIHR probate]; and the records of St. Saviourgate chapel, York [BIHR St. Saviourgate chapel], Borthwick Institute of Historical Research, University of York.

United Reformed Church History Society, records held in the Reformed Studies Centre, Westminster College, Cambridge: the Revd. John Black's MS volumes of historical notes relating to Presbyterianism in North-East England; John Peddie's volume of portraits and notes, including Sir John & Lady Sarah Hewley; R S Robson's MS and other collected notes on 'York Presbyterianism' [York envelope].

Records of Durant Unitarian church, Newcastle upon Tyne, Tyne and Wear Archives Service (Accession 1787).

Neil Glover, 'Sir Morton Peto, MP and the Lady Hewley Trust', typescript notes, 1996.

William Mortimer Baines, MS reminiscences of the Baines family of Bell Hall, n.d. c.1870.

Introduction to the Baines of Bell Hall collection, Brynmor Jones Library, University of Hull.

Craig Hornby, A Century in Stone: The Eston and California Story, A Pancrack Production, 2004 (video, narrated by Eric Robson).

Critique of sources

Many of the printed works consulted cannot be regarded as impartial, and any bias has to be born in mind when seeking to understand the long history of the Hewley Trust. This partisan writing is true not only of the period from 1830 to 1849 when interdenominational wrangling was at its most bitter, nor was it particularly confined to theological and religious authors but extended to historians, economists, and social and political commentators too. Some of the bias is deliberate and some of it seems to be quite natural and unconscious. And, of course, what is true of printed material is also redolent of the manuscripts and archives used.

It is also important to comment on the paucity of information available for the earlier history of the Trust. During the major litigation from 1830 to 1849, the respective lawyers were all handicapped by the absence of most of the Trust's significant records prior to 1760, title and trust deeds, a rough memoranda book and a few miscellaneous papers only being extant for this period. The Trust's first minute books and ledgers (which are known to have once existed) do not appear to have survived, despite efforts to track them down; it would be good to learn that these volumes are in fact still in some safe place.

Just one of the missing early sources, the first account book (1711-1760) did eventually surface, discovered in a Leeds bookshop by one of the Trustees, J R Mills, who promptly purchased the volume and returned it to the custody of the Trust. It would seem that while the early records were in the possession of Thomas Lee, sometime Trustee and Treasurer, his descendants disposed of these, the account book being retained only as a pattern for bookbinding purposes.

Notwithstanding the dearth of early documentary material, extensive research on this first account book has proved invaluable to an understanding of how the estates originally functioned and how the charity distributions were first administered. It is clear too that anyone wishing to acquire information about the stationing of ministers or indeed when particular meeting-houses and chapels were first established, would find it helpful to consult this account book as well as the later financial volumes and minute books.

Unfortunately, there was not a wide choice of excellent illustrative material, but hopefully what has been reproduced enhances the text and adds to its meaning. It should be added that it was also hoped to include a second but different portrait of Dame Sarah. The restoration of this further likeness was paid for by former Trustees, so it would have been especially appropriate to give this a place too. Sadly, however, this portrait was mislaid in the 1980s. Like the earlier records of the Trust we can also hope that this second portrait will again come to light.

Index

Personal names

Grand Trustees in bold type; Sub-Trustees in *italics*; Officers indicated thus:*. Note: Dr. Thomas Colton and John Stanley Holmes served as both Grand and Sub-Trustees.

Minster 71

North Postern 47

North Street 42

Ouse Bridge prison 28, 34

Ousegate 33

Quayside 46

Railway station 46, 47, 166

Rougier Street 41

St. Martin's Church 23

St. Saviour's 29, 30, 35, 47, 69, 71

St. Saviourgate 15, 17, 21, 29, 30, 33, 34, 35, 47, 49, 50, 56, 59, 62, 64, 69, 71, 76, 85, 119, 126

Tanner Row 41, 42, 47, 71, 72, 85, 164

Toft Green 42, 47

York House 76

Subjects

Abbeyfield Homes 81

Act of Uniformity 14, 32, 45, 164

Airedale Independent College 57, 122

Almshouses, National Association of 75, 77

Association of Protestant Dissenting Ministers In the North of England 122

Attorney-General v Wilson 62, 63

Attorney-General v. Shore 53

Attorney-General v. Shore & others 166

Attorney-General v. Wilson 166

Baptists 13, 14, 16, 17, 18, 33, 34, 35, 63, 68, 121, 147

Bessemer steel making process 166

Calvinistic Methodists 17

Chancery, Court of 22, 39, 46, 47, 53, 55, 58, 61, 64, 72, 85, 92, 94, 98, 114, 128, 130, 155, 158, 166

Charity Commission/ers 4, 5, 56, 65, 67, 68, 69, 70, 73, 75, 77, 80, 82, 96, 99, 100, 101, 128, 133, 134, 147, 166, 167, 168

Church of England 13, 14, 16, 18, 27, 29, 44, 55, 58, 131, 163, 167, 168

Church of Scotland 61, 63, 168

Civil War 14, 24, 32, 163

Clarendon Code 14, 27

Commonwealth 22, 24, 25

Congregationalists see also Independents 6, 13, 18, 58, 66, 71, 77, 133, 147

Conventicle Act 14, 164

Corporation Act 14, 15, 164, 166

Countess of Huntingdon's Connection 18

Dean and Chapter, York Minster 71

Declaration of Indulgence 15, 32, 37, 164

Dissenters' Chapels Act 62, 166

Dissenting Academies 15, 17, 21, 50

Evangelical Revival 17

Five-Mile Act 14, 164

Friends, Society of (Quakers) 13, 17, 18, 35, 44

Gray's Inn 22, 60, 84, 163

Happy Union 15, 164

Hewley Almshouses 15, 41, 46, 47, 51, 56, 63, 64, 66, 68, 69, 71, 72, 93, 130, 134, 138, 154, 156, 164, 166, 167, 168

Hewley Memorial Plaque 77

House of Commons 24, 25, 56

House of Lords 7, 60, 61

Huguenots 164

Independents see also Congregationalists 13, 14, 15, 16, 17, 18, 32, 33, 34, 35, 48, 57, 58, 61, 63, 66, 145, 147

Lancashire Independent College 58

Lord Chancellor 4, 22, 56, 60, 61, 62, 64, 166

Manchester Unitarian Academy 17, 56, 59, 60, 122, 165

Masters in Chancery 61

Methodists 17, 50, 55

Official Trustee of Charity Lands 66, 69

Official Trustees of Charitable Funds 66, 67, 69

Parliament 14, 15, 18, 20, 22, 24, 25, 32, 37, 41, 43, 44, 47, 55, 104, 146

Percy Cust District Nursing Fund 74

Presbyterians 13, 14, 15, 16, 17, 18, 28, 32, 34, 35, 44, 57, 59, 61, 63, 66, 77, 121, 133, 145, 147

Protectorate 24

Protestant Deputies (Lay) 60

Puritans 13

Quarter Sessions, Court of 34

Reform Act, 1832 18, 166

Restoration 14, 15, 24, 28, 37, 44, 45

Roman Catholics 13, 16

Rotherham Independent College 56

Salters' Hall Conference 165

Scottish Secession Church 61, 63

Schools, Blue and Grey Coat, York 29, 62, 136

Socinian Controversy 16, 55, 166

Test Act, 1673 15, 164

Toleration Act, 1689 15, 16, 34, 55, 164

Tory Party 15, 27

Unitarians 7, 16, 18, 36, 49, 55, 56, 57, 59, 60, 61, 146, 165, 166

Vice-Chancellor of England 60

Westminster Assembly 43, 163

Wolverhampton Chapel Case 58, 61

World War II 74

York and North Midland Railway 47

York city preachers 32, 33, 38, 43, 60, 120

York Civic Trust 77

York, Corporation of 20, 24, 25, 32, 46, 74

York Conservation Trust 82, 156

York County Hospital 74

York Dispensary 74

York Institute 59

York Literary Club 50

York Philosophical Society 59

York Subscription Library 59

The present Grand Trustees

Stephen Gorton is a Chartered Accountant and has worked in that profession and in industry. He currently works for a Charity on the outskirts of Durham. He is married, with two daughters, and represents the Baptist Union on the Trust.

Bryan Herbert was born in Bingley, some of whose Congregational church ministers received grants from the Hewley Trust. Educated at The Leys and Christ's College, Cambridge, he became a solicitor with a special interest in trusts. He was involved with the Yorkshire Congregational Union's joining the United Reformed Church. He is now retired, lives in Leeds, and represents the United Reformed Church on the Trust.

John Lumsden worked as a business manager for Procter & Gamble prior to retirement. He represents the United Reformed Church, and is the current Chairman of the Trust.

Dr. James Porteous is a chartered engineer who served in the electricity supply industry for 43 years, a former Vice-President of Opportunities for People with Disabilities and for the past twelve years a Vice-President of NEA (National Energy Action) working for the eradication of fuel poverty. He represents the United Reformed Church.

Muriel Proven is a retired trust administrator with a bank trust company, and represents the United Reformed Church.

Gordon Simmonds is an insolvency practitioner, and is married with two children. He is a Trustee of the Buxton Opera House {High Peak Theatre Trust). He represents the Congregational Federation.

Philip Thake is a chartered accountant by profession, and is Chief Executive of York Conservation Trust. He represents the United Reformed Church.

The present Sub-Trustees

Cathy Halliday is a member of St. Columba's with New Lendal United Reformed Church, York. She is Clerk to the Sub-Trustees, and works at the University of York.

Peter Hall is an Elder of St. Columba's and is Treasurer of the Sub-Trustees.

Revd. Graham Maskery is the minister of St. Columba's.

Revd. Revd. Gary Patchen is the minister of Priory Street Baptist church, York.

Janet Ponsford is a member of Priory Street Baptist church.

Barbara Skelton is a member of St. Columba's.

Revd. Thomas O Williams is now retired, but was formerly a minister of St. Columba's.

The present Officers

David Wharrie is a chartered accountant based in Chester, and has been Clerk to the Trustees since 1981.

Ron Perry is senior partner in Vizard, Tweedie, the London firm of solicitors who have provided help and guidance to the Hewley Trust for around 175 years. He has been Legal Advisor to the Trust since the 1970s.

Brian Wilkinson has been Land Agent for the Trust since 1976. He is a partner in the York firm of Boulton & Cooper Stephenson's, surveyors.

Duncan Brookes is investment account director with Tilney's, the Liverpool firm of investment advisors.

Richard Brown serves as Property Manager for the Almshouses (contracted from York Conservation Trust).

Richard Potts began his working life in the iron and steel industry on Teesside before making the transition, after university, to the archives profession. He retired from Tyne and Wear Archives in 1996 but retains an interest in records as honorary archivist to Westminster College, Cambridge. He is the editor of *Cornish Glebe Terriers, 1673-1735* (Devon & Cornwall Record Society, 1971), and joint author with Frank Manders of *Crossing the Tyne* (Tyne Bridge Publishing, 2001). He was baptised in a Baptist church, came into the United Reformed Church through the Congregational tradition, and now worships in a former Presbyterian church.

Design by Anna Flowers, Publications Manager at Tyne Bridge Publishing, Newcastle Libraries & Information Service. For details of a wide range of books relating to the local history of Tyneside visit *www.tynebridgepublishing.co.uk*.